THE POETRY OF PETER RILEY

THE POETRY OF
PETER RILEY

The Gig 4/5

NOVEMBER 1999 / MARCH 2000

TORONTO, ONTARIO, CANADA

For Jane and Anne

The Gig 4/5: The Poetry of Peter Riley
Editing and typesetting: Nate Dorward
Image: The Pleiades, as depicted by Galileo in the *Sidereus nuncius*.
Printed at the Coach House Press, Toronto, Ontario

All contents remain copyright © the contributors.

ISSN 1481-5133

The Gig is published three times a year; regular issues are 60–64pp, staplebound in card covers, and contain new poetry from the US, Canada, the UK and Ireland, plus a feature essay, reviews and notices. At present we cannot accept unsolicited manuscripts. The tables of contents for issues 1 through 3, along with other material (a bibliography of J.H. Prynne, poetry N&Qs, etc.), are available online at <www.geocities.com/ndorward/>.

Subscriptions for regular issues: within Canada: single issue: $6 Cdn; subscription (3 issues): $15; institutional copies: $10 each. A US subscription is $13.00 US; overseas is £8.00 (please inquire first if paying in currencies other than dollars or pounds sterling). All prices include postage. Please make cheques and money orders out to Nate Dorward. NB: A subscription beginning with issue 3 or issue 4/5 is $20 in Canada, $15 (US) for the US; for overseas please inquire first!

There is also a sibling imprint, The Gig Editions. Its first publication, Allen Fisher's *The Topological Shovel: Four Essays*, is 52pp, large format, Cerloxbound; it includes three short essays and the long piece *Necessary Business*. Copies may be had for $12 Cdn, $10.50 US or £6.50 overseas (prices include postage).

Copies of *The Gig*, *The Topological Shovel* and many of Peter Riley's books may be had from Mr Riley's own bookselling business, at 27 Sturton Street, Cambridge, CB1 2QG, UK; e-mail: <priley@dircon.co.uk>.

The Gig
Nate Dorward
109 Hounslow Ave.
Willowdale, ON, M2N 2B1
Canada

ph: (416) 221 6865
e-mail: <ndorward@sprint.ca>

CONTENTS

AN INTERVIEW
WITH PETER RILEY

❧

Keith Tuma

KT: I have just been reading your essay "The Creative Moment of the Poem" in Denise Riley's collection, and I want to begin this interview with a question or two about it, or rather about your own work as it might be set beside some of the claims of that essay. You are at some pains in the essay to define the poem as "an object between poet and reader which is both a means of communication and a barrier to communication," as an artifact "neither opaque nor transparent," a "body of light" which reflects "the need to say and be revealed crossed with the need to remain silent and secret." You set up a clear opposition between poetry and prose; unlike poetry, you say, prose has to do with a more "direct transmission" between writer and reader. "Prose, properly speaking, draws a thread from a singular past through an author and a construct to an imaginative reconstruction in the future." I want to use these remarks as background to a question about the prose in some of your own books. *Alstonefield*, for example, opens with excerpts from your letters to Tony Baker. One might read these letters as, in part, meditation on the possibility and politics of pastoral poetry, but they are letters—direct address—to a real person who happens to be a poet. Then there's the prose opening *Lines on the Liver*, which is full of provocative claims about the nature of the self and desire, industrial "encrustation" and "marine fossil energy in suspension which has men mining in their sleep," and so on. The prose there, as also to a lesser extent in the letters to Baker, sometimes takes the form of rhetorical questions—e.g., "isn't the lack which drives us into work then something from a distance, if not distance itself?" The prose is meditative but it is also propositional—much the same might be said of the poems—though the questions do suggest a direct turn to a real or supposed reader. Given what you have said about poetry and prose, I am wondering why you have felt compelled on several occasions to write prose texts to accompany your poems or, in the case of *Tracks and Mineshafts*, as a supplement to them. Why bother to frame these poems for the reader? Does it point to some lack of confidence in the poems themselves or their potential readers, to a desire to get something across that the poems by themselves might not get across? Does it suggest a need to defend or explain the poems? In what way do you mean this prose to relate to the poems?

PR: You have to remember that there is no definition of poetry. Poetry is whatever is passed as poetry, that's all you can say. In that situation, if you want to make a claim for its continued practice you enclose the corner of it you believe in. That's what I did in that piece for Denise Riley's collection, describing, rather than defining, what is practised in the corner in which I operate. It was also written from the writer's viewpoint, such was the remit of the anthology. From the reader's view I could put it more simply as: if you read prose you expect to be told something; if you read poetry you expect something else. Including, I'd now want to add, being told something. The "something else" of poetry must, as I see it, rest on the formal existence of the poem, and will be more fully evinced in the shorter, lyrical and meditative poems where the whole is always before you. Things such as rhyme and any version of poetical language exist, as far as I know, in order to maintain that sense of an entirety inherent in the slightest movement of the poem, reinforced by acts of finely judged displacement. Which is a paradigm of what happens, everywhere, which is why it gives pleasure when it is done freshly, when it touches the nerve—it offers to lighten the world.

I think there is a scale of movement away from functional prose, and when you reach the extreme of that scale poetry transfers, or fails to, in very shifted terms. What I and a lot of my contemporaries have relied on in the courses we've allowed ourselves to take is that a transference will take place in the absence of the normal transferring mechanisms of language, or in some cases by and through the deliberate blocking of them. I won't go into the theories of this which I find almost entirely posterior and suppositional. I think we have relied on an immense amount of reader goodwill.

But I increasingly think that the transfer of virtuous substance in poetry needs a midwife, and if it's left to happen of its own accord from within the poet's psychic sphere there is a danger that nothing will happen at all, because the effort required on the reader's part is greater than any promise of reward; or what is offered cannot anyway be shown not to be illusive and solipsistic. It may not be that, but in going to the extreme of its own condition it has disempowered itself from showing or proving otherwise. The constant displacement to an elsewhere in modern poetry is brought to such an intensity that it becomes an obstacle to any message there might be, there is no "return" from poetry's ecstasis. In which case it might as well not exist.

So I'm interested in prose as a support to poetry, a ground to it and a guarantor. Indeed my notion of the originary function of poetry is as a song interlude in a narrative, as in the Scandinavian epics, or an interlude of ecstasis and consolidation in a narrative called living. A static or elliptical or self-involving structure set in a continuum, which reflects greater distances than the story. I don't see what's wrong, if the poetry is going to be that wholly involving performance, in assisting the reader into it by setting it in a recognizable world of time/place/thought, as Doug Oliver for instances does so honestly in *An Island That Is All the World*. But not necessarily autobiographical or even factual. It's actually helpful, it makes it a lot easier to enter the poetical condition, and it doesn't substitute for or reduce the poem. We allow the reader the imaginative intelligence to be able to read the poem out of that frame, or indeed it might be difficult not to. The rainy piece in this collection is my latest bid at a more integrative exercise along these lines. The poetry should seem to emerge from the prose as a very distinct thing arising from the same experience. I also found that when poetical processes are embedded in a narrative like this, however trivial a one, they are themselves much less bounden to prosaic or rationalizing processes. They can be seen to be using the same materials of experience and image at other levels, and the result-ing poetical intrusions can easily be ignored if they get in the way.

Lines on the Liver actually has a purposive structure which evolved very slowly in the course of writing the book. It starts with thought-prose, the earnest attempt to state the living condition wholly and abstractly (rather too much of this, I now think) which gives way, as if out of tiredness, to personal poetry, in which the questions are not asked but the lived event is allowed to fall into its own rather short-winded language of self and world. Poems of seeming. This is then confronted with actual narrative, in that story about the tramp, the acute distance of alteriority in a desocialized dereliction. Finally that lost figure takes the self-poems and one by one answers them, crashes them against the hardness of loss and distance.

I don't fear that without these prosaic structures the poems would fail to release their substances because I don't believe the poem is a scriptural structure, that it can be expected to hold a conceptual total in its folds, as it is made to seem by the sleight-of-hand of postsymbolist artistry. The perfect poem is absolutely replete, but only with what it grasps, which can be minimal. So the poem is as particular as the prose in a different way, so that what the prose supplies in these joint structures is always additional and not substitutive. Indeed prose might be able to articulate poetry into a more extended narrative than the compacted poem could reach, into truths which are actually operative. The poem's completion is formal, invoking the world by patterns of displacement and harmony, rather than by conceptual or encyclopedic coverage. So I don't think poetry is a sacral purveyor of earth-changing messages from deep and distant unknowables. I think it's an ornament.

KT: "The Creative Moment of the Poem" doesn't pull many punches. Your claims about the relationship of poet and reader to the poem lead you to attack poetry which proposes an "*en bloc* transfer of substance" between poet and reader, that so-called "mainstream" poetry which in its "refined versions" is given to "anecdote and self-distancing" and "always implies the immediate return of the small-scale recognition which is all it offers." You also reject a poetry of "suspended suggestion, wilful fragmentation, word-salad and other negations of continuity" offered "in the name of reader-engagement," arguing that such poetry "abnegates the poet's duty to truth and leaves the reader hopelessly alone." I can't help but read such remarks against other statements you have made on the British-Poets listserv which suggest that you find yourself in a kind of no man's land between a "mainstream" and an avant-garde. Your loyalties, if you will excuse the word, seem at times to be divided. While you often declare your allegiance to the modernist small-press scene, you seem to want to speak up for an Everyman who takes little or no interest in modernist poetry, and you seem to believe that many modes of poetry are currently viable if not your preference exactly. In the essay some of these tensions are dramatized in your italicized vignettes, where you imagine a reader responding to high-minded propositions such as "The very fabric of our perception rests delicately on our love" by dismissing them as pompous and irrelevant to busy and tired readers who want you to tell a story about "your Irish grandfather." There is an ambivalence and uneasiness in that opening vignette that I am not sure you ever altogether put aside, for all of your eloquence about the "anonymous" poet and the "poet [dying] constantly into the poem." I wonder if I am right to think that a familiar kind of anxiety about the audience of modern poetry shapes your poetry and, if I am, if you might elaborate just a little on how that is so.

PR: "…no man's land between mainstream and avant-garde" and "divided loyalties"—these only make sense if you believe in the necessarily dichotomized condition of our culture, and I don't. As far as I'm concerned where I am is a normal and proper place to be, is where people like me always have been, and mainstream and avant-garde are way out on a limb, really nowhere. British culture runs to oppositional extremes—well, no it doesn't actually, but the extremes get most of the attention, and why? because they're easy, they're easily subsumed into journalistic and academic discourses, the usual TV ethos: set up a fight and you've got your audience captured. Mainstream (I'll use the word without quotes for what is normally meant, though I think it's nonsense—actually I am the mainstream) mainstream and avant-garde are no real distance from each other, they imply each other, each of their readerships is a reactive negative to the other, and from my point of view, at their extremes they're both anti-poetry. They both refuse the world-invocation of the truly poetic, in favour of singular vision, jokes anecdotes games and experiments, and politics. I haven't exactly got anything against them as such, but people start to feel threatened, or resentful that they are not widely recognized as leader, and start making exclusive claims for their pitches, sometimes on a very big scale. The worst thing is that such focused entrenchments deny the very richness of opportunity we are offered in the huge range of language uses spread all round us, the very advantage of being where and when we are.

What I do is like a balancing trick, a ridge-top walk. I want to keep in view all the possibilities, which are not just to left and right, and kind of steer a course through them. And I believe this is innovative, and does seek new movement between words, but as a renewal of truth rather than a denial of it, and so with constant check against the world. I think for instance both Hardy and Hopkins were poetically innovative and there is no point in setting them against each other. What I lapse into is either dullness or difficulty. Well naturally I waver, I'd distrust anyone who didn't waver in present conditions, but that doesn't mean I view the varying modes available as options. There are those who with an absolute singularity of purpose drive forwards in saint- or hero-like certainty, looking no way but forwards.

I don't trust it, now or ever. I don't trust the inhering disdain, and I don't know where the certainty derives from other than habitual self-confirmation. What good did saints and heroes ever do anyway, for the most part? They enforced change, and caused immense suffering.

I've always thought "audience" too theatrical a term for poetry. There's only anxiety about it when you're forced to inhabit a nationalized space in which poetry is one agenda, which is of course a fabrication, but sometimes you are forced to. Then you see extremists and opportunists getting most of the attention and rewards, and naturally you blame yourself. But really there's no reason why that seemingly unattained "poetry" audience should turn to what you do, rather than to belly-dancing or marquetry. The differences among poetical modes are as extreme as that. So there's an enormous range of activity, all kinds of different musics being produced all over the place, and most reasonably efficient performers get a band of attentive listeners, what more does anyone want?

KT: I was a little sneaky above when I worked your sentence about "distance" into my question about the role of prose in some of your poetry books. "Distance," like "completion," and the adjectival forms of these words, is a keyword in your work at least as far back as *Lines on the Liver*. I take it that it relates to your effort to construct or explore models of subjectivity and interiority which might be opposed to the reduced existence enforced by the institutions of modern culture and the modern state. Heidegger would have a language for this that involves authentic being and its relationship to everydayness. I take it that your interest in acknowledging "the gentler and more persistent demand of the totality"—as you put it in *Lines on the Liver*—might be related to such a model of authenticity, though your work also seems haunted by the prospect that efforts to grasp the "totality" are doomed to fail. You write in *Liver* that "The administration, hell bent on debasing man before his own facility, drags us across the world into nonentity as soon as we risk ourselves into its function—i.e., project human fullness of soul into the hard, crumbling, ugly and disordered outer surface of the anthill which statecraft is, and the lost souls who think they control it. We seem to accede to this political reduction, in submitting to the choice of a career or detesting the government; but then we return home to ourselves, we 'grasp the balance,' and the luxuries of denouncing wrong give place to the duties of tracing harm." Now, when I read your work, I don't find myself asking how it might be thought of as political in its wound response—you seek to expand the purchase of the human and human freedom against all that would use us, those created needs which are our inheritance. "Mining" or "excavating" in your work, for instance, is not just what they used to do more of up north but also exploration of dream-worlds; if Earth Is Us, let's dig into it to see what deposits can be uncovered, what can be recovered for use. But intellectual and poetic work as much as physical work requires tools, and what I want to ask you here is what tools you find useful for digging. It seems clear from the idioms of your prose and poetry that a Kierkegaardian language of "dread" and "fear and trembling" together with various discourses associated with Freudian and post-Freudian psychoanalysis have been useful tools. I find myself wondering, however, to what extent specific religious discourses have also informed the work. There is, after all, some talk of the "soul" in your work, occasional reference to the "Grail" and to (spiritual?) "journeys" and such. Moreover, at the same time that your work seems to want to provide models for a more capacious subjectivity or interiority, it also seems constantly to struggle with solipsism; John Dooley in *Liver* is perhaps your most famous figure of man altogether isolated amid the dump, glimpsed in a phone booth as if desperately trying to reach an outside world. He might be in one of Beckett's plays. I want to ask you, then, whether or not he is Peter Riley's tragicomic hero and, more specifically, what reading he might do to get his call through to the world or (failing that) at least live a life worth living?

PR: There are some advantages of not being professionally occupied in literature or poetry as a teacher or scholar, one of which is that what you read doesn't have to pass into a card-index and lie forever behind you. You can forget it, and you can read fragmentarily or haphazardly and it doesn't matter. You can read a book because it falls into your hands (I am a bookdealer and I spend a lot of time among old books) or you can fiercely pursue a gleam of understanding through a labyrinth of bibliography (I have one of the biggest libraries in Britain on my doorstep here). I don't either set up my own canon or subscribe to an institutional one, though I have what I call my "bearings." I'm not interested in a philosophical consistency which derives from following particular developments; I'd rather such material were spread out before me and stirred in with completely different things. I value the philosopher Alasdair MacIntyre for instance, though I never got through a whole book, but I don't think he lies "behind" anything I ever wrote; in fact I'm probably interested in him as a result of my own work, because of what's happened to my mind through all that writing. There's a kind of balanced, grounded fervour to what he does. I like to think in terms of a craft, fervently pursued but within the obtaining conditions. Knowing working musicians such as Derek Bailey or Ioan Pop has made a bigger difference, probably, to my attitudes to writing than anything I've read.

And I now like to think of that devoluted condition spread right across all the topics you prod in this question. A lot of people of my generation (especially if they come from the kind of place I came from) have probably been through all that alienation and the resulting hesitation and ambivalence, worrying about authenticity under the pressure of conformity, struggling to avoid the boredom of unproductive labour. I lived the first five years of my life through urban bombing raids aimed at centres of industrial production. That gives you a strong sense of both belonging somewhere and needing an exit. My experience has been to go on like that really, seeking an optimism and a purpose in a context which seems to prioritize opportunity and disregard, which persistently sets you aside from its centre and which claims tradition while rewarding an easy novelty; and ultimately that means seeking acts of liberation from your entire context. But it's a long struggle: you get to feel very alienated from that which also defines you, you both elevate and degrade the human image, and you seek an elsewhere which you know must be located where you are. There's a lot of this kind of struggle in everyone's work since mid-century, I think, except those who operate only within short-term singularities. You have to go through this, but it's quite dangerous because you can lose touch with how the world in fact operates in an alienated dream fuelled by resentment. If you win the struggle you reduce your context to a language, and then you can step out of it, back into where you are.

I just feel now that so much sight onto the world has become available to us that, anchored to the cohering ground of a common fate, the entire contextual question is falling apart. What we live "in" has become a shifting and multiplying term. The world sheet is spreading out, our authenticity passes through the boundaries of nation, culture, language, economy, all those things which both threaten and sustain us, they are not the only things. I think what I'm saying is that we are becoming remarkably free from concepts of importance. There is increasingly somewhere else to turn to. We are on the edge of a stateless economy, and modes of thought and creation liberated from redemptive focus are opening out. We can stop leaning on that centrality, that hope of deliverance. The pressure is off.

Some people find this complexity an occasion for a reactive entrenchment in difficulty. I find it an enriching and democratizing thing. Certainly we are still stuck in the college brain-box bashing our vocabularies against ultimate questions in the dark, but we are also outside it in the towns and hills and plains where people live just as purposefully and the beasts roam the pastures freely, and that also is "us." The priorities get dispersed. Poets, as Alice Notley said yesterday, are too concerned about the future of poetry and thus about the purpose and direction of the art rather than its presence, which must be multidirectional. What once looked like a distressing splintering of the poetry situation now looks to me like its redemption, and whatever imperatives people force on it—that it *has* to be whatever: linguistically innovative, urban, deconstructive, language-centred, critical, electronic… and pressures of another kind too, about correctness and accessibility and surface emotion… all in the name of novelty, sometimes very deeply set into a currency of despair—you can turn from these, because there is somewhere to turn, there is another music round the corner. It hardly matters what your version of that fortune is. This may be pluralism, it certainly isn't relativism because there are overriding priorities. I don't any longer view the field of endeavour as a totality but as a diversity, and a wholeness. Totality is the Platonic phantom of experimental poetry. It always lets you down.

Actually a lot of the experiment, and even the theory, is very useful (and we also need anti-poetry) but I now see its producers as inhabiting workshops scattered across the land, rather than cathedrals. You go shopping for what you need. The "religious" vocabulary—soul, redemption, etc.—remains valid as indeed it remains in common parlance, while the religious structures fall into dereliction.

All this doesn't make it any easier, and it certainly doesn't eliminate the tragic narrative, in fact it reasserts it. The "everyday" or the "ordinary" is the zone that was always free of that cultural militarism anyway, it was where you were face up against the realities of survival whatever the priests said; it can only be invaded, and exploited, by ideologues, as a self-sufficient peasant society can only be invaded and exploited by the State. It is what you seek to preserve intact as a productive space.

As for John Dooley, well, I didn't invent or program him—he occurred. I often used to drive over that particular moor because the nearest supermarket was the other side of it and I passed him five times out of ten. I didn't invent any of it, not even the telephone box episode. He occurred, and he occurred to me, as a figure of what was missing from the pastoral enclosure of personal poetry. That the potential for harm is always greater than our liberal spaces allow, especially in peacetime because we tend to forget history. His sense of total loss and calm desperation actually pushed the language towards the avant-garde, struck it into a kind of dereliction, where that book left it. But anyway that's how I like to think I operate, trawling through directly known reality as it occurs. Making a form, a whole and discrete thing out of the spread and clutter of personal experience and knowledge, the more disparate the better. "Ornamental" because it does or should form this compacted entity which adheres to the world without being a structural necessity, how could it be? But completed also in the sense that the processes involved are concluded within the piece, otherwise they can't release energy. And the best, the brightest ornaments, always hold imagery of the major entities governing existence, be it God in a mosaic dome or sun and seed on a peasant gateway.

KT: Peter, I'd like to ask a few questions in connection with your reference to "nationalized space" in your reply to my second question. I am remembering remarks you made to Kelvin Corcoran in an interview some years ago. There you indicated that an "American moment" among the English poets of your generation was of fairly short duration. You also hinted at something like an oedipal anxiety that has, in your view, made many American poets altogether unable to read English poets. As you know, there are some American as well as British readers who will think that if Cambridge poets indeed turned away from American poetry, it was to their loss. I have even heard some speak of "islandism" and "insularity" as properties or agendas of a purported "Cambridge School." This is hardly meant as flattery. It suggests that you and some of your peers have something in common with poets like Donald Davie or the current poet laureate, who writes in his little book on Larkin of an "English line." I wonder if you might take a moment to discuss the extent to which ideas of "Englishness" or "Americanness" have had an impact on your work over the last decades. You will know that I find such concepts largely empty or reified; that does not of course diminish their force. What, if anything, distinguishes versions of "Englishness" in Cambridge, or should we merely jettison the term altogether? Perhaps you would be willing to elaborate a little on the history you sketched for Corcoran;

perhaps your views have changed since you made those remarks in that interview.

PR: I don't think this is a polemical issue now, if it ever was. When you're young, especially at certain periods of history, it's natural to narrow the scope as much as you can, and to go through the motions of chucking a lot of stuff overboard. Clearing a space for yourself by prioritizing what inherently promotes your progress, junking what doesn't. Some people do this deliberately and in public, blatantly furthering a career; others do it more privately or tentatively. Some people never stop doing it and if that works you end up at the centre of a cult, I suppose. In its developed form this impulse becomes a guardianship of quality which is very difficult to sustain, because you have to conceal constantly massive acts of closure. You might recall the way Ezra Pound spoke so admiringly of the ancient Far Eastern literati who trimmed the corpus to be preserved down to one percent or something, and so set up extended standards of excellence. One might have wished Pound had trimmed a few things from his own inner library. Actually the self-wreck of the Pound enterprise is for me one of the principal signs that you cannot run poetry as a substitute university, a substitute religion, a substitute politics… —if it has any right to exist it must find its own purpose, not serve as a shortcut to more rigorous and practical disciplines. The sense of "importance" has to be left out of the equation, otherwise the whole thing runs into inhumanity and waste. I've said before in print that to academic critics and inheritors of the poet-enthroned syndrome, it's essential that there be a fewness of poets otherwise they think there can't be a history. I'm interested in there being as many as possible. It doesn't mean you tolerate dullness, it just means you seek quality (and you do seek quality) without limiting its chances. In poetry as in any other realm you seek good beyond predicated categories. You find it by result and response. This is something of a hobbyhorse of mine and I have strayed from the question.

So, yes, at one time I and others (in no sense a "school") focused on certain American poetry—roughly the kinds of writing in Allen's 1960 anthology—in the hope of sighting some kind of future; I went so far as to write a thesis on Spicer. And this did represent a rejection of an "English line" though only in its recent manifestations—it rejected a poetry of urbane talk which mainly happened in the 1950s and has gone from strength to strength ever since, now to some the official poetry of the country. (That a lot of Frank O'Hara's is also a poetry of urbane talk is undeniable and there is a lot of dishonesty among the pro-modernists in glossing over affinities such as that; but the O'Hara which interests me is a metaphysical poet.)

But what we were ditching wasn't a real "English line" at all, it was really a very rebellious impulse, an anti-poetry. Those guys of the "Movement" were self-consciously in rebellion against high culture and artiness, they were flag-waving pioneers, manifesto makers, manipulators of history. They have only precarious connections with poets such as Edward Thomas or Gurney or Auden…or Ted Hughes for that matter. And at times they no doubt touched a real nerve. The success and massive official promotion of their legacy, which I see as a shallower affair, hasn't stopped it from being always a cult of newness, of which they are their own victims. Ten years later most names are forgotten.

It was in that climate that we turned to the States, and I feel that we sought one novelty to escape from another. To me it was a quest for scope, width, size, it was to do with seeking a poetry which commanded a large sense of the world, a vast lyrical/intellectual possibility. Terms of space-time and history and geological movement, renewings of legend. It emphatically wasn't to do with the wilful disabling of language, we already had that. I valued it very highly, but at some point I noticed that some of the writers I was getting this "size" from couldn't read, or cope with, the poetical size of John Milton, or Wordsworth, or even Dante. So something was wrong. Duncan was a poet who would attend to anything that had real substance, and listen to anybody who was sincere, he didn't program himself. Others pushed themselves into crackpot messianic ravings.

But America is Novelty City isn't it? I still feel as I did when Kelvin Corcoran interviewed me in 1983 (and I was talking of a completely different set of American poets then) that they exert a pressure on the rest of the world which says not so much that we're better, but that we're more advanced. Always we're ahead, and the accusation against (I don't know why particularly English) poetry not willing to subscribe (though a few do, very successfully) is indeed like a death-wish against the parent. It sets you back as finished, outmoded, "insular," not part of the present tense or the present world. But who sets that agenda, actually, but the poets themselves?

And why should "American" be the only alternative to an insular "English"? What happened to the rest of the world? What happened to Australia for instance, where alienation seems to be less drastically cut through artistic endeavour? Or all the English-language poetry of India and Africa? I find one of the most hopeful areas is poetical writing from the war zones of the Near East, Lebanon, Palestine, Syria…such as I can get at it (in French). Modern realities engaged to a peasant cosmology. And anyway literary America is itself a much bigger and more varied proposition than the Paris–New York poetical mafia. And isn't historical time itself another vast extent, even in a very small place? And the reach that opens out when you cut through the exclusiveness of a culture prioritizing the metropolitan power-base, is another.

But England isn't a line it's a place, and that's all you're entitled to love really, a sense of settlement, which could be anywhere. It's obvious enough the way the word "heritage" is thrown around these days that the comforts of historical belonging are reserved for the very rich or the very mortgaged. To me that implicates a concealment of historical reality. But so does that blinkered modernism which would rather die than enter a medieval church to look at a beautifully carved tomb. I believe, you see, that a thing like poetry embellishes the place in which it occurs, rather than offers a critique; but how do you get to identify that place, how do you distinguish it from nation or class or theatre?—to me it is a quite mysterious location which I prefer not to call England, where the most remote provincial particular and a central accumulated resource inhabit each other. A construct, but grounded, a real place sighted at the edges of the notional place. It's easy to say all this but to perform it so that anyone else can recognize it is a different matter. My only recourse is to seek fictive experiential authenticities that set language vibrating. Or just go at it with a will.

KT: I want to bring the abstractions of my last question down to some more manageable and particular level. Just the other day I was reading your poem "Do It Again" in *Author*. There you set several lines that I take to be your own between an arrangement of words from a famous Beach Boys song:

> It's automatic when I
> Talk to old friends the
> Conversation turns to
> Girls we knew when their
> Hair was soft and
>
> whiter than star
> heavier than sea

> death white as glass
> pass over me
>
> Well I've been thinking bout
> All the places All the faces we
> Missed and then

I can imagine someone wanting to read this poem by trying to make sense of the way it juxtaposes American pop culture and a language that seems self-consciously "other" to it—lyric fragments in the high style let's call them. I know that your work often moves between registers and perhaps you do not often enough get credit for some of the comic effects produced by such movement. But here I can imagine that some readers will find you pretty far from the comic. Maybe they will think "Beach Boys songs are American popular music known worldwide, part of an American culture busy mixing with or even obliterating the particularity of the 'places' and artistic practices of the world. Riley's citation is deeply ironic; the 'real' Riley can be found in what interrupts the Beach Boys here." Would such a reader be on the right track?

PR: This depends how you read. I think I read poetry more as a particularity than a lot of people do. I don't read the Beach Boys' words as signs or representatives (of American/popular culture, or whatever), I don't figure them as ambassadors of anything larger than what they are. I read them as something which just comes along, and there's nothing you can do about it—you can't avoid it. You don't take an interest in that kind of music but it reaches you whether you like it or not, and you're stuck with it. You may indeed think its power is excessive and associate it with the Americanization of the world, but if so too bad, you can't help responding to it. I also read the quotation as something that says what it says. The whole sequence is about aging. I interrupt it because it's not saying enough.

KT: I'd like to ask some questions about two of my own favourite books of yours, beginning with *Snow Has Settled [. . . .] Bury Me Here*. I've been pondering this book as a sequence, thinking about its shape, and wonder if you might comment on that. I know that when I first read it I was periodically fascinated by the way the movement between or across poems seemed at times propelled by word-play, by rhyme as much as by discourse, as for instance when the ending of "Great Eastern" ("All right, / Opening to the earth at a guess of its plight") becomes in the next poem's opening "The earth's plight is also our delight / Lost in it, brushed awry by the night...." But I know too that the sequence has fundamental concerns not too different from those present in much of your work, the possibility of "acts of trust" as one poem puts it, or the possibility of thinking that "the mind's track on / soul-light is instrumental to the earth's / equilibrium" as the next one has it. But when I came to the last poem in the book, "Grand Hôtel du Square," I was just a bit surprised. What surprised me was the reference to "the modern state." For it seemed to me that until that point in the book the question of trust or of an ethics of "care" had been kept a little remote from specific historical circumstances, despite the book's focus on particular places. I know that there is speculation about postwar life earlier and that the Paris sequence has a poem for Baudelaire addressing him as follows: "The vertical fantasie of state O my lost brother!" And I might also have been prepared for your ending by "Causeway's" lines "My lapses from care / Are a perpetual night surrounding my mind"; I remember thinking that this was an overtly ethical and civic extension of Catullus's "nox est perpetua una dormienda"—a line most familiar to me from its adaptation in Bunting's *Briggflatts* ("For love uninterrupted night"). But in much of the book prior to the Paris poems the nation is, as one poem has it, "the nation / Of sheer being." So coming to the final poem I couldn't avoid feeling something like "Well this is what all the fuss is about then; here it is all of it finally said, all of the despair hope would lift." What had before been a fairly mysterious knock on the door turns out to be shouting in the streets and somebody being carted off to a death camp. In your note you offer pride of place to Atget's photograph of a street-singer in Paris, and the final poem has him singing against "necessity's blind chaconne." All of this is a roundabout way of asking you about that last poem and how or if it is meant to offer some kind of shape to the book, and what that shape might be.

PR: I think you're right to be surprised that the last group of poems doesn't conclude the book within the mode (transcendental, some might call it, or pastoral) which has prevailed. Rather than summating the book they tend to turn elsewhere and, the last one especially, bring all that ecstasis down to circumstance. But *bringing-down* from various mental constructs is to me precisely one of the principal functions of the movement in poems, undercutting both your own claims and those you find in the air around you, referring back to the acknowledged real however small (or unbearably big) it might become.

Because it's almost all we have. The trouble with "Grand Hôtel du Square" is actually that it doesn't do that enough, and rests too much on a sense of election. My claim for it is that it has an envoi-like function to the book, slightly like an epilogistic unmasking, revealing more of a person behind the poetry, rather ploddingly attempting to weave hope out of a dull solitude. I was so pleased that Tony Frazer managed to get that picture by Atget onto the back cover, it's such a good sequel to the poem. That remote detail of a Parisian street circa 1910, so beautifully structured, is the reality which the whole book is brought to focus on at the end, when it's read through the last poem (rather like the end of *Lines on the Liver*) and which also, to me, reinstates the lyrical daze. The woman is the singer by the way. Did you notice how their hands touch? I think the organ-grinder probably is blind.

The ordering of poems in that book was largely an attempt to avoid sequence. There has been so much stress on it, and the larger or connected construct isn't necessarily any more valuable. The quite casual sequential "arrangement" of a book like *Lustra* is a fresher act. *Snow Has Settled* is arranged chronologically, so that any connectivity or sequence there is is because it all comes from the unity and continuity of one person. Except that the poems are in groups (the sectioning of the contents page gives the groupings). Echoic progressions occur mainly within those groups. I tend to use that as a generative technique. A sense that more, or a countermovement, needs to be launched, is tackled by repetition (taking the material, site or memory on board again) or by perverting a phonetic pattern to something else, making an echoed phrase point another way. This kind of talk makes it all sound so important, but people do these things constantly in conversation and articulate thought, or while reading. So many of the so-called skills of poetry are common mental acts for the sake of presence and understanding, including those reaches the mind makes through images, which don't have a discursive function but are important definers of our condition and invite us towards possibilities that lie beyond any established discursive field. Or indeed are necessary halts to and deniers of discourse, tokens of the indolence we also survive by.

So, elements that recur through a book like this aren't structures but are more like things which I have been unable to escape from or resolve over the period, about twenty years, in which those pieces were written. So they return, like people returning. And various strategies are tried, to make them welcome or to get rid of them. And naturally major problematic terms, for me or anyone, like "state" and "care," will feature as revenants like this, in books and across books and across different poets' books and across from poetry to other things. Which is a reason I like to think of poetry as something which is able to cohabit with other discourses, if it can establish the right to stand beside them, which at present would be difficult.

So these terms keep popping up and actually, that little three-line poem "Causeway" which was mainly a bitter jibe against experimental poetry and the amount of my life and others' lives it has wasted and distracted, a little thing like that can just crunch on a major term and clinch it with a gesture of obviousness. Not by condensation, as if we inhabit a scarcity economy. Without saying anything really, because in the end it is a drama, a staged act. The drama is fragmented these days, but mostly it still is one.

KT: I see now in looking again at *Distant Points*, which has the first two books in your ongoing *Excavations* sequence, that there's a reference on page 24 to "hope wrought across transport in the occulted rhythm where the nation evades the state." Let that reference function here as my own transition between *Snow Has Settled* and *Excavations*, sequences that, formally at least, seem different, the latter of course having the appearance anyway of prose and being a little more open to modernist fragmentation and juxtaposition within its sections. You might comment on any of that if you'd like, but it's somewhere else in particular I'd like to push you with regard to *Excavations*. I'd like to hear you say something about your use of the found and treated text there—not only the Mortimer and Greenwell but also, say, the Renaissance lyric or song. Now there's a rumour afoot that much of what sounds like Renaissance lyric in the sequence is actually Peter Riley. Then there's also the occasional moment when the purportedly cited text seems to have a comic function—I don't think you get enough credit for puns and such in general—as when on page 28 you write "Every step I take is on the soles of your feet," which I can't help hearing Sting behind. Having looked at the Mortimer some, I know that his massive text is used in an idiosyncratic way too, so that what appear by virtue of italics and such to be boundaries between incorporated text and your own writing are actually quite fluid: Mortimer's own tropes are picked up here and there. But in my most recent reading of the poem I was more struck by how often what you pick up from Mortimer has to do with direction, the way the bones are positioned. I'd like to ask you about that in particular, about what the point is regarding disposition of the bones and other materials in the gravesites. To toss just one more issue into this heap of observations designed to provoke some commentary I want to quote something from Andrew Duncan's essay on London and Cambridge in *Angel Exhaust* 8. I don't know whether he had you in mind when, mentioning the Cambridge school of archaeology (Ian Hodder and Mike Parker-Pearson) he wrote of an interest among Cambridge-based poets in "psychic and cultural trash" and "the subsoil as the ruins of Time." (He names only Out to Lunch.) Here's a passage from Duncan's essay that might be worth pondering beside your interest in the contents of the prehistoric graves as catalogued by the Victorians: "The distinction between pits with animal bones (kitchen refuse) and other pits with human bones (religious & hallowed ground) [is] not necessarily observed." I wonder if that blurring of the everyday and the religious pertains in this case, and if so if you have any interest in it.

PR: *Excavations* arose from a very long and detailed study of a subject which was obviously going to yield nothing because it was just too far away and would echo back only one's own ignorance and inarticulacy. The archaeological interest had always been there, long before any Cambridge school, I've studied it since I was a child, and for me it slotted straight into the quest for an expanded poetic in the 1960s, the possibilities of a researched poetry participating in an expanding sense of where and what you are, or a much larger sense of what was sayable. This prehistoric aspect of it was always bound up with those antediluvian neuroses which we can't seem to free ourselves from, through the seventeenth century, Blake, Ruskin, all kinds of modern versions, Pound, Olson…always trying to get "behind" some historical point to a primal integrity…which is some more or less vacuous dream of course, or an inflation of the self as agent of recovery. Always refusing to take into account the demographic facts integral to that perceived "wholeness" in a predivided vision. My project brings that to its ultimate, its absurdity, you apply yourself to the furthest away you can get, the furthest behind anything, where there's virtually nothing left, which says nothing to you except a few tantalizing particles dragged up from the soil. "Modernist fragmentation" is merely a useful handle on a condition which imposes itself anyway, making the whole dramatic projection possible because in that history I can begin to suppose people willing to read it. So it's not a matter of dreaming the self into a modern visionary capacity to tackle an ancient or mythological entity, but of drawing on techniques projecting uncertainty and inarticulacy to tackle an irrevocable negative, which nevertheless still concerns what we are and have been. Because… Because because. Why because? I don't know. Because it's there, because you can't just have the world as a present given, it's not made that way, there's always something else, lost, destroyed, pulverized, spoken and perished four thousand years ago, which makes a kind of edge to what we are. And as Jeremy Prynne said, "Only at the edge does it chime…" (or was that shine? it doesn't matter), which is true, as I take it not in the sense of the broken middle, and I don't believe in the multiple worlds theories or Beckett's rather dishonest fringe essentiality… but only from the edge does any wholeness become contemplatable and achieve reverberation. Like the meanest image, like a single grass-blade, seen as something on the very verge of nonentity.

The sixteenth- and seventeenth-century lyrics got in because, I suppose (and I don't know, they just started sprouting up like budgerigar seed on a waste dump producing African violets) there was a vacuum between me and this recalcitrant material which needed filling. Because I wanted this contemplation of utter remoteness and concealment to read as a normality, like the way we have bits and pieces of songs, always, floating round in our heads, fractions of sung language, or of poetry itself, odd phrases and half-lines, which descend on us when we need them or when we don't, but are in a sense most of what we've got from our "culture." That particular period predominates (though there are many others) because it felt like a middle placement between here-now and the prehistoric nowhere, like something we half have. And I valued the obsessive melancholic focus on love-loss in those songs, as an edge of refusal against human will and desire.

As for authenticity, almost all those verbal units are either quoted or remembered, and sometimes the misremembered version was preferred. But it was very important to retain the original orthography, these things had to show their age as part of the whole structure, where the most intimate or immediate thing is also remote and untouchable, buried in time. Unfortunately it wasn't always available to me, especially with words taken from madrigals, you just can't get at unmodernized texts of madrigals, so sometimes I had to invent it from my familiarity with the orthographical habits of the period.

Not so different from ordinary poetry anyway. I mean poetry isn't just to do with being highly intelligent and knowing what's happening in the world and using every word at its maximum. It's also to do with being stupid and getting it wrong and not knowing what to do with a word, being defeated by it. It's also where you take a word and turn it this way and that and try it one way and then another in the hope it will show its true worth. Particularly, as you picked out in the previous question, the terms for the human communality and its occupation of earth-space: nation, state, community, country, land, territory... These words get pasted up into the construct as the question marks they have become. Or they are risked in a bid for positive meaning but subject to contradiction or revision elsewhere in the text. My only allowance to "difficulty" these days is to let a thing occur in a text like *Excavations* as a partial, unfinished or ununderstood thing which is retained in the text's mind and completed or extended or revised on another occasion, in a different picture.

This kind of progression by trepidation is always there but *Excavations* stresses that side of things: it entertains conditions where you find yourself not saying what you think you meant and also find yourself saying things you don't understand at all, because you're caught up in the theatre of it, which is a trusting to a poetical instinct or something.

Like that material about direction, the cardinal points. Even the earliest reports are full of it, they seem instinctively to have realized that it was important: which way the body was made to face both locally and terrestrially. And there's plenty you can read about it in anthropological literature, about the direction of the land of the dead in relation to migration for instance. But I just let it be there, I slotted such details in where they seemed unobtrusive and let the repetition of them in writing and reading build up its own signification to the point where, somewhere or other, I more or less say what has become obvious: that the east–west tensions concern living and dying, beginning continuing and ending, settlement and economy, whereas the north–south tensions concern something else, like possibility and impossibility, comfort and hurt, politics, science, hope and despair... And these cardinal tensions are still there, translate them as you will.

Otherwise, there is a theory behind *Excavations*—briefly, that the tumulus grave in the period when burial first became individual was a site of communal observance and graphic representation handled by those with the know-how, which expressed in semipermanent form through a variety of materials most of them now lost, the end state and result of the individual's life almost diagrammatically, both in particular and as participation in a history. I think that some of them are the way they are because the person in question had qualities demanding these projections; but in others the tumulus ritual was simply needed, for historical reasons we cannot even guess at, and maybe the next person to die served, even if it were a baby. I can't know this and in supposing it I don't want to fall into the antediluvian dream-pool again, so that too is broken and scattered into the text, and I also speak from amazed incomprehension or even fear of what those things might mean.

But I'm no expert on *Excavations*. That's the kind of thing it is.

KT: Okay, Peter, I'll give you a break from my long-winded questions about your books. What I want to know here concerns Nicholas Moore. I've read what you've written about his work—its great variety for instance—and about the man. What I want to know is how Moore's work has informed your own poetic practice.

PR: It was my only real encounter with poetry of the pre-academic era.

(I think that's my answer to that question. I can't think of anything else to say. Except that if I imply a freedom from interference there, as I do, I also imply a quite appalling lack of support. A proud man, a craftsman, living in awful circumstances, his life-work crushed by the whims of an alien power structure on which we are thank God no longer dependent: the poetry book market, official culture, all those experts, all that vaunted success. But at the same time free, free to write what he needed to in the full range of an acknowledged modern poetry. And that freedom and professionalism is there in the very syllabic detail of everything he wrote.

It wasn't so much the intrusion of the academy into current poetry, interference by interpretation becoming prescription; though there has been that. It was when the poets all stood up and said, "Hey, we're intellectuals too! We know all about Derrida and all that stuff, we're just like you…!" Or otherwise began to write as someone else said was necessary. That was what really wrapped the art in briars. I contest that all the time, and its contrary.)

Well, poor old Moore. It made me feel that all the stuff about importance, all that "leading poet" blather, whether it comes from the academies or the poetry newspapers or the inordinate soul itself, all that discrimination, all that favouring, of which the poetry world is crammed full—it's just another and rather subtle way of exercising the human capacity for cruelty. And I think it knows it is.

LLŶN IN THE RAIN,
SEPTEMBER 1998

Peter Riley

1) Over two mountain passes to meet up with Barny at Blenau Ffestiniog station. Already it's raining. *For Sale* signs all over the town. I think we have uncovered the depopulating source of the Eastern England house-price boom. Indeed Barny's been round the town's estate agents pretending to be interested in properties, and says they're almost being given away. But who wants to buy a corner shop for ten thousand, live here surrounded by dereliction and go barking mad in a town with a miniature railway running through its centre? Old slate quarries looming over the houses, the books in the bookshop all damp, the tired pastries in the bakers' windows. Later we learn how these places return to their true identity in bad weather, but as yet it is dull and depressing. We get through to Mrs Jones from a 'phone box: yes, it's all right to go straight there and arrive a day early. We do the supermarket shopping (an interesting-looking beer from Warrington!) and drive off, plunging behind the town into the granite vale that opens down into Cardigan Bay at Porthmadoc.

> Rock and fibre glowing wet, brown and green,
> estuarine light blue under trees:
> a bright rail alongside—we fall between,
> buying the future an earthen dream.

2) A take-away curry from the Tandoori at Pwllheli, which is a white-washed brick shed just off the sad white rain-washed sea-front, across the road from a boarded-up beer hall. Sit there waiting for it, nodding at the staff: young Asians living out here, so far from the city communities, I wonder what that feels like. Run through the rain to the car with the wrapped curry. Which when we get to the caravan with it (a shock coming over the rise towards the farm—it's a new caravan! this is the third) is the most strangely weak, barely curry at

all, strangely sweet stew, which must be what is expected in far west Wales... but we're here. We're all here again.

> Solid cloud over land / blue-white sea
> black-tipped waves / threading back to us
> all here all busy / eating and thinking
> small in the rain / patched histories

3) Mrs Jones had a heart attack but has been all right since. So she tells us, in that cool matter-of-fact Welsh style as if talking about the price of soap. In exactly this tone she told us of her brother Geronwy's death from throat cancer eight years ago; who had been our tutor here, shyly greeting us every year, tending our spaces, naming the rocks, taking us out in the boat... No more boat. The fishing is all finished. Government licenses have become so prohibitively expensive for the one-boat farmer they have all stopped and their boats rot in coves. Kathy says the same thing happened in Mozambique at about the same time.* The sea is left to its captains. Also Mr Jones (up the road, no relation) has died: said to have been the last man who knew how to make Aberdaron-style wicker lobster-pots. We look at his small, tight, weatherproofed house and peer through the windows. The little triangular lawn with tall banks round it, the shed with the pots hanging up. Who will buy it? Young people don't want to live here any more: the '60s pastoral dream collapsed before the new hard domestic economy and its inhering conformism; the rich want their extra houses abroad; the locals have had enough: fishing prohibited, no use farming, sheep two a penny. House prices have not fallen, but they might.

> Raging apart the need and the cost
> hollow distances where the gull sits
> and laughs and the tides roar back
> small change wash hands take it.

4) Days of persistent rain. Reading books or playing chess as it beats on the metal walls. It's been like this all summer, and by September no one around at all. I've never seen the place like this. Porth Or a

---

*And at CCCP9 Robert Adamson said the same thing had happened in Australia.

big empty bay, the shop almost abandoned: two young girls in charge
of a few racks of leftovers, you can't even get a cup of tea. And every-
where you go the same quietness, raining or soon will be, Aberdaron,
Nefyn, Abersoch, a few stragglers in macks passing from newsagent
to grocery store and hurrying back to the car.

I remember going on holiday with my parents to places like
Llandudno and Rhyl, and in those days you stayed in boarding houses
which gave you breakfast and chucked you out; you weren't allowed
to return until the evening meal at six. So if it rained for the week
you'd had it, you stared at the shop windows for as long as you could,
you lingered in tearooms and amusement arcades but basically you
sat in the leesides of the sea-front shelters. You sat on a bench with
half a roof over you wrapped in coats and watched the barren sea
frothing or the shops opposite and the battered tulips inbetween un-
til it was time to go back. And this was people's only holiday, they
worked 50 weeks of the year in factories offices and shops and this
was their one annual break from it. And they spent it sitting in the
wind and the rain while the kids sulked and sucked sweets and cried.

But now it's a victory, a restoration. The rubber dragons sitting
unsellable in the corner novelty shop while the sea wind shakes the
glass door, the guides to Celtica Mystica and works of the previous
vicar dampening on the shelves, the watercolours unlooked-at, the
candy-floss machine unplugged, the luminous pinks and yellows de-
flated. It is such a relief, that the place stands so solidly there while
the season's sordidities shrivel away. Places arisen for an economic
purpose and a spiritual relief, turned into nonsense depositories. And
thank God it rains and rains until you think it can't rain any more
and then it rains again and the truth finally unwinds: there is actually
no reason to come here.

We dart about in this unreason. We nip in and out. We sit with
the shore expanse before us through the window of the hotel bar in
Aberdaron, the rolling waves rinsing the brown sand and the standard
beer in the glass. We pause before the slate tombstones the biggest
crowd seen in these parts for some time. Tea and Welsh pancakes at
Carreg Plâs under Mynned Carreg, surrounded by people talking
Welsh. Superb little salty-sweet buttery mouthfuls, and no English
earner-snobs spreading their ignorance in the air, their paid-for-it-
and-entitled, their contempt for the locals and the language. Outside,
rain sweeping the fields and no one on the paths. Bareness over all
this peninsula, but native, speaking softly to itself of the music it
lacks.

Because an alien centrality took it away and replaced it with a trade in fakes which, predictably, let everyone down when fortune's pink smile faded in the slowing of the Gulf Stream. Fair-weather traders, find something to sell that people need.

And the wind on top of Uwchmynned is magnificent, you can hardly stand up in it. The concrete road curls up to the top, you get out of the car and whirl round and the door slams, it blurts across your ears, it hisses round the corners of the coast-guard shed (closed) information centre, the heather tight to the ground vibrating in its passage and you push through it coat flapping to the top of the slope to see Bardsey before you, riding the turbulent ocean two miles off. How the true locations are still there in all the changes of weather and the prosperity badges ripped off, how the sites were made solid enough to pass by all that, and the structures that talk us into it. And us ourselves, certainly.

> Viewing the green theatre behind the rain
> knowing our little cares will increase
> year by year and the red of the petal
> and the red of the fire do nothing but gain.

And no, we shan't get to Bardsey this year either, clearly, but the time will come. The space between it and us is too full. Like the space between prosperity and purpose, full of all that weather and most of what we are, and the silence when everyone's gone away.

> Then green takes its fair shine
> we wondering what we need
> freely twine red thread on
> walking stick maybe the last time.

5) Porth y Nant under rain, the deserted village rebuilt as a Welsh language centre, and with a café, which even has a few people in it, staring out at wet slopes through steamed-up window, macks dripping onto floor. Signs have sprouted everywhere like mushrooms: *For Sale* in the towns, *Keep Off* at the edges of the land, and there is no one to keep off, and nothing to keep them off. *Private* in front of a bracken-coated cliff, and big red *Danger / Keep Out* all over the remains of the gravel works on the shore and the quarries further on. Institutions protecting themselves from claims, worried before the privatization of law, plastering warning messages on everything in sight.

Later walking alone up the cliff steps at the south end of the bay because I want to photograph an old farmhouse I remember on the top pastures, the rain really comes on. The stone steps in the cliff, which the workers made for themselves to get down to the gravel loading bays, are little cascades. On the top the wind drives the rain hard against me from landward, it soaks my trouser legs and gets down my neck front and back and into my shoes. I pass that strange wooden dwelling like a cricket pavilion which I'd almost forgotten, and which does look lived-in, but the stone house is silent as ever, sitting there on a shelf of the sloping pastures. In rain or sunshine, the waiting house stands its ground. Standard Welsh thick-walled small farmhouse, two storey with central porch and slate roof, furnished and curtained but never anyone there, exactly the same for twenty years. So the family, somewhere, that owns it remains elsewhere, and the fact that this is one of the few houses without a *For Sale* sign means they at least survive, whatever they are for good or ill they haven't been dispersed or eradicated by death and change. I stand in front of a house which is a kind of sign saying "We continue" and take a photograph of it.

And walk behind it across the fields to the clifftop and back down the diagonal path across the face, another workers' route, to the north end of the bay again. Stone sills over red mud. A buzzard hovering over the cliffs, and two choughs on the beams of the derelict quarry house. A mountain goat noticed high up the cliff through the café windows. A lot of seals around, one usually appears whenever we get down to the sea, and two regulars in the left cove at the farm. And there was a raven behind us at Porth Ceriad, the first I've ever seen — this noise from the cliff like an irascible and bronchitic old woman approaching an adversary and there was the great black bird. People moving in as people move out.

> People moving on, people turning,
> rooks circling the green pastures spotted
> with bright red sores / armies of remorse,
> protect us also from armies of single cause.

6) Let the rain do its worst, we perform the whole routine, we shirk none of it. We do the full Morfa Nefyn sequence first established circa 1983: drive there (along the coastal tract south of Nefyn which is one of my strongest images of this terrain: the land coming down from the central ridge and striped with stone-walled fields rebound-

ing in a gentle wave before stopping suddenly at the cliff edge, the light always taking it horizontally—a great scroll of land up the coast…), get the fish and chips (the F&C shop itself is for sale! this really could be the Last Time) and take them down to the sands to eat on the boulders, dump the paper in the same green oilcan provided for such purpose for the last fifteen years and then walk over the wetness a mile to Porth Dinllaen. Low tide, we pass close under the stilt houses, some of them showing signs of habitation, mostly not. And the quietness that's everywhere has settled here too: no one in the pub, a boy in leopard-hair serving. Then walk on, the little shore-side path along the edge of the headland. The wooden hut in the cliff niche, still there, someone still getting there maybe a week a year and keeping it going, bottle of washing-up liquid on side window-ledge. Somehow people keeping a few things going as desertion settles round them like rain. And on past the lifeboat station to sit on the cliff-edge of the golf course no golfers and watch the seals coming to roost out there on the rocks. And they do, again.

And in our hearts we shout over to them, "Hey, seals, remember us? You haven't seen us for four years now but we always came here. And you were here in those days, seals, we watched you and waved at you out there on the rocky pinnacles, your home for the night. Every year we came here since the baby was born, eighteen years and now the twenty-second. How you getting on, seals? It looks good, there's more of you than ever. Big ones and little ones, rolling about on the sharp rock needles with nothing but seaweed to comfort your hides. Snorting and puffing and calming down as the light goes. And being there, at rest on a known point, being there tonight again. We think it's a great achievement, seals. Can you hear me? We think it's the answer."

> Don't forget you were once a newly born baby
> as helpless as a seal on a rock just
> rolling around while war effort flew
> green and red banners over the entire city.

7) Reading books or playing scrabble while the water hurls itself at the thin walls and the whole edifice shakes slightly. The few sheep in the field outside looking perfectly happy about it all, just standing still in the rain. They have names: Peter and Emma, two hand-reared lambs who run up to you if you enter their field. Two friends, two siblings… Two notions of what's happening in the world, birth-

joined in a hatred of injustice, but rigorously opposed to each other.
The buyers and the sellers.

Sharpness of the tannin against the sweetness of the sucrose. A
balance, a conflict taking place between them which generates the
tension on which the song is sung. It is rare to find a good bottle of
wine in far west Wales, or a curry for that matter. But out here we can
easily do without these habitual conflicts and look around again at
our victory, hidden behind the pouring rain.

> Only the song stands high to see
> on stones of the yard on the message wire
> stands and calls, brushes water from coat,
> everything said returns to the throat.
>
> Making there its nest, red cell cluster that
> closes the light and leaves the land
> quiet under vast rain vast under spread pain
> lapping the edges of a modern caravan again.
>
> Later it won't matter what these words mean
> in the light of what these words seem a cat
> on a wall a rook on a wire a sheep in a field a
> hope lost in the pink world home to its believer.
>
> And the long land with white houses proposes
> a symmetry to your warring poses and the answer lies
> all round you. A little flock of some little bird or other
> over the rain beaten bushes flares and falls together.
>
> Do so and melt. *Zerschmiltz, du felsenhartes Hertze!*
> Everything said runs back to the throat, and
> works there a form of gain. A security brighter
> than the fields, and harder than the rain.
>
> A solitude which is gained, a safety in a shortness
> of time, curved to the sky and turning round and
> round again a chaconne which we bird voices
> trill over in flight, settling to the bar of night.
>
> A solitary night together, all of us. Towards
> the end of which a passing luminous creature
> spreads a call over the roof concerning death that cause
> of fear. Wrapped in distance we count it ever more dear.

ON *LINES ON THE LIVER* AND *TRACKS AND MINESHAFTS*

❧

John Hall

I am constantly bugged by something I think I'm supposed to be saying: the philosophy of poetry or the joys of wisdom or the truth that snaps the world back into place. Where is it? It's easy enough to focus on nothing like a missing pilot and set absence into the text just to have it there before us, newly reflective; but you are elsewhere and it's very uncertain that something human is actually there at the end of this dispersed line wanting or waiting for anything on earth. Surely the fire is getting low; if we don't signal our love there will be no reason for dying. I turn to the simple sky-trapped animal, the *looke in thy heart and write*, bit. Plentiful and expensive. The heart, of course, is a nonexistent book in which we read the education of the world. The Adventures of Bugs Hunter. What rubbish. *I am not I, pitie the tale of me.*

From (v) of "Eight Preludes," Tracks and Mineshafts

I can only begin to give an account of my reading of these texts: my own reading so frequently contradicts itself and the texts are themselves so self-knowing that they accommodate into themselves a number of contradictory self-readings: they acknowledge both the inadequacy of saying and deal as a recurring concern with the inadequacy of the need to say.

I am not in my attentions going to distinguish between the two main texts for I am more interested in the voices and preoccupations that connect them. In particular I find myself responding to a gathering dependence on prose, to the way that layers of prose are made the home of an errant poetic: under the guise even of explication a

This review of *Lines on the Liver* (London: Ferry, 1981), *Tracks and Mineshafts* and *Two Essays* (both Matlock: Grosseteste, 1983) first appeared, untitled, in *The Many Review* 2 (Spring 1984), pp. 12–18. Many thanks to John Hall and to John Welch, editor of *The Many Review*, for permission to reprint it.

prose attaches an intentionality to an abstract image of "the self" that the poems then try to outwit.

Lines on the Liver begins with nineteen pages of prose, by the "Self-lecturer" who is also author of the thirty poems that follow. The variations that end the book are preceded by two pages of prose descriptions and contextualization. *Tracks and Mineshafts* includes many prose passages (like the one quoted above) and one long prose sequence and comes with a sibling prose text "published to elucidate some of the imagery of the poems in *Tracks and Mineshafts*," which are further self-lectures, extensions of the primary metaphors of mining and dreaming that confirm that Peter Riley is dealing with knowledge and its informations, not with mining but with readings and dreaming of mining, and with living that knowledge and those dreams so that the miner becomes a figure of the self, economically, ontologically—an economic function embedded in all human purposes and equivalent to those other individualized metaphors of the self, the hunter, the gatherer, the pastoralist, the cultivator.

I don't want to engage in the detail of these prose explications but nor do I want to brush them aside as distractions from the "poetry." I want instead to try to respond to their purpose and language as part of the substance of contradictory desires that I find to *be* these texts. For despite the wish to have a world, there, despite any speaking of it, there is also a wish to talk a world into being. Around the corner of each utterance is not any kind of silence, but the poet talking, talking, self-lecturing. And just as the reading that meets it is a lonely reading—no one in my daily life talks to me about the latest Peter Riley text—this is a lonely writing that knows its own urgency from within and has lost any easeful nonchalance about the political vacuousness into which it might place itself.

There is a fact of our lives that these writings are helpless within: that we may recognize the desire that is us, that we may find a speech inseparable from the forms and substance of this desire, but that this sensed power is not returned to us in the confirmations of social power; it is all source, and solipsism and desperation. For example I have just used a "we" that universalizes a fundamental phenomenological self. *Lines on the Liver* and *Tracks and Mineshafts* are writings caught up in a sense of the writer's destiny to be in the fullest imaginable sense "a person," and in the paradox too that this destiny to be a full person moves within a language that makes of the pronoun "we" a despairing term, one that has to deflect a whole series of collective meanings.

In the first place there are the simpler versions of "we," two homophonic pronouns, semantically and existentially intertwined: the "I" who desires and the "I" who knows what it is (he) desires; the one on whom the light falls when it does, the one who digs for it. These are two identities, contradictory, dialectical. They correspond to two other first pronoun uses, both singular and plural. There is the everyday self, the one who is domestic and is more or less employed, who moves house and gets overtaken by the owners of faster cars. This domestic "we" is often present, especially in the "poems," and where present is often threatened, guarded, cryptic in the way that the namelessness of pronouns allows. Where the other language of the self, with its primary metaphors of economics and spirituality (both manifestations of *essential value*), deals in a notion of "home," these domestic people live in a house with windows, bookshelves, wallhangings, a telephone and a car outside in which to go to work. And in this domestic economy desires get in each other's way. So this is an "I" and a "we" caught up in contingency, each move provisional, hopes in transcendence ironically modified by the desperation of circumstance. The voice is colloquial, talkative, occasionally capable of expletive. Within a larger linguistic space that relies on magniloquence, that hopes for so much from metaphor, there is a voice that can be sarcastically antimetaphoric, "down-to-earth."

The second identity, already implied, is the plural form of the person assiduously involved in the rhetorical transactions of metaphor, in transformations willed by desire—by love, hope, belief, lack. It is not a contingent "I" but "the self," the very type of human consciousness. This figure shifts around too. Sometimes it is a collective sense coinciding with the idea of "the town" as a specific social and emotional forcefield within the landform, as extended *home*, a specific community lived from within rather than sociologically describable; or it might be the human figure implied by an archaic term like "the plain" or an understanding of humans in which geology is socially incarnate. As I say the figure slips around and usually the speaking voice is outside any social gathering, is implicated only in the sources of behaviour, not necessarily in the mannerisms. At any moment this "we" can either be caught up in history or transcend it.

I think that there is always in these texts this contradictory, paradoxical duplicity of identity: the historical "we," Western, postindustrial, living out the technology of mass-production and massreproduction, not so much victim of capitalism as accomplice through and through. This "we" is in all the nets of power—not only technology but geology too, as though the technology were absolutely determined by geology so that "we" are "used" by metal and its "exhaustion."

The other is of course the pure figure of human possibility, desiring, dreaming. And of course I do not speak as if I have caught Peter Riley out in some way. "We" are all these "we's" and to keep them all in play without abandoning the possibilities of utterance to an absence of intention, to claim and to disclaim, to reach for love without denying circumstance—well, these are very considerable achievements, are records of a battle with the angel of language that most wouldn't have dared begin. His moves are more or less as follows:

The angel drives him into the homiletic. He becomes the lonely wayside preacher.

The angel drives his attentions down chthonically, below the surfaces open to perception into the tunnellings open only to specific experience, knowledge, dreams. The poet's knowledge mediates dreams of the underworld and the miners' labour becomes merely emblematic: the true labour here is metaphoric.

The angel suggests that a wished-for world can inhere in an unwished language.

The angel insists on his writing as a social attention burdened with responsibility for the future.

The angel suggests that in play the signifiers of language can turn away from their responsibility for the future without sarcasm.

The angel's last play: to outwit the Law, which is Language and Knowledge, there is only Language and Knowledge.

There is nothing to be except clumsy in the face of what he tries to take on because he is not interested in a manner of stoic elegance but wishes instead to write his way through every move, through the whole net, and through it all, despite everything, runs the hope of a redemptive power of (a notion of) selfhood and language. As so often when there is the idea of "self" at work, there is a strong and consistent metaphor of redemption, with its implied loss or failure—that gap that pertains to desire rather than an easily redeemable lack— and also there is that familiar questing self, burrowing it seems into otherhood out of sheer ontological destiny. In some strange way what "the self" tries to redeem is an irredeemable economic and social loss, so the discursive task is experienced like that of Sisyphus.

And this is the desperation I find in these texts. I find in them an unhappiness, but more than that they deal with an experience that is of its nature incomplete without grace and yet is dogged by a refusal to accept the conditions of a grace. How to act, how to be in the world: these questions are obsessive. Loss is seen to pervade the material world: relationships and employment are contingent destinies, haunted by inadequacy; materialist politics are seen to evade the profound metaphoric verities of the self. There is only one place to get it right and that is "the person" and it is perception itself which must be right since desire joins, is joined by, perception to all other behaviour. But perception opens onto a world conditional on language and history: history has lost nearly everything; there is no prelapsarian self set apart and rescuable from history. So the world is loved and not loved and the self cannot disclaim the world or seek through power to change it. Grace which is necessary is impossible.

I put this too simple-mindedly, I know, but I want to get at what troubles me and to put simple-mindedly what has its formal substance in a particular archaic rhetoric which is to be found often in the prose. I do not doubt for a moment that perception and shared mental images in the form of collective metaphors are of ethical importance but when this becomes the basis for a hesitant self-contradictory and doomed transcendentalism I am worried. What is at stake is as usual what poetry or writing can offer, how attentions within the language can work ethically as well as aesthetically. These are texts of strong ethical intention which keep, on the very point of political clarity, reverting to a psychic theology of original sin. Between the person and "the world" there are only just perceptibly the mediations of culture. Although the poet can use a dismissive and despairing tongue about "motor-way communities" and "the stupid hordes," which places a commentating self somewhere outside the dialectic, he insists that the "self" is implicated, that what is desperate in culture can only work by finding its original permissions in selfhood.

This is fine. Of course there is no pristine and potentially "whole" self outside culture. But apart from the notions of "the world" (how this word recurs!) and "alteriority," both of which weight everything in favour of the isolated perceiving, desiring and knowing being—because they belong to it—there is nothing to offer as second term in a social and economic dialectic in which the configurations of power might be considered. What could the mechanism of such a transformation as that stated in the following be? "Every human act genetically modifies the species, since it is only at the new point (of access and departure) that we gain our formal existence, and the moment is absolutely decisive in the future of the world and the fate of its bearers." The "act" for a writer, the doing, is the written production of language to meet the force of occasion. Is it just hope to say that "the world" returns this act, enfolding the person who writes? Who does? A sense of an economics of language or of labour, in which each act acts on another and responds to the acts of all the others, moves in and out of metaphor, which is another sense of determinism leaving the *world* open to the acts of the *person*. The miner is of course one such economic metaphor; but also more loosely, less tied to such a specific form of labour, throughout the texts is a string of rhetorical figures having to do both with material commerce and the commerce of the soul (gain, profit, loss, coinage / furtherance, redemption, salvation, loss). The very possibility of there being a *false* language relates to these figures as something like counterfeit notes and coins.*

We are told in *Lines on the Liver* that all this "might look like a theory of election but isn't." It isn't, only because all are elected (or doomed) in the face of the universal destiny of selfhood—death— or in the face of the aim of all labour which is "for the speedier decay of nature."

And yet despite the disclaimer—and the reason why there needs to be a disclaimer—there continues to be a feeling that there *has to be* a redemptive behaviour; that although it might be "our" destiny to be "used" by fossil fuels in a kind of inverted humanism there is a way of living with destiny, of attaining an anonymous presence in the world, in which as it were the desires of the self can become contiguous with natural *light*, that might constitute a salvation. "Light" is a very important term, particularly in *Tracks and Mineshafts*, and is one of a number which link these pieces back into an earlier (Christian) tradition of spiritual exercises and battles with meaning. It wants to be a theory of election and is but isn't because it also has theoretical and temperamental reasons why it can't be. Whatever it is it is given to language and is allowed to take place there.

P.S. Anyone who has tried to write about texts that are humanly and linguistically complex knows the frustrations. In order not to shower on a second set of readers the radiating fragments of a fragmented reading, in order not to reconstruct the confusion and half-ignorance of the going, the pleasures and distractions of the ear, I have ended up with a partial reading. Of course. But I want to say so. And to register that in this piece I have lost my first response to *Lines on the Liver*, which now that I register it remains important, which was excitement about how right that book seemed to be, how wise it was about living in England now and how welcome that was, given the scarcity of things in any form that gave me that.

September 1983

* *A note to the paragraph starting "This is fine…"*

Our attentive editor [John Welch] asks me if I could clarify this paragraph and I wish I could because it is the nub: if you look for "the truth that snaps the world back into place," if what you are after is "the philosophy of poetry," where do you look? Poetry can have wisdom which is joyful and how easy it is to confuse this with the eager "philosophizing" of the self of the poet. By working in what frame analysis would presumably call a multiple frame, Peter Riley's texts hope that the two can be one. In my article I've hardly attended at all to the wisdom of the poetry but instead have listened to the "philosophy"—particularly to the terms that have been in use within phenomenology—and to the ways it is embedded in the texts as a whole. Of course in these texts the "philosophy" isn't systematic or academic; the steadily held "I" of the phenomenologist is cut into the multiple text, both into that frame that can be typified by punning where a domestic meaning dances with a play of sound, and into that wavering "I," the talkative one, who shifts about, authenticating the whole as having been experienced.

Now although the "philosophy" isn't systematic (in fact it is carried and placed within a larger structure that is literary—in a fiction it might be assigned either to a character or to the authorial voice; here it is assigned to the character of the author who has other characteristics too) the philosophical statements do imply a systematic philosophy that could be reconstructed by someone more knowing than I am. The paragraph that causes the difficulties is a far too hasty attempt to take the outlines of the philosophy and lay it over a few parts of the text that point up a mismatch. Beyond these texts, and very much within them, I am very interested in the poetic and philosophical term "world," which can be claimed as the environment for a speaking self: it can become the loosest of all generalities, the global spread and naturalizing of "otherness" (here "alteriority"). To the extent that the recent notion of selfhood implies an important dimension of the person that transcends any social, cultural or historical context, this term "world" becomes a necessary context for the self. As terms they are nothing without each other. (They belong to each other.) Anything so large is both ecstatic and deceitful as a context: of course at times a "self" will be dislocated and lonely.

Although the large term, in the quotation from *Tracks and Mineshafts*, is not "world" but "species" the statement implies a means by which the acts of the self are integrated into that larger space as more than context and it turns out that the mechanism is biological ("genetic"). Such a claim is edifying for the lonely speech of a self and without stating a mechanism it obliterates all the intermediary groupings between person and totality of a species if such a scale could be thought even to exist. This is not just a case of faulty philosophy or bad theory: it is the silencing of a writing in the desperate search for its own necessities, for as a writer a person's chief "act" is writing.

I wanted to connect to this operation — this specious connection — the second-order transformation of labour into metaphor whereby features on the economic plane can be entirely taken up into global desire; it is to do to mining what happened extensively to agricultural labour when that too was naturalized into landscape.

I am caught here: my explanation, which has become a commentary on my own words, is still far too hasty and, again, simple-minded. To expand it would be to take us into something else.

BEFORE YOU FALL:
POSTLUDE ON A PRELUDE

John Hall

This brief article starts life as a postscript to an earlier article on Peter Riley's *Lines on the Liver, Tracks and Mineshafts* and *Two Essays*, written for John Welch's *The Many Review* 2 (Spring 1984) and reprinted here. I wanted to respond to more recent writings with some of the thoughts left trailing in that article in mind.

The books I have particularly been reading are *Alstonefield* (1995) and *Snow Has Settled [....] Bury Me Here* (1997). Apart from some brief general remarks, not tied to any specific reference, my focus is going to be very narrowly on a line-by-line reading of the first poem in the second of the two books—called "Prelude"—in the belief that that very short poem offers ways of reading the two books.

Hasn't it been a feature of Peter Riley's writing that there is always some shaping urgency behind the texts—a purpose in respect of something to be known, or found out, some intuition to be pursued, some ethical quest to be undertaken? This urgency has been such, it seems to me, that no single voice—no single persona for "Peter Riley"— could carry it; nor could he live easily with what poetry all on its own might be assumed to *know*, without recourse to the knowledge frames of, for example, palaeontology, archaeology, social geography, industrial history.

He has seemed to want a writing that could be instrumental in the endless business of recovering an image of human vertue, of grace, of love. At the very least he has wanted to lend himself to struggles for disengaging harm. There are ironies in this but not at all the ironies of supposedly agency-free utterance. There is a play with first person modalities which seems to me tactical: the author allows himself to be ignorant, foolish, banal at times, like one of Chaucer's dreamers, because this is the wisdom that outwits ignorance by allowing it back in as another valid mode of knowing.

This play between personae often sets up some explicit or implied narrative, often the kind of journey that is burdened with a question—perhaps even a question which itself needs to be found rather than answered. He sets up narratives or lyric moments where the swooning limits of the phenomenal call for the linguistic strategy that Keats called negative capability. A wide-eyed literalism—grace in particulars, the pleasurable resistances of the real—runs alongside a sleepless hermeneutics, treating the world as an interpretable text. It is the movements between these that seem now to characterize Peter Riley's work.

Take "Prelude," the first poem in *Snow Has Settled [....] Bury Me Here*. The poem invokes a particular poetic (and painterly, photographic and filmic) register which finds an elegiac melancholy in the perception of landscape, a charge of affects not accountable for by the surface of particulars. This landscape is usually empty and at the same time filled with loss. Where there is human presence this is as a trace or memorial or is a figure silhouetted in the redolence of loss.

> Snow has settled in the lines

I am reading this off the page and already my ear is responding to a familiar metric, a way of both hearing and seeing the language as coming in lines. (This of course means "hearing" what can only be seen. Lines are visual.) This line is keyed to a soft sibilance, reinforced at each end with an *s/n* relationship, symmetrically arranged. The only consonantal breath-stops in the line—the *tt* and the *d* of "settled"—add up to no more than a brief caesura after the *d*. A line in the landscape is being observed through a markedly prosodic line, implying a pun that cannot be spelled out—in Saussure's sense of the term, a *motivated* relationship across the bar of the sign, linking associated signifiers, linking implied signifieds, overdetermining poetic cohesion.

> Of an old ridge-and-furrow system

The metric is sustained as are *s*'s and an avoidance of stopped consonants. But where the first line belongs to percept and introduces the tone that invites associative reading, the second moves into knowledge code. Snow has settled on a *system*. Perhaps the ridge-and-furrow system of what became the Elizabethan line is also settling snow.

> Striping the gently sloping dark

"Gently" was already there, carried in the means, and it slopes into that "dark," whose privileged position in the line system catches it temporally as a noun. The dark. Once you slope into it, that's what there is: the dark. It can be where fear is, or ignorance, or where sleep restores colour in readiness for the light. It is where there is relief from the brute repetition of objects.

Then the noun is recuperated as an adjective, a relatively innocent attribute of the environment:

> Green fields, engrossed scripts

Scripts are supposed to be engrossing not engrossed. What is this enlarged and fattened writing, already associated with the fields? The double signification of "line" continues.

> Of duration, repetition, authority

Duration—old; repetition—system of lines, insistence on the constitution of the same; authority—the systematic anonymity of power. Who is the author of these lines, whose "system" was there ahead of them, ensuring a dialectic of same and different? What is the time of their authority? What is the duration of the system of correspondences which links the two kinds of lines, given that the dark, in its alternating pattern with light, is eternal. Light/dark—another ridge-and-furrow system, replicated synchronically in any set of ridges and furrows seen at an angle.

Up till now, answering my own question, the authority of the poem derives in part at least from a literary tradition of duration and repetition. The "author" is no more than the person on the spot, the conduit of a repetitive wisdom. And then what happens?

> At which that calm baby in the self

Which calm baby? The demonstrative precision of that "that"! That one. There must be a term in the old rhetoric for this device which invokes the phenomenal authority of deixis in pointing at the emperor's new clothes. In the earlier lines metaphor is implicit in the figures used and is underpinned with the same kind of photographic literalness at play on the front cover of the book. Both "baby" and "self" are troublesome terms, the latter very much a figure in Peter Riley's narratography. More than that, though, "that" and "the" reach out to some "system" that might need to be separately learned. It has no immediate link to percept.

> That finds it so difficult to speak

Is difficulty ever calm? This baby is not an infant. This baby can speak but finds it difficult. And is calm. Is there any evidence of difficulty of speaking in these lines? Are the signs of difficulty not subsumed within an authoritative coherence?

> Lowers an eyelid on the shrinking day
> And suddenly says outright
> The entire brochure of love and all.

The metaphor moves into narrative. Is it George Herbert who is somewhere there? The baby, given to silence, breaks into the spontaneous "brochure" of love. A brochure in my book sells or specifies something. In this case, love. But no not just love. Love and all. Oceanic.

And finally, the form that begs for rhyme gets it:

> Stay here before you fall.

There is such satisfying completion here. Not the shrinking but the closing of the day. The sense of calm closure is prosodic entirely. What does this all mean? You are going to fall—swoon perhaps in the oceanic dispersal of particulars into love and all—and since you are going to fall you might as well stay here to do so. In which case the strictly temporal "until" would be better. "Before" can be either spatial or temporal or ambiguously both. But "before" does bring with it the colloquial authority of a form of parental or teacherly imperative: *Shut up before I make you!* This reading could be:

> If you don't stay here, you will fall.

"Fall" is like "dark," so habituated as a word to metaphoric use that alternative readings can't be kept at bay. The fall. Perhaps there is a third reading that can be pointed up by adjusting the "you" to "your":

> *Stay here before your fall.*

This one comes to me from other readings of Peter Riley, where versions of the self take on adventures against primary harm, finding it everywhere, and staying there because that is where, paradoxically, these selves find love and grace.

July 1999

THE SUBSTANCE OF
TRACKS AND MINESHAFTS

Peter Middleton

Frühe Geglückte, ihr Verwöhnten der Schöpfung,
Höhenzüge, morgenrötliche Grate
aller Erschaffung, — Pollen der blühenden Gottheit,
Gelenke des Lichtes, Gänge, Treppen, Throne,
Räume aus Wesen, Schilde aus Wonne, Tumulte
stürmisch entzückten Gefühls und plötzlich, einzeln,
Spiegel: die die entströmte eigene Schönheit
wiederschöpfen zurück in das eigene Antlitz.[1]

Rainer Maria Rilke, The Second Duino Elegy

Deep conviction or preference can seldom
Find direct terms in which to express itself.
Today on this shingle shelf
I understand this pensive reluctance so well,
This not discommendable obstinacy,
These contrivances of an inexpressive critical feeling,
These stones with their resolve that Creation shall not be
Injured by iconoclasts and quacks. Nothing has stirred
Since I lay down this morning an eternity ago
But one bird. The widest open door is the least liable to intrusion,
Ubiquitous as the sunlight, unfrequented as the sun.
The inward gates of a bird are always open.
It does not know how to shut them.
That is the secret of its song,
But whether any man's are ajar is doubtful.
I look at these stones and know little about them,
But I know their gates are open too,
Always open, far longer open, than any bird's can be,
That every one of them has had its gates wide open far longer
Than all birds put together, let alone humanity.

Hugh MacDiarmid, "On a Raised Beach"

47

When the history of British late-modernist poetry is written, *Tracks and Mineshafts* will occupy an important and to a considerable extent self-appointed role as an extended reflection on the fate of modernist poetics during the 1970s in Britain.[2] The opening lines of its first poem, "Material Soul," project a vision of the human condition which recapitulates a persistent modernist preoccupation with time and matter.

> Given to death and life, no choice,
> fallen into these terms, borne as the
> tide bears the wave to its strike,
> cut to bedrock, crest, charge the shore.
> Given to this, life carving itself out
> of its knowledge and the earth
> is like a cup, to which the lip fits,
> and the senses' final construct moves
> relentlessly through substance to the houses
> of light, mutual, devotion (7)

The universalizing proposition resonating with modernist antecedents states firmly that our existential condition is to be "given to death and life, no choice." A series of images dominated by metaphors of the wave breaking on a rocky shore, articulated in Heideggerian terms of holding and clearing, culminates in the last stanza's assertion that the "world" ends in every moment. Only in the final lines does the elsewhere ubiquitous collective pronoun "we" make an entrance, to be followed by a framing statement in the language of Freudian desire—"so I wish it"—as if this is not after all the actual human condition but the ethics projected by the poet. Then the metaphor of rock resurfaces once more, and the self announces that it will "plunge / into the stone" never to be seen again.

The question a reader is then expected to ask is what a late twentieth-century British poetry could mine from this flashback to the modernist ruins of time and matter. There is D.H. Lawrence explaining that free verse is the poetry of the unfolding instant: "The whole tide of all life and all time suddenly heaves, and appears before us as an apparition, a revelation" (70). He represents the movement of such poetry as a bird in flight: "The bird is on the wing in the winds, flexible to every breath, a living spark in the storm, its very flickering depending upon its supreme mutability and power of change.... Now, *now*, the bird is on the wing in the winds" (73). There is T.S. Eliot. The "cunning passages, contrived corridors" of history in "Gerontion," and the footsteps echoing in the memory of "the passage which we did not take" in "Burnt Norton" (Eliot 40, 189), reappear as the "unlivable corridors and arcades / of transitional time." There is Hugh MacDiarmid contemplating the ruins of matter on the stony beach in the 1930s:

> These bare stones bring me straight back to reality.
> I grasp one of them and I have in my grip
> The beginning and the end of the world. (175)

Just as Lawrence's "wing" will become one of the recurrent motifs of the sequence, so too will MacDiarmid's idea that birds and stones have "gates" of perception that are much more open than those of most people, "though through them no man can see." Rilke's question at the start of the Second Duino Elegy to the angels, whose substance is both light and stone, and who mirror creation so much better than human beings, will be a guiding question for Riley's sequence, one provoked especially strongly by what is probably the most poignant moment in the entire book, when one of the prose poems asks what we can do if the "upper sense of the heart furnace, in the end fails, scatters and dies into featureless geology," and the resulting slag no longer reflects any significance back to us: "these things we have given our lives to... finally sit there on the desk staring back at us entirely void of expression or promise, unsellable un-mirroring exhibit, mere tools which we have set at the focus of increment and exhausted—vehicles of communication from which we expect oracles" (28).

The book is not, as this opening poem might seem to herald, a nostalgic continuation of modernism. It does not evoke these earlier poetic achievements in the same spirit as an Ezra Pound demonstrating how the technical skills of global cultural allusion might inspire a concerted national effort of recivilization by restoring absent traditions and re-establishing symbolic exchange on an ethical foundation. Its context is a cultural politics of the 1970s whose starting point is the belief that "it was a 1960s confusion from which several derived lasting damage, to think your fate would respond to a conditional, shorn of act" (32). Opening the gates of perception by emulating stone will not be enough if it does not issue in praxis, and so the possible terms of such vision will be the concern of the following poems. Even one of the most cited guiding concepts of the new post-structuralist theory of the late 1970s, Victor Shklovsky's "defamiliarization," might not be sufficient if all it meant was merely that modernist art would enable one to "recover the sensation of life" (12).

He had claimed, with prerevolutionary fervour, that without the modernizing effect of art we would gradually sink into a cognitive oblivion of the everyday: "art exists that one may recover the sensation of life; it exists to make one feel things, to make the stone *stony*," and without it the stone would lose its material essence, its stoniness, which depends upon the quality of perception. Art keeps perception fit. "The purpose of art is to impart the sensation of things as they are perceived and not as they are known. The technique of art is to make objects 'unfamiliar,' to make forms difficult, to increase the difficulty and length of perception because the process of perception is an aesthetic end in itself and must be prolonged." Providing the occasion for its audience to feel the resistance, the grainy, solid endurance of the stone, its rough-edged reminders of the deeper rock it is broken from, its slow almost eternal time, is what the stone is for, in perceptual terms. This stony aesthetic does not assume that art will assist in extending ethical insight or general knowledge, because what matters is that *"art is a way of experiencing the artfulness of an object; the object is not important."* Shklovsky's emphasis underlines this surprising conclusion. The stoniness of the stone is not a gate to its importance as matter; the more we plunge into stone the more we are able to immerse ourselves in the art of perception. The stoniness of the stone is a measure of our freedom from the locking of the gates of perception: the stonier the freer—the stonier the more aesthetically fulfilling. And so in a curious way stone drops from significance as stone; the materiality of the substance that is given to our senses is what really matters, and the stone is merely a fixed marker as the accelerating human condition rushes by. Riley is skeptical of all such disavowals of substance (this word is his magnetic north), saying that "we are beset by hypnotic clouds, dispersals of substance, / drawing us towards the void of artless existence" (61), yet he is all too aware that the alternative to the stony aesthetics of modernism may be another form of antimaterialism—the poetics of the personal lyric which came into ascendancy during the 1970s.

Stone, time, and landscape were preoccupations of many of the most prominent—because promoted by the leading publishers— poets of the late sixties and the seventies, whose characteristic poetics were cleverly anthologized by Fred Inglis in an educational anthology of poetry and prose, *The Scene: An Anthology about City and Country* (1972), a title whose pun aptly captures their hegemonic ideology. Donald Davie, Ted Hughes, Philip Larkin, F.T. Prince, R.S. Thomas and Charles Tomlinson are presented as the inheritors of a sense of English landscape that can be traced back through Eliot's "Little Gidding" to Edward Thomas, the Romantics, Crabbe, Pope and the builders of the great country houses. A passage quoted from Lewis Mumford's *The City in History* (1961) optimistically looks forward to the global village, and says that "the city of the future" should create "a visible regional and civic structure, designed to make man at home with his deeper self and his larger world, attached to images of human nurture and love" (90). But as the poems suggest, these ideals are not met in the modern world. Instead, Charles Tomlinson finds the ruined hall in Stowey damaged both by time, weather and, worst of all, the "barbarous mean" of modernity visible in the wrecked rooms redecorated to fulfill a "suburban whim" (160). Only the stone of the buildings remains as a reality beyond symbol, and the poem repeats the word twice as if it directly presenced the material itself. Stone "cut, piled, mortared, is patience's presence," and this poem imitates the masonry with its own carefully cut stanzas of eight lines piled to overlap like mortared stones in these walls. The sentiment is not too distant from Riley, who is capable of echoing Tomlinson's dislike of the abandoned refurbishment done on a "suburban whim" with equally antimodernist remarks of his own about such excrescences of modernity as the "talking photograph in the / living room to which there is no possible reply" (61). Where they differ radically is both in form and stance. Tomlinson can assume that his formal stanzas emulate the dressed stone of a lost civic virtue, and even more significantly, that he can place a figure of the author within the poem who can stand there and act as a mirror of its decline.

> Saddened,
> Yet angered beyond sadness, where the road
> Doubled upon itself I halted, for a moment
> Facing the empty house and its laden barns.

Riley doesn't believe that such witness can be so easily achieved, even when he "picks his way among hollows and craters" of the old mineshafts (50), also finding signs of decline, because he is implicated, through language, perception and material being, in the condition of what he sees, in a manner which Tomlinson's poetry is unable to acknowledge. Riley knows that even our most careful judgements can help create this ruin we deplore: "The fuzzily scanned futures of our acts / become a chalky rubble under our feet" (55). The problem is that, as Heidegger explains, "our going back to 'the past' does not first get its start from the acquisition, sifting, and securing of such material; these activities presuppose *historical Being towards* the Dasein that has-been-there—that is to say, they presuppose the historicality of the historian's existence" (*Being and Time* 446). Tomlinson's type of poetry fails to acknowledge its historicality.

By 1982, the hegemony of Davie, Hughes, Larkin and Tomlinson was being challenged by younger poets who took their lead from the Irish school of Seamus Heaney and Derek Mahon. Two of the most entrepreneurial figures in recent British poetry, Blake Morrison and Andrew Motion, introduced *The Penguin Book of Contemporary British Poetry* with a familiar modernist claim to represent a new wave, saying that a decisive "shift of sensibility has taken place very recently in British poetry" (11). Their insensitivity to the full implications of the reuse of Eliot's modernist language of sensibility (they also employ the phrase "objective correlative") shows how little had changed. They justify their claims by pointing out a move away from "naked" expression to greater subtlety and obliquity, and they cite as an example one of Heaney's bog poems about the preserved corpses of people who, it is suggested by some archaeologists, were ritually murdered before burial in the peat that pickled them. They afford Heaney a means of suggesting that the Irish troubles have a timeless quality to them, that other societies also created scapegoats and exiles, and to prove this by admitting his own readiness to be complicit in such denials of reciprocity: "I almost love you / but would have cast, I know, / the stones of silence" (29). The editors also cite Derek Mahon as a determining influence on this new sensibility, and print Mahon's best known poem, "A Disused Shed in Co. Wexford." This poem about mushrooms growing in a forgotten shed begins with images of mines and indigenous peoples ("Even now there are places where a thought might grow— / Peruvian mines, worked out and abandoned") as locations of memory of the past, and then makes the mushrooms into bathetic, comic images of the "lost people of Treblinka and Pompeii," the faces of a history trying to gain the attention of those who finally enter the shed and take photographs (79–80). In both Heaney and Mahon, the damaged lineaments of bog corpse and emaciated fungi serve as a judgement on the immediate history of Irish civil war and Second World War. History is puzzling, violent, and only apprehensible indirectly through the landscape that reveals tracks to where, in Heaney's poem, "each hooded victim" was "slashed and dumped," and in Mahon's poem, to mineshafts into the darkness where the lost souls of disaster call out to the confident intruders from the prosperous, peaceful future: "Let not our naive labours have been in vain" (80). The key word here is "naive"; these souls lacked the sophisticated irony to recognize their own insigificance and the humour of the situation. However offensive it now seems, Mahon's poem was immensely successful at a time when, as the editors note, in Heaney's own words, poets and readers felt like "inner emigrés"—"not victims but onlookers" of their own lives (12).

Riley's poem is determined to reassess these discourses and their tracks and mineshafts; "stones of silence" need to be met with the recognition that, in Riley's words, "we mould the materials of earth to our own rhythms / ignoring the backlash" (55). He deeply mistrusts the assumptions at work in both Inglis's collection and Morrison and Motion's anthology, knowing more of the modernist history that these hegemonic poets seem both entramelled by and unconscious of. The plunge into stone is a re-entry into the lost history of British modernism made necessary by the continuance of modernist ideas of substance in such unreflective ways. He is committed to tunnelling deeper into "the message that exceeds us, the concept not grasped, the emptiness of total being, pure sign of itself to which such substances as metal, poetry, history, can only be tools of an interim script" (27). His guide into these underworld regions will be Heidegger,[3] as is probably already evident from the quotations, and he will work through a wide range of poetic forms, notably the prose poem, a form of which he is a leading exponent. Nor will he feel constrained to say nothing ill of his conceptual master whose language permeates the volume. Towards the end Riley observes that "nobody is writing the Phenomenology of Evil" (62), and this marks a decisive turn in his relations with Heidegger: Heidegger would have thought that his own descriptions of fallen, ontic life were just that, but subsequent historians of philosophy have found his own proximity to the evil of Nazism a dangerous component of his own phenomenology, as if certain aspects might be both a phenomenology and an advocacy of evil without knowing it.

Materialism was the essential politics of the cultural left in the late seventies and early eighties, a talisman against the hallucinatory charms of bourgeois ideology and sixties mysticism, more fundamental than Marxism and more intellectually sharp than Socialism, although in practice Marxists and Socialists often called themselves materialists too. To be a materialist was to be committed to the view that the world was neither some natural outcome of evolutionary process nor a material inspirited by ideas which were the ultimately determining force. History was powered by the transformation of the bare ore of the world into the metallic exchange systems of capitalism, a transformation made possible by the progressive changes in the organization of material production. *Tracks and Mineshafts* questions the stoniness of this materialism. When Riley explains that the world of office employment is limited because it cannot "mine into light" the way poets and lovers can, he is pushing against a particularly narrowed concept of material world. The persistent problem for the materialists was to theorize their own relation to substance, not least the substance of their own being, and the dilemma was perfectly caught by the ironies of a hit single issued the year before Riley published *Tracks and Mineshafts*. "Spirits in the Material World" (1982) by the band The Police included the repeated line "we are spirits in the material" and then climaxed with the affirmation that "we are spirits in the material world." The brilliance of the lyric derived from the repeated withholding of the final word, so that adjective became noun, and suggested that this collectivity of performers, and perhaps listeners too, were animating energies in the song itself. Only after this possible interpretation was reiterated for several refrains could the "world" appear, as if its manifestation were dependent upon the prior achievement of the song's large and inclusive empathy for listeners. If the material world is the bourgeois world, then those who oppose it can represent themselves as free spirits soaring through it, perhaps powerless because of their lack of substance, but at least able to reach beyond it. This was a more comfortable estrangement than Punk had offered a few years earlier, more fitted to the ambient concern with the tension between two forms of materialism, those of radical politics on the one hand and the consumer ethic they opposed on the other. The song's material world is presumably the bourgeois world of what Riley calls the "overtakers" who "glide past in their dream wagons" (19), but its willing embrace of the antimaterialist discourse of the sixties to make its point shows how problematic these issues had become.

One of the icons of the materialists was the miners and the miners' union, which had successfully helped bring down Edward Heath's government by striking in the early seventies, and continued to represent a left-wing politics capable, many imagined, of kick-starting a political revolution. Miners were symbolically the ultimate materialists, because they plunged deep into stone every working day. Inglis is alert to this connection in his anthology, where he reprints a short essay written by D.H. Lawrence near the end of his life, when he was no longer as critical of the miners as he had been in his youth, and now could recall them as a positive force (but as abstractly as this phrase implies): "They brought with them above ground the curious intimacy of the mine, the naked sort of contact, and if I think of my childhood, it is always as if there was a lustrous sort of inner darkness, like the gloss of coal, in which we moved and had our real being" (150). The Derbyshire landscape of *Tracks and Mineshafts* is scarred with "abandoned mines, standing out like sores through the rough mingling pastoral surface," and the poems repeatedly return to meditate on their significance, and on the fate of the former workers, whose houses and chapels are now empty too, "inhabitants blasted to nonentity" (23, 50). Riley's book appeared just as the National Union of Mineworkers began the first stages of its disastrous strike under Arthur Scargill. In 1981, the then president Joe Gormley had extracted significant concessions from the Thatcher government, but Gormley retired in 1982 and Scargill was convinced that he could use the power of the striking union to overthrow the new, and hated, conservative government of Margaret Thatcher. Key to this strategy was the plan to starve the country of energy by denying power stations sufficient coal to continue to provide electricity, but the government was far-sighted enough to encourage the Electricity Boards to stockpile coal, so this threat never became a reality. Meanwhile enormous numbers of police were drafted in, and the main strike of 1984–85 was eventually defeated by brute force, the manipulation of the courts (the union's funds were seized) and the demonization of Scargill.

Riley's poem could not have been written after 1985. What the conservative government set out to destroy was a sense of national moral debt to the mineworkers and, by implication, manual workers generally. The nature of this obligation is sharply expressed in David Storey's novel *Pasmore* (1972), in which a university lecturer visits his parents to tell them that he and his wife have separated. His father, a miner, articulates the emotional debt with crushing force: "When you were at school…and I was working, at every bit of coal I dug I used to say to myself that's one bit he won't have to dig" (86). This familial legacy remains strongly within his imagination, and after a second more successful visit once he and his wife are reconciled, he makes another visit to his parents, and walks to the pit with his father, who is on mornings. Later, on the train out of the town, Pasmore looks at the sunlight and thinks: "Somewhere, underneath, was his father, lying down" (170). Not surprisingly, the novel ends with a reference to the pit: "He still dreamed of the pit and the blackness. It existed all around him, an intensity, like a presentiment of love, or violence: he found it hard to tell" (171). Storey's anguished intellectual could stand for an attitude to working-class life widely shared during the 1970s and early 1980s, a sense that this work with the raw material of rock and energy somehow represented the essence of an industrialized, capitalist nation. Left-wing intellectuals shared a largely unexamined sense that their imaginations were made possible by the work being done by those underneath the landscape, by those who tunnelled into the bedrock substance of their nation, and this was destroyed by the Miners' Strike.

Riley's poem remains on the far side of that pivotal cultural moment. The abandoned mineshafts he is referring to are lead workings, but the question raised throughout the poem—how we should understand material, or substance as represented by stone—is a deeply political one, although Riley's poem only works indirectly around it. This politics is also now remote from current readers and therefore needs to be read back consciously into such features as the mineshafts. Like Tomlinson, Riley also visits sites of historical memory, but his are read with more allegorical consciousness of the political implications of decay and therefore less one-sided regret: a "royal garden," now ruined, has "no spirit, no presence, no memory," so that "all this / material, stone, fibre, with no one to hold it, / rots, swirls, and tumbles into hell" (79). We should recall that the monarchy had recently attempted to revitalize its image with the wedding of Prince Charles and Lady Diana Spencer. Republican sentiment is also there in the recall of the long forgotten miners who worked the local Derbyshire mines, their labour a symbol for Riley of a work that is needed even more urgently today—that of hewing a way through this material world and working out what its substance is. A haunting echo, "endless hammering inside matter," won't let up (82). What Riley's poem wants is to find a way for flesh (not spirit) to transform this stoniness without denying its being:

> Organic energy tends towards regularity
> and law is the end of that dream, the final
> symmetry, the insistence of flesh against stone.
> For stone resists order and pushes down into
> chaos and sameness. Flesh clears a space, a small
> travelling theatre at the heart of substance.... (76)

The "resistance of / matter" is such that only the unremitting work of body and imagination through love and creativity can find the "stone in the heart" and transmute it, although Riley is insistent that this ethical call to the reader does not just require a decision of will, or some access of passion (74, 68). It requires a transformation of the way we inhabit the world conceptually and materially. Without such change, the outlook may be bleak. The old mineshafts stand for a possible fate "into which this whole substance, not just / life, not just you and me, this whole physics / will one day be tipped, light and all" (60).

The problem with substance is therefore not just the economic materialism which denies spirit and imagination, and so it cannot be countered by the conjuration of empathies and passions through the music of a band like The Police. Science, our modernist orientation towards the future as an impending temporal outcome, our forms of work, and our politics, all collaborate in the making of this material world for which the old mineshafts remain a powerful symbol of possibility and loss. The care for those former manual workers is part of what is needed for change, as is the concern for the present-day miners, but for the poem, there is another necessity too: the ruins ultimately result from an unwillingness to learn the lessons of mining and recognize that modern society is ground down by a false understanding of matter. Substance does not need to determine our lives in the way it does. A momentary *deus ex machina*, a "saint on his tiny island," is offered as a utopian image of the possible:

> love
> like this meets constantly the resistance of
> matter directly as a gardener where every shrub
> is won from nothing into the ancestral shield,
> and the stones rise to the hand. (74)

Love, passion and flesh, three terms embodied in the poetry, are capable of a materialist production that would not simply turn the world into commodities and eventually blank, unmeaningful, unmirroring substance.

At the heart of Riley's meditations on stone is not only the danger of developing a heartstone (the "stone in the heart" that echoes Yeats); stone's own heart or substance is itself in question. This is where the book is most ambitious and most at risk of denying its own materiality, because it would appear to rely so extensively on the authority of Heidegger. A conceptual scheme from outside the world of the mineshafts and the poet's daily life would disperse the substance of an embodied world as effectively as any of the other processes of modernity, but fortunately this is largely avoided by the book's resolute care to think through the dilemmas of materialism. Part of the risk is down to readers' likely confidence that they know these Heideggerian arguments, since what they are most likely to be familiar with are Jacques Derrida's persuasive rereadings of Heidegger's work on time and language, which have overshadowed Heidegger's own ideas on material culture for the past twenty years. A recent polemical reading of Western theories of matter may help correct this, and certainly helps illuminate Riley's ambitions in this book. John McCumber argues in *Metaphysics and Oppression: Heidegger's Challenge to Western Philosophy* that an idea of substance that first found full articulation in Aristotle's work (it was already current in Greek culture) has persisted for millennia, despite efforts of philosophers, most recently Heidegger, to set it aside. Aristotle proposed the concept of *ousia* to describe the basics of a thing. A thing has a boundary; it has, at the most fundamental level, a unity or essence; this essence determines the thinginess of the thing (the stoniness of the stone); and the thing cannot change without changing this essence. This *ousia* "is what we understand, seek, and make. It structures our sciences and societies, our loves and lovers. It is what we 'really' are; it is our essence" (45). It is "lurking in the lowest depths; the shrouded Alpha from which all things come, and the dark Omega into which they must return—…the ancestress of the id and the proletariat, of body and *différance* and of all that is colonized or seeks liberation: matter" (45). European thinkers appear to have completely rejected the idea of *ousia*, of things that contain within themselves their reason for being, their controlling essence, and expelled *ousia* from the natural world, which is now considered to consist of bodies in motion, but what really happened was that the concept relocated itself in the human world of subjectivity (108). The Cartesian subject is an *ousia*: "it is independent of any cosmic order, capable of knowing only its own contents, and governed by the immanent activity of its will" (126). From there, and in the work of many thinkers, it was possible to find justification for oppression, because what was outside this privileged subjectivity was mere matter, even at times the colonial others or women in marriage (205). Heidegger reviewed this history and showed that a metaphysical image of subjects still persists, a belief that Being is manifest as presence. Unfortunately, according to McCumber, this was both triumph and failure, because Heidegger misconstrued the consequences of this persistent metaphysics of the subject: *ousia* is a problem not because it assumes that substance equals presence, but rather because it thinks of substance as power.

To be a being for Aristotle, was to contain a structure in which one part dominates the whole, via the three axes of boundary, disposition, and initiative. Equating such structure with Being itself meant writing domination into the basic nature of the universe, and that has in Modernity been seen to be in complicity with a variety of evils: with patriarchy, colonialism, and slavery; with absolute status for private property and for state sovereignty; with the melancholy "triumph" of the individual. (206)

Heidegger did, however, show in his later philosophy what matter might look like if it was no longer conceived as an *ousia*. In essays like "The Thing," he enacts a realization of the jug, for example, that is not determined by one fundamental property, and arises out of a convergence of different realms, none of which are determining or take priority. The jug holds emptiness and that enables it to pour forth its contents. A poem by Holderlin becomes an "interplay...the play of a set of mutually irreducible meanings; and it is that which, in being gradually revealed by the words the poem contains, exercises such 'disposition' of them as obtains" (248).

This is exactly what Riley's poem attempts to do with its instabilities of tone, its varieties of form, its implosions of metaphor and its avoidance of resolution. Yet always pitched against this is the promise of a new collectivity capable of creating a "travelling theatre at the heart of substance," a promise indicated by the poetry's willingness to address this liminal collective condition and warn that it is always at risk: "unable to sustain love we succumb to the strata" of inert matter (76). Substance, matter and materialism are not themselves the difficulty. It is the false materialisms of government, dominant poetries and lazy hope that have to be resisted.

There are, unsurprisingly, problems with this ambition in the poetry, especially in the climate of neglect. Sometimes the collective visibly shrinks to the poet and his lover, the couple who "run through the list of jobs / and go to bed," an irony that can make the larger address seem strained (75). The authority of Heidegger's language is largely established by careful attention to contextual, geographical and historical rendition of the philosophical metaphors, but not always. The status of Heidegger is also not as unquestionable as much of the text appears to assume (despite its ruminations on "the Phenomenology of Evil"), although this is a risk that every interlocutor of Heidegger runs, as McCumber also recognizes (he notes how much of Heidegger's thought about science is "warmed over cant from the European right wing" [9]). The hardest question Riley's book faces is whether it was or is readable within the continuing suppres-

sion of modernist literary history and practice in Britain. My ar-
chaeological essay suggests that it can be, but like so much of the best
poetry of the past three decades, it risks attenuation through the lack
of the shared readerly attention necessary to let it take on the "flesh
and detail" (to borrow McCumber's words about the concept of *ousia*)
that could really place it where it belongs, in the public spheres of
English-speaking cultures. Do we need to share Heidegger's hope
that this poetry, "being a work,...always remains tied to preservers,
even and particularly when it is still only waiting for preservers and
only pleads and waits for them to enter into its truth," as he puts it in
"The Origin of the Work of Art" (67)? It is a measure of Riley's
major achievement that twenty years after publication, and despite
considerable neglect by reviewers, publicists and canon-formers of
British poetry, *Tracks and Mineshafts* can offer to readers truths and
insights which are more substantive and timely than ever.

Notes

1. In Stephen Mitchell's translation:

Early successes, Creation's pampered favorites,
mountain-ranges, peaks growing red in the dawn
of all Beginning,—pollen of the flowering godhead,
joints of pure light, corridors, stairways, thrones,
space formed from essence, shields made of ecstacy, storms
of emotion whirled into rapture, and suddenly, alone:
mirrors, which scoop up the beauty that has streamed from their face
and gather it back, into themselves, entire. (157)

2. Riley's book was published in 1983 by Grosseteste Press; readers unfa-
miliar with the press should look at its associated magazine, *Grosseteste Review*,
which offers not only a good cross-section of the late modernist poetry of the
period of its publication, but also consistently published the best essays on a
pertinent poetics.

3. Charles Olson and later the influential journal *Boundary 2* under the
editorship of William V. Spanos—Riley contributed to the Jack Spicer issue—
had made available a certain aesthetic reading of Heidegger in the US, and
J.H. Prynne had done so in the UK. The Heideggerian language in this
volume of Riley's is as much a dialogue with these writers as with the phi-
losopher himself. Nevertheless the image of Heidegger as a Virgilian guide
to the underworld of the mine captures something of what is happening in
Riley's poetry at this time.

Works Cited

Eliot, T.S. *Collected Poems 1909–1962.* London: Faber, 1963.

Heidegger, Martin. *Being and Time.* Trans. John Macquarrie and Edward Robinson. Oxford: Blackwell, 1962.

————. "The Origin of the Work of Art." In *Poetry, Language, Thought,* trans. Albert Hofstadter. New York: Harper and Row, 1975.

Inglis, Fred, ed. *The Scene: An Anthology about City and Country.* Cambridge: Cambridge University Press, 1972.

Lawrence, D.H. "Preface to the American Edition of *New Poems.*" In *Poetics of the New American Poetry*, ed. Donald Allen and Warren Tallman. New York: Grove, 1973.

McCumber, John. *Metaphysics and Oppression: Heidegger's Challenge to Western Philosophy.* Bloomington: Indiana University Press, 1999.

MacDiarmid, Hugh. "On a Raised Beach." In *Complete Poems 1920–1976*, ed. Michael Grieve and W.R. Aitken. 2 vols. London: Martin Brian and O'Keeffe, 1978.

Morrison, Blake, and Andrew Motion, eds. *The Penguin Book of Contemporary British Poetry.* Harmondsworth: Penguin, 1982.

Riley, Peter. *Tracks and Mineshafts.* Matlock: Grosseteste, 1983.

Rilke, Rainer Maria. "The Second Elegy." In *The Selected Poetry of Rainer Maria Rilke*, trans. Stephen Mitchell. London: Pan, Picador Classics, 1987.

Shklovsky, Victor. "Art as Technique." In *Russian Formalist Criticism: Four Essays*, trans. Lee T. Lemon and Marion J. Reis. Lincoln: University of Nebraska Press, 1965.

Storey, David. *Pasmore.* 1972. Harmondsworth: Penguin, 1976.

ON *UNTITLED SEQUENCE*

Peter Robinson

First, some literary history: at the April 1977 Cambridge Poetry Festival, Peter Riley read from a sequence of poems which began:

> And then we..
> No.
> Not "we."
> I.

It was later broadcast on the BBC Radio 3 program devoted to the event. I attended the reading and heard the poem again on the radio. The same sequence was published in *Perfect Bound* 4, the Autumn 1977 volume. This was a little magazine based in Cambridge, England, which ran for seven issues between Summer 1976 and June 1979. Poetry (and in one case a review) by Peter Riley appeared in four issues. Perhaps the sequence he read at the festival was published in *Perfect Bound* because I requested it, or maybe it was offered to us. Twenty-one years later, asked to contribute to this special issue on the poet's work, I remembered the sequence and thought it a possible text to discuss. Had it been reprinted in a separate volume during the intervening years? It must have been. However, when I contacted the poet, it seemed that after its magazine appearance, he had all but forgotten the work. Parts 3 and 10 had been taken out, lightly revised and given separate titles with the idea that they be included in a projected selected poems. Peter Riley sent me "In a German Car-Park" and "Is this Düsseldorf or Kiel?"

I was surprised he hadn't put the entire group into a more visible publication, and said that perhaps I'd write on the sequence in its magazine form anyway. Some time later a further message arrived, which included the following:

Concerning that sequence which you "discovered" in *Perfect Bound.* I've tested it on a few connoisseurs and it seems to go down rather well. I might include it in the "big book" I'm preparing—I had provisionally selected the

3rd and 10th poems. Anyway I've tinkered with it a little and below is the text as I have it now.

The main problem with my proposed contribution seemed to be that, with the exception of those few people who had filed away copies of *Perfect Bound,* no one would have read the work (in either unrevised or "tinkered with" forms). What if it were republished in my contribution? Back I went to ask for permission. Here is part of the reply:

The only thing about the *Untitled Sequence* and *The Gig,* is that I've now agreed with a small press to produce a separate edition of it (revised version of course) — Wild Honey Press in Ireland.... Perhaps it would be profligate to print it again in *The Gig,* or might interfere with Wild Honey's sales? But on the other hand this means it will be in print, so if you wrote on it you wouldn't be addressing a vacuum, as it were.

In what follows, aside from a few observations about the changes made between the magazine text and the revised version, or when history dictates that the earlier one be quoted, I cite from the revised text of *Untitled Sequence* — so the following comments can double as a review of the Wild Honey pamphlet.

Untitled Sequence is, as its author's note states, a remnant of a larger project. Written in 1970, it was abandoned two years later, only to be taken up again, revised and made public, in 1977. The work was then described as a "set of poems worked from materials formerly the fifth and last section of *The Linear Journal,* subtitled 'Germany.'" The *Perfect Bound* text also includes the information that "This is likely to be no longer that fifth section," making it an outtake of sorts. An end of line bargain, or *disjecta membra,* this title-less or untitled sequence carries with it an unentitled air of dejection, of unpropitious circumstances borne over from the unpromising situation which it intermittently narrates and out of which it came:

> What happened was the hiking schoolboys got older
> and became a college dramatic society taking *Macbeth*
> round Germany on a coach, playing in gymnasia halls
> and cinemas before large but entirely
> compulsory audiences. I played Seton.

The opening poem in *The Linear Journal* (1973) announces: "My regard, of you, takes the form / of a band of adolescents in shorts /

setting out on an alpine ramble." *Untitled Sequence* marks a continuity in the narrative gesture with "What happened," but the phrase may have proved the indication of a rupture, one in which the enclosed coherence of the later sequence's story and the graver tenor of its concerns may then have made it not seem fitting as the earlier work's fifth part.

Nevertheless, *Untitled Sequence* signals its ancestry with a series of echoing quotations from the book. Part 6 of the later sequence, for example, echoes a phrase from the opening of *The Linear Journal*: "the / Central Gardens of your presence, your / image, that I hardly know":

> Suffice it to say,
> here I have you in mind,
> the calm and fearless
> Central Gardens of your presence
> asleep or at the other end
> of the continent gives me
> some chance of weathering
> the obscurity, even if it denies
> most of what I think I know.

This calmly dependent second-person invocation of a loved presence-in-absence imagines emotional security as a city park. It's a vivid touch to bring the casual phrase "have you in mind" alive in this way. The theme is further drawn out at the start of the following section of *Untitled Sequence*: "Wind seeps through cracks in the park / and woos the inner female." This strikes a chillier, grimmer note than the playfully aware manner of *The Linear Journal*, section 1, where "your presence" appears to be glossed as:

> a fixed-term loan of variegated parklands
> known as "continuing to exist"
> or all of the past and all of the present
> "Have fun," they say, "Goodbye."

Despite its echoing recollections of the earlier book, *Untitled Sequence* developed away from its sponsoring occasion in an apparently ongoing work—only to be left aside for decades in one back issue of a small magazine.

Riley's recent tinkerings with the *Perfect Bound* text can be improvements: "I played Seton" is better than the original "I was Seton." Both are repetitions of previously used verbs, but in the revised versions the play on "played" is more resonant and suggestive about the predicament of the bit-part student actor, because the poem tells us that he wasn't at all, in a Stanislavskian sense, Seton. However, the older poet's modesty in saying he has "tinkered with" the text may also inadvertently express a weakening of the original impulse: the earlier version's "large but largely" is better, I think, because more crushing in the collapse (an important word in both this sequence and its sponsoring book) of "large" into "largely / compulsory," while the avoided repetition in "large but entirely" is efficient prose, but no more. Similarly, "a troupe of students" (felicitously echoing "a band of adolescents") has become "a college dramatic society"—which is not far short of authorial vandalism.

Untitled Sequence includes at least one allusion to the play these students are taking around Germany. Part 8 begins:

> The tour is not going well or badly,
> the tour is just going. We have not
> whistled in the wings. We have spoken
> a language we barely comprehend but in
> fits and starts, but we have spoken it
> as it stands. We have murdered it.

"Macbeth does murther Sleep," of course, but one of the students has helped murder the play by saying it in act II, scene ii. Seton (Seyton in the Arden edition) is one of Macbeth's attendant lords. He has about five lines to speak during his two appearances in the play's last act; his great moment is when he announces "The Queen, my Lord, is dead"—the line that cues Macbeth's "all our yesterdays" speech:

> Life's but a walking shadow; a poor player,
> That struts and frets his hour upon the stage,
> And then is heard no more: it is a tale
> Told by an idiot, full of sound and fury,
> Signifying nothing.

Seyton is on stage as Macbeth, night after night, repeats one of Shake-speare's most quoted and borrowed pieces of dramatic verse. Even the "poor player" who has to stand there reacting is likely to know it off by heart. The narrator's role in *Untitled Sequence*, not surprisingly, borrows from its gloom and insight into a flawed life's mean-inglessness:

> I played Seton.
>
> I
> had very little to say. And the scenery,
> the scenery was quite different: it was
> a set of collapsible platforms of hardboard sheets

> and perforated steel struts which towards the end
> of the run began to buckle, and swayed
> like reeds in the wind
> when Duncan leapt on his prey.

Here, an imperfect rhyme on verb and noun sounds a close to the stanza, where the play's denouement and the floppy scenery are figures for a series of collapsing structures—the flopping play itself, the narrator's sense of himself, the idea of the players as a coherent group, and on to more inclusive structures such as Europe, humanity, or that one noted in section 2: "we are divided, and reach across / by magic, which in schools is called / sympathy, and in universities, structure." But what sustains the poet's claim here to give the authentic, yet more mysterious, explanation for what allows us to reach across division while other explanations are denigrated as (to exaggerate for salience) humanistic clap-trap in schools and theoretical clap-trap in universities? Here lies a key issue that the sequence tours around.

The makeshift scenery of the student players also has an echo in the collapsed and temporary-seeming landscape of a bombed Germany—the Germany that was a key ideological battleground for the Cold War world through which the student players are travelling. One of the original footers to the sections ran: "a British officers' mess in a small town somewhere in the Rhine valley":

> Is there a war on? No.
>
> But there has been. A photograph
> on the hall-stand shows it, a sweep of the arm:
> all these was new builded, he was flat.

Riley's poem evenhandedly acknowledges both the disorientation of hearing your language garbled by non-native speakers, and of mangling someone else's language when abroad, as here in 8:

> So now I feel the need for a particular drink.
> It's called something like flughaven mit schmalz
> no, that's ridiculous, so I don't get one, and
> the local bearer of Hölderlin's language looks at me
> in blank dismay.

It *is* ridiculous. The *Perfect Bound* text has "Flühock mit schloss," which gestures towards flying in "Flü-," essays a wine with "hock," and then inexplicably qualifies it "with" the fortifying "castle" or the claustrophobic "lock"; the prepublication text Riley sent me to work from has "flughaven mit schlosen" in which, haplessly felicitous, "flughaven" means "airport," "mit" is still "with" and "schlosen" sounds like a badly defective participle of the verb "to close": "geschlossen." So is this attempt at ordering a drink, in which only the "mit" might be correct, a hopelessly garbled version of "The airport is closed"? Re-revising "schlosen" to "schmalz" on the Wild Honey proofs looks like a misjudgement; the Yiddish-derived loanword for sentimental art is worse than ridiculous: it's impossible, as the student player would surely have known. That lost echo of a sense in "schloss" or "geschlossen" had added to the serious air of entrapment in *Untitled Sequence*, as more sardonically here in 9:

> It's also quite exciting
> staying in a hotel without windows.
> You could really work here: you could
> steer the whole bunker into victory.
> The varieties of reflected light
> suddenly seem a paltry affair to this
> concrete corridor and threadbare carpet,
> the tiny, empty bar, the porter in his
> alcove with his accounts.

The ghastly hotel momentarily conjures up a memory of Hitler in the Berlin Führerbunker, or of the winners in their blastproof shelters after a nuclear exchange. "You could really work here" away from the distractions of the natural world, but would you really want to, and for how long? Riley's choice of German poet to register his implicit point about art and language-competence is hardly accidental. Hölderlin (rather than the obvious candidate for the role of language representative, Goethe) has been a favourite of some English poets since David Gascoyne translated from his work. Though Michael Hamburger had also published a large volume of his poems in English translation by this date, Riley is probably making acknowledgement of the interest in the disturbed visionary's writings shown by Tim Longville and John Riley of the Grosseteste Press, publishers of *The Linear Journal*.

However, having evoked the shadow of the pathetic fallacy so as to figure a relationship between the poor players and their collapsible scenery, or between the students when not called upon to strut and fret, and their disorientated experiences of knocked-about cities, the poet distinguishes the actors and their surroundings by concentrating, perhaps a little melodramatically, on the dejection of the young theatre company in 8:

> But all that was really damaged
> was the fiction of ourselves,
> shattered. The ruins of empire strewn
> around us were works of art compared
> to what we knew we weren't qualified
> to be. The buildings are now all razed and
> grass grows in their spaces, for a time.
>
> Ruins of a war, ruins
> of a reconstruction scheme, the vast
> acreage of wonderful rubbish lying
> still in the day, meeting the light

Thus in "I played Seton. / I / had very little to say" the lineation plays up the romantically isolated vulnerability of that "collapsing structure" ("the fiction of ourselves") by detaching the subject pronoun from its verb and allowing it a line all of its own. The task of the poem will be to give validity to this "I," distinguished from an inflated and presumptuous "we," by finding means for bringing it into relation with those others and things from which it feels separated— its main implement for achieving this validation being the stylistic flexibility of the phrasing, lineation and diction.

Such a task, in such unpropitious circumstances, is in need of permission. Riley ends the first section of his sequence by finding this in the heart of pointlessness and indifference:

> Knowing at last how little it mattered
> whether this show was on. Making it possible
> to continue.

Coming at the end of part 1 this is inevitably reflexive, expressing the poem's sense, at that moment, of how a poet may also be able to continue—one which acknowledges the real difficulty of attempting to do something substantial when you are very much unacknowledged. And no legislator either. The benefit of that minimal self-permission is that if you can find it there, you can find it anywhere. A reader might also notice how much the poem denigrates and minimizes the language competences of its protagonist, and yet in this unpropitious situation that protagonist will try to rise to some memorable speech and significant utterance.

The unpropitious situation is registered for us by an unpropitious subject, overtly vulnerable, but not appealing for sympathy, intent on registering the subjectivity of the view, its singularity:

> Walking this bright boulevard which really
> could be anywhere, any big place,
> I seem made of insubstantial elements
> like a leaf in the wind, an unsteered ship,
> small bird lost in the sky roads:
> weightless, of no authority, moving
> on the stream of my, or someone else's
> wakefulness

The figures for the self here ("leaf…unsteered ship…small bird") sound like much-circulated lyrical tender, and "I seem made of insubstantial elements / like a leaf in the wind" (a phrase worked into John James's poem "Sister Midnight") draws on the medieval Latin of the Archpoet; but the phrase "or someone else's / wakefulness" asks what is staked by this literary subjectivity. How important is it that this is happening to this person? Is the subject a blank counter for what anyone might feel, but which someone specific will have to if it is to be part of a lyric sequence? If the collapsed sense of self that the sequence writes from signals a crisis of purpose for the poet, it is not a crisis unique to those composing poetry. Riley's "I" character in these poems shares some of the cultural characteristics of the classic Cold War figures "waiting" in theatrical settings like Beckett's most famous play, or Stoppard's Shakespearean one. Section 26 of *The Linear Journal* announces this theme too: "waiting also, for the next phase of waiting" and "waiting for what you say, what you bring / into the air."

Untitled Sequence, though, has the spiritual condition of waiting in history, waiting in an individual life, built into its narrative situation. Riley's "I" is someone—

> Waiting
> for a 5-minute cue in Act IV. But we become
> contracted, there's a strength in it, we drag
> the most collapsed notions of our stature
> around with us for years regardless and then
> we behave like people after all.

Here's the phrase "collapsing structure" from 1, transmogrified into "collapsed…stature." This word "collapse" and its variants had echoed throughout *The Linear Journal*: "people's legs collapse, habitually, it's alright / everyone is sub-standard, artistically speaking"; "the development section collapsing on me in the night"; "and maybe an entire life / is waiting to be collapsed in the next phase." Part 7 of *Untitled Sequence* narrates just such a fall:

> Sometimes I like myself very much
> and think I'd make a first-rate detective.
> Except for the bits that involve courage.
> and expertise. and enthusiasm for the whole thing.

The Marlowe-like detective, *in* a nasty situation but not *of* it, is a familiar role model for the junior poet. Riley makes skillful mockery both of liking "myself very much" (a sure sign something is wrong) and of this poet-as-detective idea—for "courage" and "expertise" and "enthusiasm" are required of someone engaged on a case, whereas the poet-detective is usually just an isolated waiter and watcher. By the end of that sequence of marked sentence-close revisions, there's little left to speak of in the "first-rate" gumshoe musing.

A person who sometimes likes himself "very much" is concerned about whether others share the same opinion. Hence the problems of group identities and subjectivities in *Untitled Sequence*, a note struck by the sequence's opening, its isolated "I" and the problem of a relation with pluralities:

> And then we… No,
> Not "we."
> I.
> (Can't I get rid of that inflated pronoun?)
> What was I going to say?

What's telling about this is that while others were wondering about how to reclaim poetry's cultural centrality by abandoning the limited, lyrical subject in search of a communal voice, or by effecting an absence of pronoun-marked subjectivity, Riley writes with the specified aim of reinstating the singular subject, anxieties and all:

> All this is a method
> of avoiding looking you in the face
> because I'm shy or nervous or I'm
> a latent homosexual (ouch) or something
> distracted me, a crash or two outside,

> something one of us dropped in the grass a
> collapsing structure.

In the *Perfect Bound* text "(ouch)" had been "(oh)": the surprise of a recognition has been turned into the twinge of a revelation. And who is the "you" here? It must indefinitely include the reader, the audiences of the play, other actors in the troupe. The same could be asked for "one of us," where that first person plural raises its head again. The sensed problem of whether the players are a group or a collection of isolated individuals is directly addressed at the opening of 5:

> Evenings off we drift and scatter,
> wandering round a foreign city,
> we re-certify small agreements.

If you specify who "we" are then you make no necessary claim to speak for others, merely to report on the behaviour of a limited group. However, if you don't specify, then the pronoun will likely balloon out in its reference to include any readers and even humanity at large. Part of the rhetorical device of Riley's sequence is to keep both "we" and "you" pronouns hesitant between specified and unspecified options. So his narrative dramatizes the post-romantic/modernist problem of the relationship between the poetic subject locked in a private life and putative willing readers (a public), for the student actors are "playing in gymnasia halls / and cinemas before large but entirely / compulsory audiences."

Riley's "I" character is practically obsessed with what can or may join us together. The use of intimate-milieu detail, *à la* Frank O'Hara, is here put to a more overtly moralized purpose:

> At times like this questions such as
> I wonder what John's doing now?
> assume a hitherto unrealised importance
> and tenacity, as a matter of, oh — survival
> even.

In the light of a work like *Untitled Sequence*, Riley, far from being an explorer of marginal possibilities, seems intent on performing culturally central tasks:

> The wonder is what does survive here
> of the eye-light
>
>   in a metropolis meaning
> we are divided, and reach across

by magic, which in schools is called
sympathy, and in universities, structure.

In this passage already referred to, the poem grows sourly smart about the cultural role of English Literature, Shakespeare's *Macbeth* being a prime recruit, and how it has been moralized to function, often implausibly, as a substitute for religion in the inculcation and maintenance of social relations. But if Riley seems sardonic about an "only connect" liberalism, it may be so as to smuggle a more mysterious version of it back as…magic? Shakespeare's play, its weird sisters and their prophecies, gives little positive timbre to that word.

Riley is not one of those writers drawn to a desiccating of the human subject in poetry, not one who assumes it must be expunged so as to rid culture of that pasteboard enemy, the bourgeois subject. Rather, he attempts to sustain the poetic subject on other grounds. He is able to approach the issue of our relatedness only and precisely because he includes himself in as a vulnerable and damaged part of the material which can find itself in or out of relations with others and things. The sequence follows that crushed self, the student actor; but tracking him across Germany is an ambitious poetic subject embedded in the writing who takes his all-but-rhapsodic chances when they are suitably prepared in the casually sketched circumstances.

What's underplayed is the notion of a guiding consciousness other than the inscribed subject, but this can be heard as present in the sound of the lyrical flights:

> Ruins of a war, ruins
> of a reconstruction scheme, the vast
> acreage of wonderful rubbish lying
> still in the day, meeting the light
> where the mind stops urging itself
>
> O the bright world is harder than horn.

The seeming address turns into an exclamation. The "bright" turns into the "harder": lyricism both evokes a surface pleasure and recognizes an obdurate resistance. The obduracy is a thing equally to confront and be grateful for. The poetic voice in its ambivalences can render both for our benefit. The last line of this section is remarkable in its change of register and pitch. It manifests the poet's true self-image as distinct from that of the student actor who is its stand-in within the narrative. Our being divided and the possibilities for connectedness ("we…reach across / by magic") constitute a drama played out in the poem at a level some way above the mimetic fallacy, in the terms of the poem's lineation—as in that line-break above—and the sustained syntax. For this sequence, the idiom that Riley develops takes the text a distance from the "fracturing" gestures of *The Linear Journal* (such as this from section 30: "a littered field / beautiful refuse of the mind / O / the possibilities!") towards a style distinctly more continuous and declarative, as here once more in the hotel with no windows of part 9:

> To speak of love and point
> to the nearest blank wall
> and the rest is extra,
> deserved, and won, but extra,
> my own love of you, and you and you…
>
> When all that was damaged was the map itself
> of what lies between us.

In its self-correcting mannerism ("love of you, and you and you…") the passage does break off and take up again with a syntactic disjuncture, but barely a semantic one. Once again, what Riley brings to that stuttering way of proceeding is a fairly articulated, founding moral urgency. We can interpolate it across the gaps—by magic, or, if you prefer, by sympathy, or, again, by implicitly construable structure.

So the personal feeling of collapse is made to bear the sense of a more general collapse and the vulnerability of the "I" comes to represent a condition of the social and human fabric. The poem instances a desire to do repairs to this, and attempts what it can at the level of its structured voicing, but is wide enough awake not to think that this effort can be made to register on the hard world by an act of afflatus, or aesthetic fiat. *Untitled Sequence* is awake in its casual registering of circumstance on a map of Europe during the Cold War, in its sense of Germany: "It is a country turned against its own borders, / falling in double light across the streets." And a few lines later:

> It is very much Europe, this,
> very much a tattered bar off-centre to
> a sense of realised spaciousness now inhabited
> mainly by retail chains.
> Where in the lower stratum
> of a converted warehouse a horizontally
> elongated structure dimly glows in the
> night of dereliction.

What is the "structure" that "dimly glows" here? Decentredness, far from being a state to aim for (so as to throw off the spectre of collusion with a theoretically constructed notion of the hegemonic subject), is represented in the sequence as a condition of disempowerment. Its opposite, a "realised spaciousness" like those "Central Gardens" or parkland, has been bought up by the "retail chains"—with their quiet pun from the slogan at the end of *The Communist Manifesto*. Unsurprisingly, the sequence articulates a predicament that it can't begin to transform, not least because of the terms in which the problem is set. But what it can do is to mitigate the consequences of the problem with its style, that elongated structure (linear journal) dimly glowing "in the / night of dereliction"—and with this the strategies of the *Untitled Sequence* come into sharper outline.

Roy Fisher's sketch of Riley's poetic in the later *Lines on the Liver* from a recent interview with John Kerrigan ("Come to Think of It, the Imagination" in *News for the Ear: A Homage to Roy Fisher*) praises its contrariness:

I think Peter's hard/soft/hard, straight/twisted/straight poetic is a valiant attempt to duck out from under the Impossible Poetics plastic sheet, and he's good enough to have something to show.

What this indicates is that Riley has been attentive to the siren calls of "Impossible Poetics"—the risk being that you reduce your creative options to zero by imbibing too much from the prevailing theory-driven accounts of what, if you dare to go that way, will make you fatally incorrect, politically speaking. Yet Riley has cut them with some shamelessly flexible methods and obdurate materials from his own history and sensibility. The results, as Fisher's sequence of slashed concepts implies, can be heterogeneous and at odds with themselves.

Riley's poetry, at this point and later, has been composed from far-fetched allegiances whose implications can run to conflict and contradiction within the textures of the poems. Yet this is as it should be, since it both testifies to his poetry's restless ambitiousness and to the crisis in the 1960s which supposed that the old models would no longer work, but left the new models somewhat short of a broadly acknowledged cultural role. In retrospect, it may appear that the sense of a cultural purpose was too readily assumed, while the poetic means to that supposed end were never sufficiently appreciated in their consequences and, as a result, never widely absorbed. Riley's sequence exemplifies both the benefits and problems of its pluralism, not least in the attempt to get a modest and historically beaten-up English sensibility ("This would never have happened / if I'd stayed in Stockport," as section 25 of *The Linear Journal* notes) to take on the brashly enthusiastic and culturally engagé tones of the American models that the author followed and championed back then. The 1970 Cape Goliard edition of Charles Olson's collected poems, *Archaeologist of Morning*, for example, acknowledges and thanks "Mr Peter Riley, who gathered early."

A reader may hear the tensions and conflicts of allegiance in the uneasily self-dramatizing behaviour of the seemingly improvised, thinking-on-your-feet lines in part 2, when Riley writes how

> questions such as
> I wonder what John's doing now?
> assume a hitherto unrealised importance
> and tenacity, as a matter of, oh—survival
> even.

That "oh—survival / even" attempts, quite effectively, to have its flip cake and profoundly eat it too; and it's with the inherent precariousness of such a literary "collapsing structure" that I want to conclude:

> So you see there is no solution, this web
> of tensions is what we are going to live in,
> into the future; to talk of breaking it
> is to damage more than us; it is what
> also we act by, and with, raising
> messages to the ends of the earth holding
> intact each working space. A spreading
> light moves to the land's edge.
>
> Where a ship is always waiting.

"This web / of tensions" and "to talk of breaking it / is to damage more than us" carry an improvisationally structured sense of our separations and connectednesses via their syntax and enjambments—in the style itself. There is a certain lack of attunement in the breath-driven iterativeness—suggesting the benefits and drawbacks of a jamming manner, the sense of the poem as preferring (with its "better to travel than arrive" poetic) to seem more a performed "gesture" than a finally made structure.

Yet the sequence has brought to articulation a dilemma about the grounds and sources of poetic authority—to which Riley brings a native charm and wit, self-deprecating and modest, but with an ambitious lyrical impulse concealed, Trojan-horse fashion, within it. His poem avoids the occasionally fatal self-importance of the late-modernist high moral style through its informality, and the included subject's recognitions of itself as a seemingly collapsed source of insight that, nevertheless, proves thematically up to its task of articulating both its dilemma and a poetic context for the larger cultural consideration of that material. Thus, in *Untitled Sequence*, a complex of aesthetic, moral and cultural problems related to the role of the individual subject in life provides the terms for its provisional amelioration in coming to see the world as necessarily more benignly structured, a "web / of tensions" not to "talk of breaking" or that "waiting" ship which, unlike the "waiting" student actor but in concert with the poet whom he partially represents, is about to reach across geographically separated pieces of terrain. *Untitled Sequence*, like that ship, has, to borrow words from W.H. Auden and Roy Fisher, somewhere to get to and will arrive with itself.

MINING THE HEARTFOLD

Nigel Wheale

Grasmere Youth Hostel, April 1965, snow and mist in that old-style spring, and the folly of a tough walk over Helvellyn along Striding Edge and down to Patterdale, soaked through and shaking by the end of the day, perhaps a Near-Thing. Don't tell Mum and Dad. The mixture of young in the evening, and vividly, two lads from Manchester, puckish land-walkers, free through their almost-nothing status, walking out of their conurbation, old beyond their years thanks to a class-history of sharp attention. Predictably they were also army-struck, Junior Leaders but graced with the military virtues, no vices, boy-soldiers on the free high fells and laws, occasionally condescending to drop into the cushy Hostels below them. This was the mid-1960s, yes sure trembling with involuntary excitement watching the Beatles on the Sunday Palladium, but in the Youth Hostels there were older cultural traces still hanging on the air, a kind of Fifties National Service ethos, and then bright veins of Forties New Romanticism offering some mysterious allure yet to be explored, and further back still, negotiating through a black-dark thicket, the rumour of Thirties mass-trespass and the promise of a people's pastoral freedom. Those working-class boys just escaped from the TB generation, but still hollow-chested and birdlike, with a passion for the beauties of egg collecting, burning by the light of their own rare knowledges. Laurel and Hardy, Morecambe and Wise, David and Jonathan, Oberon/Puck, fourteen and fifteen, father and son. We are all held there in that full moment of what we will become, already knowing how to grow up, just waiting for the details to accumulate, the gracious pattern of our adulthood perfectly achieved. Let's go over and say hallo to those three interesting girls from Sheffield.

Reading *Love-Strife Machine* in 1969

Here was the new thing. The very pure excitement of a seriously clear format, light and square, a set of terms for the whole works, "how to sustain the music beyond / the first bright hope" (66). The way that the Courier font lies on the raked weave of the bright laid paper, genius in the design which is somehow also intimately the poetry. The make-up of the collection suggesting new possibilities for how lyric might inhabit the page, Michael Craig-Martin's structure of an envelope plotted on the untitled cover offering a diagram of how to despatch poetry to its precise readers around the nation and beyond. This is the New Occasionalism, a way to write the convincingly fleeting moment on which the largest questions are borne. The provincial truth of life in corners of England, but now in a larger kind of frame, no metropolitan condescension or smugly snug northernism; ways of living written into a texture of places, the organum of poetry, a musical gift. This poet plays his typewriter like a spinet. I'll never be this good.

"Poems written on 11th May 1968." This is the night following the "Night of the Barricades" in Paris when the French government begins to make concessions to student demands. But of course the poems don't tell you, you have to intuit the presence of those other noisier *événements* between and within the line-turns and breathings. But the weft of the writing is such that you can find your way to that unnamed material, caught invisibly within the same weave. These are respiring webs of "projective" verse which loop our British person into new kinds of context and question through persistent pressures of the frequently suspended syntax:

> a morphosis the colour of blood
> and winter sunsets   out of
> dreams of limestone   coagulates
>   into
> a device capable of speech (19)

So many poems eloquent of that moment, and still so, "the wind across the chimney top" (54), or the ordinary truths of "One Day,":

> and quite honestly
>
> turn my head and close my eyes
>
> into the hard, tall valley,
>
> the strong road, the currents that sweep
>
> across the earth (76)

Contact, 1974

"21st May. 63, Lord Street, Macclesfield. Dear Nigel Wheale, Roy Ashbury recently showed me some poems of yours, which certainly interested me… & if you'd let me know if you haven't got a copy of the magazine COLLECTION, No. 7, I could send one. In fact I have several hundred of them here so if you have any friends who'd like one…. With regards, Peter Riley. P.S. Quite incidentally—I'd be pleased if you could let me have some time a full bibliographical reference for your source for that quote about the site in North Uist— large eggs inside stone cists are the sort of thing I get excited about…." Enclosure: Statement About Poetry: "…The purpose of poetry is to de-bewitch."

Writing the Material Soul

During the 1970s Peter Riley's pamphlets and chapbooks further developed the bright lyricism of *Love-Strife Machine*, taking on more sustained modes, and mixing with the creative stimuli of improvised musics—John Tchicai and Cadentia Nova Danica, for example, in *The Whole Band* (1972), then Derek Bailey, Evan Parker, Lol Coxhill and others in *The Musicians The Instruments* (1978). Living in terraced streets as we do where the houses mostly open directly onto the mostly social pavement, it's a blessing to be able to share in the communal piano-practice hour, by simply walking by; and it's always worth pausing a little longer outside Peter Riley's front door, though more usually in the later evening.

A really rewarding connection was made with *Ground Absolute*, a selection of translations from the work of Lorand Gaspar, a Hungarian-Romanian-French-Tunisian poet-traveller-surgeon; the resulting Great Works pamphlet in 1976 was "a construct of the author's from the poem *Sol Absolu*, published by Gallimard, Paris 1972." This creative friendship has developed over the years to produce Peter Riley's "versions" of Gaspar in *Four Poems* (1993) and reciprocally, Gaspar's translations (with Sarah Clair and Claire Malroux) in *Noon Province et autres poèmes* (1996). There is an unembarrassed luxury of metaphor and reference in Gaspar's desert songs which just cannot be managed with anything like conviction in current English poetries, and Peter Riley's versions of this Franco-Judeo-Arabic vein enable a voice which couldn't otherwise sing, but which it is then possible to hear at times as a lost echo within Riley's more strictly British registers. Peter and Beryl's forays into Transylvania, partly enabled through links with Gaspar's family remaining in Romania, promise further rewarding developments along related axes.

Tracks and Mineshafts and *Two Essays* (both beautifully designed and published by Tim Longville) appeared in 1983 when the Cruise Missiles arrived in Britain and Margaret Thatcher gained her second term of office, the main question being by how big a margin she would win. Grim times but, perhaps not fortuitously, a productive moment for the New English Poetry: J.H. Prynne's *The Oval Window* appeared towards the end of 1983, also at some level a quest-poem through remote terrain (compare the cover-photograph of the first edition with the tipped-in photo of *Tracks and Mineshafts*). John Hall's 1984 essay on *Lines on the Liver* and Riley's two linked books is a thoughtful account: "These are texts of strong ethical intention which keep, on the very point of political clarity, reverting to a psychic theology of original sin. Between the person and 'the world' there are only just perceptibly the mediations of culture" (39). The poems and prose wrestle with the latest forms of social rapacity, but continue in their search for another order of being in this world:

> And famine of the earth in pictorial wars, false
> tensions, monetarization of time whereas the emptiness
> is real and there is no return, no restitution
> oh keep intact the underwing starts, the
> cup through it. (12)

"Material Soul" is the thesis-poem which constructs a distinctive kind of attention to lives led in marginalized poverty, at the edge of almost nothing. This prologue establishes the way in which the whole poem will examine the traces of human effort labouring to create the space of life:

> perception opens
> onto a cleared space, a settlement, holding
> people of all ages together,
> the whole of life, is this shift
> back, this rearing
>
> and arrival, which leaves a mark.... (7)

The paratactic glide here reads like one of Charles Olson's ambitious tropes, but a more immediate British writing-context could be Douglas Oliver's *In the Cave of Suicession* (1974), an "imperfect Derbyshire nocturne" (76) where the inquirer "Q" parks "his beige Austin car on the moorland verges of the road through Winnat's Pass in Derbyshire's Peak District" to enter an "abandoned lead mine, generally called Suicide Cave" (71). Here he will consult the oracle, infolded "in a rock of memory" through writing (69). Like the questing persona of *Tracks and Mineshafts*, who plunges "into the stone, you never see me again" (8), Oliver's inquirer enters an "earthly swallowing-up" (69). The inquiry is urgent—Q: "Alone, how do I reach the possibility of good here?"—and one of the central categories throughout Oliver's ethical poetry is again present: "Can I still continue without harm?" (78, 86). The search for "the good" conducted in the "Cave of Suicession," an allegorical space which confronts simultaneously the phantasms of succession, suicide and recession, is transacted through dialogue with visionary presences and ideal (female) others, as also in Oliver's later poem *The Infant and the Pearl* (1985). By comparison, Peter Riley's *Tracks and Mineshafts* is a more seriously incoherent text, a reading-through of what seems to be a complex series of re-scriptings, perhaps an increasingly characteristic manner of working (and so reading) for Riley's poetry from the 1980s onwards. The writer will never be able to acquit his text via this way of working, and nor will his readers—we all struggle and moil at the face-veins, anything else would be a travesty. But now and then there is the view of the day-sky turned to night through the depth of the shaft's eye, "intrusive holes in the landscape / or star targets" (18).

The "Eight Preludes" begin to exploit the vein of mining and ore-bearing promise as a working towards fullness; the landscape is streaked by manifolds, some exploited, others still unknown, which figure as the image of a "stake" which might be taken, a value and fact at odds with the failing life of the cities below. Simultaneously a relation is sketched at the edge of a northern conurbation in desperate times and as "the overtakers / glide past in their dream wagons" the climate sours (19). We encounter a lock-out at the front line where the social heart seeks warmth from oil-drum brazier fires: "someone is stockpiling sugar in an abandoned theatre across the road from where we live" (16). There is unpunctuated switching among apparently hopeless options, *à la* Beckett: "Carry on go here there make a note of it what for" (11). The mode-shifting is simultaneously fluent and desperate, from ballad strophe verses with appended tails (12) to diurnal prose notes like improvisations from *Kora in Hell* (13, 16). But there is also the alterity of a material world which is simultaneously obdurate and full of promise, the "far reaches of the upper manifold, where /

is it, what is it, green chapel if it rains it rains" (11). Gawain's en-
counter also promised to be dire, but the blade swerved and lessons
in courtesie were taken:

> I also think of you as fairest before sight
> in a vocabulary which is generally considered
> nonsense out of a 13th Century context and still
> fairer dark by the light that glims beyond. (17)

(But this chapel gets rescripted in the bleak midsection of the poem-
book, as "the dim green light of an industrial chapel," locale for a
"seemingly endless presentation dinner" [55]).

"Kings Field" is a superb prose sequence of paragraphs which hews
at the nature of expressive effort, a Blakean figure whorled within the
rock, "fingernails tight in the engravure" (24). How this commit-
ment may then inform the daily life back home becomes another
question, together with the way in which the vision can again dissi-
pate among "the world of ordinary things, that stand for personal
redundancy" (27). Yet this horror at the rubble of life is further trans-
formed in the exultation of the two final paragraph-strophes, incar-
nated like Glad Day in "a spiritual figure, full of beauty. / Completely
answering the world" (29). It is around this systole/diastole near the
heart of Peter Riley's writing—and not only his—that John Hall's
review-article attempts to analyse the nature of the poetic gesture in
Tracks and Mineshafts. How can this poetry create a discourse which
is both aesthetic and ethical, if it is in some fundamental way caught
between two such radically polarized spheres in its description of life
and the *appui* of poetry to existence?

> apart from the notions of "the world"…and "alteriority," both of which
> weight everything in favour of the isolated perceiving, desiring and knowing
> being—because they belong to it—there is nothing to offer as second term
> in a social and economic dialectic in which the configurations of power might
> be considered. (39)

Hall's review is also alert to "a feeling that there *has to be* a redemp-
tive behaviour" motivating key moments of the three texts, a direct
consequence of this traumatic dichotomy in the terrain of the poem;
"It wants to be a theory of election and is but isn't because it also has
theoretical and temperamental reasons why it can't be" (40). It may
be that John Hall's argument here circles around questions central to
the 1970s writing of Douglas Oliver, Peter Riley and J.H. Prynne,
questions that their poetries attempted to resolve in various ways,

and with varying degrees of success. *Tracks and Mineshafts* makes an immediate reply to these genuine questions in "(Letter)," which addresses the issue of being disengaged from social process. The page of welcoming correspondence to another who now feels adrift, having lost a "relentless intensity," could as well be addressed to the poem's persona: "Welcome in fact to the world, where you go on, and the images with their double edges do not at once tear at the heart, and objects no longer (fencepost, omnibus, feather, crystal) recede.... And so you move on, past the defeated and the defeating questions of who you are by reflection and accession; you move to a wider, more social and apparently firmer sphere" (32). Yet the final sentence of the letter seems to return to the remorseless desire for an ethic which will "save" through its integral stance: "Surely the whole of life is the issue at every point by obtention—your crisis is a metaphor—you are focussed (scissors, maypole, tumulus, gun) on a redemptive centre." Poet and correspondent are left where they began.

At about midpoint in the sequence it may be that the cost of this ethic begins to take its toll as the poems address the obduracy of lonely and exacting enterprise:

> To see one thing clearly we distort
> the entire landscape...
>   [yet] the one thing being known
> at once radiates back its own illumination,
> splaying up the cleft towards day. (44)

But I'm less sure of what to make of the final third of the text, an intensifying despair perhaps, prompted by discovery of some "stone in the heart" (68), flesh against stone, but that's an agreed element of the reader-risk in negotiating these poem-books which are so much more than aggregrations of lyric moments. *Tracks and Mineshafts* concludes with an elegy, "Adonais," for the miners and their works, and for the labouring persona; a "Procession of tail-lights on the motor-way arm" becomes our dome of many-coloured glass, staining the white radiance of these pages (82).

"On Cautley where a peregrine has nested, iced heather hurt the knuckles."

I began this effort intending finally to walk us back to the late 1920s and early 1930s via W.H. Auden's preoccupation with the lead-worked upper fells of Northumbria, as one poem-vein which might also run down through the Derbyshire moors of *Tracks and Mineshafts*. We might have taken in other arias to the pregnant fantasy of stone: Adrian Stokes, *Stones of Rimini*—"Under certain climatic conditions, limestone is the formation of workman-like fertility in which agricultural interference not only is, but looks like, a work of art" (32); Jacquetta Hawkes, *A Land*, perhaps even Alan Garner, *The Stone Book*—and these would have been nation-moments too, where writing caught its times in a particular fashion. And maybe it could still be true, but that route seems less convincing now. I'd wanted to say that there is a kind of consonance between Auden's massy, confident perspectives on the ways in which his world was tending, and Peter Riley's constant invocation of the whole, the whole of life, the earth, the inhabited city, which lends the work a grandeur that perhaps translates smoothly across languages—"rien de plus déconcertant que cette quiétude vigilante, aiguisée, tendue" (Labrusse 9). And that the lyric hauteur of both poetries needs to look down on the inhabited cities from the worked-out and isolated places of this world to maintain their particular strength of purchase, an edge which is also double-edged. This effortful burrowing, self-burying is what we all do, and this writing is a consummate day-book and night-book to this quality of our labours. But after days and nights on the fells and laws, let's go back down to the hostel kitchen and the mixedness of human company in the bothy, which knows perfectly well that it's only on temporary leave from the prose of the truly social, in the cities and the streets below.

Notes

"On Cautley where a peregrine has nested...": spoken by John Nower in Auden's *Paid on Both Sides*, second version (*Plays* 29).

Works Cited

Auden, W.H., and Christopher Isherwood. *Plays and Other Dramatic Writings by W.H. Auden, 1928–1938*, ed. Edward Mendelson. Princeton: Princeton University Press, 1988.

Garner, Alan. *The Stone Book*. Fontana, 1979.

Hall, John. "On *Lines on the Liver* and *Tracks and Mineshafts*." See pp. 35–42 of this journal. Reprinted from *The Many Review* 2 (Spring 1984): 12–18.

Hawkes, Jacquetta. *A Land*. London: Cresset, 1951.

Labrusse, Hughes. Preface to *Noon Province et autres poèmes*, by Peter Riley. Bilingual edition, with translations by Lorand Gaspar, Sarah Clair and Claire Malroux. Saint-Pierre-la-Vielle: Atelier La Feugraie, 1996.

Oliver, Douglas. *In the Cave of Suicession*. In *Kind*. London: Allardyce, Barnett, 1987.

Riley, Peter. *Love-Strife Machine*. London: Ferry, 1969.

———. *Tracks and Mineshafts*. Matlock: Grosseteste, 1983.

Stokes, Adrian. *Stones of Rimini*. London: Faber, 1932.

A BEARING POINT ON HURT: THOUGHTS ABOUT *OSPITA*

James Keery

I intend to follow the poem on its interpretative quest:

> Seeking a bearing point on hurt I find
> Hollows and rooms in the thick of the night,
> A building hard at work flashing its bright
> Offers into the star dome. Consigned
> Forward I bring my name in a sealed jar
> To the steps up, pay the slight fee, assent
> To slow harm by the covering letter;
> Entering into purpose distance springs
> Back from the horizon to hold the cup
> The bitter cup but true, of flesh-driven earth
> (This night is the day outside the dream, his
> Tableau my government, or family wish)
> And deep in the brickwork think of asters
> Blazing on the far links in slow birth.

I find this a compelling opening. There is little danger of any "unseemly rush from words to world" (Forrest-Thomson xi), yet the intensity of the speaking voice is palpable. It would almost be true to say that it "has a palpable design upon us." Riley has always been a poet of positive rather than "negative capability," a solemn, even at times a didactic one. *Lines on the Liver* (1981) begins with "prefatory prose" which "represents a wish to discover the meaning to my own states of a welter of enviable wisdoms clinging to my mind from the work of others." Admirably scrupulous as it is, this is clearly not the statement of "a man…capable of being in uncertainties, mysteries, doubts, without any irritable reaching out after fact and reason." Rather someone more like "Coleridge, for instance," who (according to Keats) "would let go by a fine isolated verisimilitude caught from the penetralium of mystery, from being incapable of remaining content with half knowledge." *Tracks and Mineshafts* (1983) was accompanied by *Two Essays*; and *Sea Watches* (1991) by four pages of "Topographical Notes," an exegetical "Note on the Verse Form" (which elucidates an occult "grammar of rhyming") and a programmatic flyer:

A person finds him/herself, year after year, in an ancient landscape. It is a peninsula in North Wales pointing to an unreachable island. Pilgrims' goal, rock of ages, ecstatic finality. What do you do about that? What do you bring to bear on this sense of ageing purpose begging to be renewed?

A "bearing point on hurt" might be a point where "hurt" can be borne, or endured; but it is also the point at which "you bring to bear" accumulated "wisdoms" in order to "discover the meaning." The speaker undertakes an inquiry into the problem of pain with a discursive cogency that the Age of Reason might have approved. Yet "bearing" can also mean "bringing to birth," suggesting artistic gestation rather than rational analysis. Accordingly, a tendency to illuminate and present ("bright / Offers"; "Tableau"; "asters / Blazing"), even to qualify and explain ("The bitter cup but true"; "This night is the day outside the dream"), becomes involved in images of obscurity and concealment ("in the thick of the night"; "my name in a sealed jar"; "the covering letter"; "deep in the brickwork"); and there is a curious tension between images of passive inexorability ("slow harm"; "slow birth") and active immediacy ("hard at work"; "distance springs / Back"). The rhyme-scheme follows a similar course, beginning with full-rhyme *abba* in the mode of the Petrarchan sonnet (as befits a poem entitled *Ospita*) but then forsaking any scheme until the final word "birth" picks up "earth" in line 10 (as well as, semantically, "bearing" in line 1). Both imagery and rhyme combine, at this stage, to attenuate any sense of firm ground underfoot.

Unless, of course, the "building hard at work" is simply a hospital, as in Larkin's "The Building," an extended riddle to which he provides a definite solution. The images of "lucent comb" and "clean-sliced cliff" are gestures towards indeterminacy, but clues such as one across ("what keep drawing up / At the entrance are not taxis") and two down ("Like an airport lounge") leave nothing to chance. By the fifth stanza, in which "Someone's wheeled past, in washed-to-rags ward clothes," Larkin appears to have tired of his own game: "a kind of nurse" becomes, in fact, just "The nurse." Toying rather half-heartedly with the technique of *ostranenie*, he achieves little more than coy pathos, except in the memorable contrast with daily reality: "Half-past eleven on a working day, / And these picked out of it."

"Bad naturalization," to use Veronica Forrest-Thomson's appealing jargon, exploits everything that comes to hand and ignores any inconvenient surpluses or countercurrents of meaning. It is the "unseemly rush from words to world" in action, as follows. The staff are, as usual, "hard at work," even "in the thick of the night," when the brilliantly lighted building appears to make "bright / Offers" of care and alleviation of pain to sufferers. The speaker is a patient with a "covering letter" from his or her GP and a sample in a "sealed jar." The "slow harm" is a course of treatment with cumulative side effects and the "slight fee" is a prescription charge.

Yet Riley's title is rather more cryptic than Larkin's. "Ospita" is Italian not for "hospital" (as I confess to having supposed) but for the third person singular of the verb "ospitare," to house, shelter or entertain ("ospite" = guest). The non-English title insists on the need for translation, or allegorical interpretation. What about that "slight fee," for example? I can't persuade myself I don't hear the words of another sonneteer, Hilaire (Pierre René) Belloc: "The world's a stage. The trifling entrance fee / Is paid (by proxy) to the registrar." Belloc? Why not? Riley's answer to an inquiry about the tradition present in his writing elicited a "Gasp!" from Kelvin Corcoran, in "Spitewinter Provocations," the best interview of a poet I have ever read:

English poetry. All of it, good bad and indifferent, popular and unpopular, overvalued and neglected, the lot.... The tradition is more than you can read. It's an entire climate. It has to be total...the total of what as a poet you belong to and can learn from and contribute to. Some poet might be there because of one line.... The academics insist on a fewness.... It wouldn't be so bad if they read enormous amounts of writers and then reported back on their choices but they never do that.... (14–15)

(*Only* "English poetry"? Riley quotes from languages I don't even recognize, let alone read, as in the epigraph to *Noon Province*: "Jag sjunger om det enda som forsönar..."!) It is, to anticipate, remarkable how many of the echoes I hear in the poem are of *sonnets*. It is almost as though, in order to contribute to it, Riley has indeed ingested the entire sonnet tradition, "good bad and indifferent...the lot." I find the thought of doing that inspiring, and I wouldn't put it past him (besides, "The world's a stage" appears in Larkin's *Oxford Book*). Belloc's allusion to Jacques' speech from *As You Like It* (and its bitter reprise in *Macbeth*: "Life's but a walking shadow, a poor player, / That struts and frets his hour upon the stage") is also suggestive: perhaps *Ospita* is an allegory of the "bitter cup but true" of life in time?

Macbeth's actions have "put rancours in the vessel of my peace," but the bitterest of all is the nil signification of life in time. It might be sour grapes, but that's what he says. At any rate, the hospital imagery, with its possible allegorical interpretation, brings us to the halfway point of the first sonnet, the semicolon after "covering letter"; precisely halfway, and no further.

From this point on, the "bearing point" sought by the speaker proves elusive; and so does the speaker. The first septet is syntactically simple, the subject "I" governing declarative present tenses and participles giving no cause for alarm. The second septet is more complex. The subject is no longer the lyric "I" but, apparently, "distance," which exerts itself "to hold" and also, across the parentheses, to "think." It is as hard to see what else can be the subject of "think" as to construe the syntax as it stands. If "distance" can suddenly fetch up close and hold a cup there seems no reason why it shouldn't "think of asters," though its "purpose" remains as tantalizing as the "cup…of flesh-driven earth." Are the "links" those of the great chain of being or golf "links"? Are the "asters" flowers or (etymologically) stars? "Tableau" and "family wish" have overtones of the Freudian primal scene, consistent with the oxymoronic equivalence of day and night, and "the dream" encrypts the contents of consciousness, in which the alternatives of "government" and "wish" are poles apart, not almost synonymous. The "covering letter" also begins to sound like something out of *The Interpretation of Dreams*. "Entering" begins, or as good as begins, a new sentence, in parallel with "Seeking" in the first; but in this looking-glass sentence, the lucid "I" is estranged into "distance" and distributed amongst a "family" of pronouns. The "star dome" is no longer comfortably overhead but inside-out. The syntactic doubling of the septet-sentences is a reminder of the textuality of the seeker after truth. Perhaps even the word "speaker" makes an unwarranted assumption.

At any rate, the lyric "I" reappears at the beginning of the second sonnet:

> I bear my coat and cast to a senior,
> A new-old faithfull, who should know the coils
> And corridors of the heart, the slender
> Ghost smiling to the third tune. What is false
> Be set into a pestle, what rings be
> Represented as an inner garden
> Open to Syrius, one and the same be
> Ground and broiled and spoken as your answer.

> The house is quiet, old radio music
> In the walls, scissors on the table, streaks
> Of blood in the sink. A call in the night;
> I get up, white coat, glance out at the rain
> On the glass, attend. What do I exchange for pain?
> Holding a stranger's thin arm I turn down the light.

At the end of the first sonnet "a bearing point" has been brought to "slow birth," but there are no grounds for calling off the search. The first line of the second appears to introduce another sense of "bear," an archaic synonym for "carry" or "take"—but what about "cast"? Possibly another stilted verb? With grammar in difficulties, bad naturalization tries its luck again, reading "cast" as in plaster-cast, "senior" as in professional rank, "coils / And corridors," "scissors," "blood" and "sink" as familiar hospital phenomena and the "call in the night" an emergency which a doctor in a "white coat" must "attend," giving the patient something for the "pain." Knowledge of the "corridors of the heart" might imply a "senior" heart-surgeon (though "new-old faithfull" has overtones of the patronizing periphrasis for an evergreen retainer, reinforced by the archaic variant spelling of "faithfull"). The "third tune" might be "old radio music" on Radio Three, formerly known as the Third Programme. This time, hospital imagery brings us rather more than halfway. Again, however, there is a non-negotiable sentence. The "pestle" might be requisitioned as a superannuated piece of dispensary equipment, but its religious suggestions ("the mills of God grind slowly…") are more to the point. As in the first sonnet, the emphasis is no longer on "hurt" but on truth, on "What is false" and "what rings" ("true"?). Are "hurt" and truth interchangeable, even "outside the dream"? They are almost anagrammatically interrelated:

> we learned to mouth
> Old truths, and to forget them when they hurt,
> Hurt us too much: truth became true as that.

> (Burns Singer, "The Transparent Prisoner")

Perhaps Riley, like Burns Singer, seeks "a bearing point" on both. Has this any "bearing" on the role-reversal between doctor and patient? What of the stage direction: "The house is quiet"? There is the term "house-surgeon," but a hospital is not a "house." Again, there is a Freudian hinterland. I was reminded of Macbeth's mocking request to the doctor, a "new-old faithfull" about to desert him, to "cast / The water of my land"; but also of the amazing prolepsis in his earlier inquiry about the possibility of psychoanalysis:

> Canst thou not minister to a mind diseas'd,
> Pluck from the memory a rooted sorrow,
> Raze out the written troubles of the brain…?

The "answer" he receives is compassionate, albeit negative: "Therein the patient / Must minister to himself." *Ospita* might be considered as Riley's attempt to do so. If the unconscious is structured like a language, it makes sense to consider its "troubles" as texts. "What do I exchange for pain?" Freud's "answer" was "common unhappiness," the equilibrium state of the human psyche: "Holding a stranger's thin arm I turn down the light." Ultimately, this equals acceptance of death, as Belloc accepts it in the last line of his sonnet, which might almost follow on from Riley's: "On with my coat and out into the night." The "stranger's thin arm" is reminiscent of Hardy's "hand of friendship down Life's sunless hill" ("She, to Him" I) and also of Larkin's "answer," in "Toads Revisited," to a deceptively inconsequential question: "What else can I answer…? / Give me your arm, old toad, / Help me down Cemetery Road." Larkin's reason for considering happiness out of reach was that "you know that you are going to die, and the people you love are going to die" ("An Interview with *Paris Review*" 66). What if the "stranger," the "slender / Ghost," is death itself? The synthesis of all contraries, in which "night"–"day," near–"far," "new-old," "false"–true are "Ground and broiled and spoken as your answer," becoming "one and the same"? Perhaps "what rings" is a death-knell?

It might be, if it weren't for that "inner garden / Open to Syrius"! Whatever it is that is "Represented" in this startling image, it is an ineluctable part of "your answer." I take it the reference is to Sirius, the dog-star, the brightest in the "star dome." I find the combination of "dome" and "garden" reminiscent of "Kubla Khan," with its drug-induced "vision" of plenitude and sublime denial of nil signification. Coleridge's poem culminates in an hallucinatory self-portrait with "flashing eyes," awakened out of the state described in the "Dejection" ode as "Reality's dark dream." The reality principle is powerless against the Orphic rapture of the inspired poet.

The third sonnet introduces Orpheus himself:

> Calcium night light. Suddenly a man
> Shouts, "Orpheus!" and the dying die,
> The sick sleep on, the deserted bitterly cry
> And I count the call as best I can across

The fogs of routine silence; word that holds
The earth into a chiming whole, enfolds
Love in a capsule coated with loss, never
Cedes to wishful death but calls us to drop
Our trades and be again that whirring top
On the mountain ridge, screaming down river a pain
Of incompletion, fall medallion, cut
The human heart to song. And it will, don't
Turn the light out, see to the day's wounds, won't
Stop our good hands tying, that sweet moan again.

"Calcium…light" might refer to calcium carbide, used in making acetylene gas and thus in obsolete forms of institutional illumination, in which case the stage direction might suggest a (decrepit) hospital. "Suddenly a man / Shouts" is in the same mode of naturalistic drama—but as for his shout! "Morpheus!" (the god of sleep) would be more in keeping. "Morphine!" (named after him) would be more likely. But "Orpheus!" It is nothing less than a magnificent disruption, with apparently climactic results: "the dying die." "The sick," however, "sleep on": perhaps, on second thought, "die" is a continuous present, so that "the dying" continue to die as the sick to sleep and "the deserted" to "cry." The shout, on this reading, is unheard or ignored amidst the "routine silence" in which cries of distress are muffled by familiarity as if by "fogs." Except by the speaker, whose response is to "count the call as best I can," "count" as in "count the cost" but also, I take it, as in "account for" or "give an account of." At any rate, that is what happens, assuming that the "word" is "Orpheus," whose music could charm the inanimate "earth into a chiming whole." In apposition to "the call," "word" governs an extraordinary series of increasingly high-pitched and asyntactical tropes. The "word" that was in the beginning is dejudaicized, and "Love" as a capitalized attribute of God is dechristianized, in the mythopoeic landscape of "mountain ridge" and "river" in which Orpheus met his fate. It might be Christ who "calls us to drop / Our trades" and follow him, but it is unmistakably Orpheus, dismembered by the Maenads, whose head is thrown into the River Hebrus and borne "screaming down river." Hysterical one moment, orgasmic the next, the "sweet moan" of Orphic inspiration "never / Cedes to wishful death" (cf. Keats's wishful thinking about "easeful Death" in "Ode to a Nightingale") or to the "pain / Of incompletion," possessing the power not only to redress "the day's wounds" but also to confer immortality. To "cut / The human heart" is to produce dithyrambic "song." The "fall medallion" is minted out of extremity, an "exchange for pain" that provokes a repudiation both of the "stranger's thin arm" and of the stoical intention to "turn down the light" or to endure the guttering of the "brief candle." "And it will" is a triumphant assertion.

Stoicism suffers a final defeat in the third sonnet, but there is another voice to be heard and reckoned with:

> A man shouts in pain, the voice constructs
> A door. The god batters his forehead
> On our simple attendance, the fruit
> Of centuries' observance. But to eluct
> Wisdom from hurt—any hospital bed
> Would burst into flame at the mere thought.
> The music coils within: a long solo,
> And the final voice squeezed from a lump
> Of flesh held over a sink said and we tried
> Our best to stifle that singing, "Do
> What you will to ease me over the hump
> Of death I belong to the great outside.
> My burning lust courses at the last through Hell.
> The pain of what I couldn't manage spreads like a bell."

This sonnet is a climax, but also a palinode. It begins with a rebuttal of triumphalism, a harsh insistence on the fact of suffering. The rhapsodic image in the third sonnet of "a capsule coated with loss" suggests that, just as a coating of sugar sweetens the bitter medicinal powder, so "loss" and "pain" are mere extrinsic and deceptive guises of "Love." Now, however, what I take to be the same shout of "Orpheus" is heard only as an expression of physical "pain." It "constructs / A door." That the door is closed goes without saying but is implied by the terseness of the phrase and the way enjambment confronts the eye with a full stop. Against it "the gods themselves / Contend in vain"; the assault for which Donne pleads in the fourteenth "Holy Sonnet" ("Batter my heart, three-personed God") is reduced to head-banging futility. The accumulated "wisdoms," "the fruit / Of centuries' observance," cut no ice. Despite the unspecified lowercase "god," both "observance" and "attendance" have connotations of Christian worship, but at this point the speaker rises to a prophetic pitch of indignation at the quintessentially Christian idea of wisdom through suffering. I think the image of the hospital bed bursting into flames at the thought is just utterly wonderful. Has the pathetic fallacy ever been put to better use? Or the neologistic archaism? "Ineluctable" is the only familiar formation from the verb "to eluct," to struggle forth, recorded by the *OED* as "Obs. rare," with a single citation: "They did eluctate out of their injuries with credit to themselves" (Bishop Hacket, 1670). Three of four citations of the noun "eluctation" ("obs.") carry similarly pious and triumphal connotations: "There is nothing more acceptable unto the ingenious world, than this noble eluctation of truth" (Sir Thomas Browne, 1682); "I shall be with him in his Eluctations, in his Victory" (Donne, 1627); "At last we…find our selves freed by a comfortable and joyous eluctation" (Bishop Hall, 1656). An apothegm on "the eluctation of wisdom from pain" would not look out of place. Taken together, the citations represent a whole seventeenth-century wisdom literature. Riley cuts it off short ("eluct" is unrecorded), giving an edge of curt puritanism (sharpened by the strongest rhyme in the poem) to the imagined reaction of any right-thinking "hospital bed." The image of spontaneous combustion has mordancy and wit to match its brilliance.

The sestet is followed by a "long solo" of an octave, a grotesque, almost farcical re-enactment of the third sonnet. "The human heart" becomes "a lump / Of flesh" to be "squeezed…over a sink," a variation by Francis Bacon on the theme of "Love." In this hospital-sink drama, the choric voice of recoil ("we tried / Our best to stifle that singing") is intrinsic to the "coils" of "music," just as the passionate refusal to "eluct / Wisdom from hurt" is intrinsic to the quest for "a bearing point" upon it. The image of "the hump / Of death," highlighted by the inelegant rhyme and effortful enjambment, strikes a strangely bathetic note, together with the deathlessly rhetorical gesture towards "the great outside." Though awkward, however, the first sentence uttered by "the final voice" appears to make an extraordinary assertion. I construe it in parallel with "we tried / Our best": "Whatever efforts you make are bound to fail; you cannot ease the pain of my terminal suffering any more than you can stifle my singing. It is my very agony that enables me to go beyond the bounds of mortality."

It is at this point that *Ospita* comes uncannily close to Burns Singer's "Sonnets to a Dying Man":

> To talk to you in all moralities,
> Each to its true end mastered, till all one
> Their intertwining helpful verities
> Collapse across the gesture of your pain,
> And then begin, replete in my whole tongue,
> Each blind persuasion searched and hidden in

> Its language luminously, at last begin
> To tell you that, impossibly as you clung
> To what you could not keep, what clings to you
> Claws at its own ghost also yet to be
> Created by your death, that though it try
> To filch the pain which you are living through
> It cannot take it: nothing can undo
> The immortality of the day you die.

This is the first of fifty. Like *Ospita*, Singer's sequence combines positive capability with extreme textuality, in which a family of pronouns conducts a compelling argument in a flowing combination of "mere thought" and *symbolisme*: "Time's acres kindled in the sort of way / That could not burn us back to what we…merely thought we knew" (XXVIII). Singer also makes intermittent use of the hospital scenario, but his "Dying Man" is no more specific than Riley's "man." As in *Ospita*, the ultimate scenario is the "ecstatic finality" of Orphic inspiration:

> Love was the unconditional condition
> Of peace in heaven or of hope in hell….
> From all your deaths love floats its worlds, and cries
> To you to follow by the million on
> A fugue of footsteps of immense replies. (VIII)

Singer's direct treatment of the theme, "The Love of Orpheus," was preceded by an inchoate poem, written in 1947 at the age of eighteen, in which Orpheus is the unnamed protagonist:

> I who have been a listener in the halls
> Of universal anguish, am become all things
> I listened to and loved. Wherever falls
> The guillotine of time my dead head sings.

Not even Peter Riley could have read "The Circle of the Sun," which has yet to be published, but had he needed an epigraph for *Ospita*, he could have done worse.

The couplet of the sixth sonnet is a jangling aria from *Orpheus: The Remake*. Bad naturalization supplies the libretto, in which the "god" (Orpheus was mortal, strictly speaking, but only just) "courses… through Hell" like the River Styx, which he negotiates by charming Charon the boatman. Equally charmed, Dis allows Eurydice to follow him out of Hades on one condition, but he "couldn't manage" to avoid a backward glance. The "bell" tolls a knell for Eurydice.

Also, perhaps, for the parallel search on which the speaker sets out in the first sonnet. How could a "bearing point" be found when "pain" is reverberating through the system? The fifth sonnet is at once a poetic collapse and a brilliantly constructed expression of moral and formal exhaustion:

> This house constructed as an escape
> From harm is unlikely to escape
> Its own folly as a new escape
> From language and source of new dolour.
> A woman shouts down a corridor
> A real name: "Sidney! Sidney! Sidney!"
> A door slams bone shut. I am sorry
> To have life shot through by her call
> I can't dream any harder the fall
> Of light onto the wet leaf, the stain
> Of nurture on a simple erection:
> In the end she is right: the rape
> Of endless joy and everyone's to blame.
> Out on the lake the long boats wane.

"This house" is a construction of language, a sonnet in a house of sonnets, like Rossetti's "The House of Life," and a house of cards. The collapse of confidence is complete and undermines the whole poem: "to house" is one of the meanings of "ospitare." The stepped repetition of "escape" constructs a concrete fire-escape as well as a subliminal warning: it is almost as if the building has "burst into flame." The "door" that "slams bone shut" suggests a coffin-lid, and I can't help thinking of Rossetti's burial of his manuscript alongside Lizzie Siddall, only to retrieve it by exhumation some time later: a story as macabre as "The House of Usher" and a grotesque imbroglio of "folly," "dolour" and desecration if not an act of necrophilic "rape." A complex response to "life" in this "house" finds expression in "A real name" shouted by a woman. The name is that of a noble English sonneteer, another inhabitant of "The House of Fame" that appears, from this elevation, nothing but a grandiose "folly." It is also, of course, an English Christian name, which happens to have been common in the recent past amongst working-class middle-aged men. The woman who shouts "Sidney!" eclipses, at this point, the man who shouts "Orpheus!" "Sidney" is a "real name"; "Orpheus" is not. His "voice constructs / A door"; at the sound of hers, "A door slams bone shut." Illusorily, it would appear, his voice held "earth" spellbound "in a chiming whole"; now "life" itself is "shot through by her call." The "house" of English poetry is a "source of new dolour," but such a poeticism has a hollow ring when set against the plain-spoken response to the woman's "call": "I am sorry..."; "I can't..."; "In the end she is right." Finally, the fact that it is made by a "woman" and not by a "man" intensifies the speaker's despair and guilt.

It has to be said that "rape" is a bitterly loaded metaphor, particularly if "everyone's to blame." What, exactly, is the woman "right" about? Inferred by the abject speaker from the repetition of a name, the indictment is nevertheless a comprehensive one. It is as if all cultural constructs, all experience at a higher evolutionary level than "the fall / Of light onto the wet leaf" or the "simple erection" of an innocent primate, everything belonging to "nurture" as opposed to nature, were tainted by the sexual aggression of men. There is no "bearing point on hurt" in (traditionally misogynistic) poetic language, which will always "escape / From harm" into the anaesthetized nullity of "dolour." Insofar as I can make anything of the last line, it strikes me as a detumescent murmur of dismay. This is truly the nadir of the poem.

The sixth sonnet manages an extraordinary "escape / From harm":

> At night the walls are blank but we can hear
> The plovers crying in the dark fields, their
> Wings beating over waves of wheat. Downstairs
> Someone opens the piano and strikes a chord
> That tenses the flanks of hope. Again there
> Is a silence in which the lapwings graze
> The ear tips and clouded underwing
> Swoops across the sky. Then where and where
> In this globe of health we balance and bear
> From room to room, where is a lasting thing?
> Where is a good done that also stays it?
> Someone attempts the new soft swing but out
> In the earthglow between mind and chest
> Brilliant metallic birds like kisses dive to rest.

The opening might appear to be in keeping with the sequence: "At night the walls are blank but we can hear...crying." Yet the sonnet as a whole is in a very different vein. The cries are those of lapwings, not distressed people. It is as if Riley has accepted an offer by Michael Haslam:

> Here, take these token wings,
>   an interruption to an argument,
>   a stop upon an outrage and an anger;

> may they carry you through areas
> of Spiritual Danger —
>
> the infernal haunt that hurts internally (79)

Continual Song begins with "WINGS / in a *blank* white shining room"
with "white … *walls*" (italics mine). The "wings" are those of a kes-
trel, but I'm sure I can hear Haslam's lapwings too:

> Lapwings hanker spectro-sexually, flap
> against the blanks in cross black clouds.… (101)

Continual Song, "a sequence of improvisations upon double-sonnets"
(163), appeared in 1986, the year before *Ospita*. Riley reviewed it in
Reality Studios 9 (1987), beginning, "… for, *ists Orpheus, wenn es singt*"
(in allusion to Rilke's *Sonnets to Orpheus*). Applying the term "Orphic"
to Haslam's "mode of high transformational lyric," Riley describes "a
record of progressive self-realisation which patiently … gathers each
assemblage of imagery together and rides it forwards in the search for
cohesive summation" (93–94). It takes nothing away from Riley's
generous reading of Haslam to make a connection with his remarks
in the "Readers' Poll" of the same issue of *Reality Studios* "concerning
the actual proximity of one's own new hopes and quite obsessive wor-
rying focus on what has just been bequeathed to the world," namely,
Ospita.

It is clear that Riley identifies with Haslam as "a poet determined
to continue [the] central tradition of poetry, against all the odds of
favour and fashion": "After all, most British poets of the last 50 years
who have dared a mode even tentatively 'Orphic' … have had their
knuckles severely rapped" (93–94). By Kingsley Amis, for example,
in his anti-Rilkean "Sonnet *from* Orpheus" (italics mine): "And now
I'm tired of being the trade-name / on boxes of assorted junk.… /
Speak for yourselves, or not at all; this game / is up — your mannikin
has had enough" (Morrison 193). Or by Larkin: "I am not going to
fall on my face every time someone uses words such as Orpheus or
Faust or Judas" ("Interview" 69–70). Riley and Haslam reopen com-
munications with the Apocalyptic poets of the 1940s at whom Larkin
and Amis, and their Movement confederates, were directing their
fire. Riley's editions of Nicholas Moore and publication of Dorian
Cooke were early stages in the rehabilitation of the Apocalyptic poets,
a rehabilitation now gathering momentum: four were featured in *Con-
ductors of Chaos*, Iain Sinclair's anthology of "elective outsiders" pub-
lished in 1996, and at the recent University of London conference on

"Larkin and the 1940s" there were papers on, amongst others, W.S. Graham (by Tony Lopez), J.F. Hendry (by Andrew Crozier) and Burns Singer (by me). According to Peter Riley, in a letter to me of 4 June 1991, it was Singer's work that "kept some sort of flame alive in the late fifties which links Graham and Prynne," a flame with which Haslam and Riley continue to burn.

It is at this point in *Ospita* that Riley is closest to Haslam. I think the key word is "spectro-sexually." The sonnet seems to me to be suffused with spectro-sexuality, an eroticization of landscape, perception and gesture that is perhaps the last thing one would expect to find in any sequel to the fifth. The simile in the last line, "birds like kisses," colours the whole. It is indeed "an interruption to an argument." It might even be described as an "assemblage" of non sequiturs. Waves of lyrical images arrive out of the blue. Or almost. For there is, as I have noted, a deceptive continuity in the opening lines ("night"; "walls"; "blank"; "crying"; "dark"), a continuity extended to a series of ominous verbs ("beating"; "strikes"; "tenses"; "graze") which, however, in context, all denote something evocative or pleasant. As a musical transition, in fact, it is skilfully managed, the striking "chord" and ensuing "silence" integrated into a plangent passage by alliteration and enjambment. Still, the disjunction remains. "A door slams bone shut": the two spondees are weighted with utter dejection. "Someone opens the piano": soft sounds, open vowels and light stresses give "hope" by a kind of onomatopoeia. A "simple erection" is tarred by association with "rape." Music "tenses the flanks of hope" with what else but desire? Life is "shot through" by the woman's shout like a ricochet in an echoing "corridor." The mirror-images "ear*th*glow" and "**glo**be of heal*th*" evoke a sense of rosy plenitude. "Sidney" is specified by agonized repetition. An unspecified "Someone" strikes a chord and "attempts the new soft swing," which sounds delightful.

We seem to be proceeding on different premises. It takes considerable aplomb to introduce "this globe of health" when the sequence has been preoccupied with suffering, pain and death and to all intents and purposes set in a hospital. But the quest, or question, seems to have changed, too. "Then…where is a lasting thing?" arises out of a desire to perpetuate or immortalize all that is "good" in life; the quest for "a bearing point on hurt" from a desire to come to terms with all that tastes "bitter." One implies that life is too short; the other that it is difficult to endure. Perhaps most disconcerting are the echoes of Hopkins's anguished lines from "The Wreck of the Deutschland" ("where, where was a, where was a place?") and "No worst, there is none" ("Comforter, where, where is your comforting?"). This strikes me as nothing less than a comprehensive repudiation of the "world-sorrow" of the "terrible sonnets." There is a lack of urgency to the two questions that verges on the complacent, almost a sense of the satisfied sigh: *Ah, would that 'twere possible....* Even the word "bear" has lost its connotations of suffering or endurance: in combination with "balance" it carries suggestions of elegance and formality, of the value and magnitude (not fragility) of the all-encompassing "globe of health." The "Brilliant metallic birds" have a symbolist erotic sheen but also a Yeatsian inhumanity. They are a bewildering "exchange for pain," a far cry from the compassion and vulnerability of the gesture that concludes the second sonnet: "Holding a stranger's thin arm I turn down the light."

The seventh sonnet appears to pick up the narrative thread from earlier in the poem, but again only momentarily:

> The man dies and the bell sounds across
> Grass and sea and mixes with the gulls.
> The dream sleeps into the morning, turns
> On its side and drifts along the coast
> Under the great grey cliffs and buildings
> Dedicated to healing but now
> Empty and dark at dawn, the sharp keens
> Of the white hens warning us to be slow.
> We comfort as if there were no cost,
> As if pain could be stilled to patience
> Separately, and the story lost.
> Good men have died in empty time
> But loading their bite on th'intrinsic nation
> Steady as grade of light, or yellow chime.

The assumption that the same man makes the "call in the night" in the second sonnet, shouts "Orpheus!" in the third, "shouts in pain" in the fourth and now "dies" seems to be reinforced by the clear association of "the bell" with death. Yet the second line has a sense of alleviation and serenity that represents a further relaxation from the sensuous arousal of the sixth sonnet. The "gulls" strike me as an emblem of risen souls. The "waves of wheat" prefigure the "Grass and sea" as the lapwings the "gulls," but the intensity of that "crying" and "beating," striking and tensing, appears to be dissipating, an impression amusingly borne out by the image of a dream enjoying a lie-in, turning over and drifting along a rather scenic "coast," perhaps the border of consciousness. Yet the fifth line takes a less picturesque and again increasingly ominous path "Under the great grey cliffs." It even seems to regress in time, "into the morning" suggesting a later hour than "dawn," and both the "buildings" and the "hens" are disconcerting. The collocation of "cliffs" and "buildings" in the context of a riddle to which the answer seems to be "hospital" reminds me again of Larkin, no less so because the answer is wrong. Hospitals are neither "Empty" nor "dark at dawn." Those "buildings / Dedicated to healing" must surely be churches, like Larkin's "accoutred frowsty barn," complete with keening "hens." Hens neither wail nor mourn "outside the dream." They do give "warning," of a kind, "at dawn," but "sharp keens" has a dreamlike blend of tautology ("keen" as adjective = "sharp") and oxymoron (it's hard to wail sharply).

The dream-ominousness of the octave then modulates in the sestet into a "warning" of another kind altogether. The lucid admonition on the subject of pain is abstract to the point of sententiousness. The tone is no nearer to Hopkins's writhing anguish than in the previous sonnet. The sententia might be interpreted as a rationale for suffering, finding the loss of poetic power a poor "exchange for pain." The "cost" of "comfort" is to be condemned to life in "empty time," from which poets, but not "Good men," redeem themselves by the transmutation of unstilled "pain" into Orphic song. "Separately" seems to do little for its keep, and a phrase opposite in meaning to "the story lost" would admittedly make more consistent sense, but even so that hospital bed is beginning to smoke a bit. Surely a warning of the cost of comfort implies a desire "to eluct / Wisdom from hurt"? The twelfth line is transparent but also "empty," a discard from "Do Not Go Gentle…" ("Good men, the last wave by, crying how bright…"). Except for a suggestion of an affinity between "their bite" and Thomas's injunction of savage resistance to death ("Rage, rage…"), I don't know what is meant by "loading their bite on th'intrinsic nation" at all. For once, the effect of the archaism seems purely arbitrary, not least because it fails to perform the traditional function of eliding an extrametrical syllable, as in an arbitrary variation: "But load their bite upon th'intrinsic chime." As it stands, the line is as rhythmless as it is opaque, in marked contrast to the one that follows, in which the initial trochee and four iambs constitute a model pentameter, complete with final rhyme. "Steady as grade of light" might refer to the wattage of standard bulbs as opposed to natural (or spiritual) light, perhaps returning us to an institution. Similarly, the synaesthetic "yellow chime" recalls the "chiming whole" of Apocalyptic inspiration in the fourth sonnet, but the adjective "Steady," the metrical regularity and the rhyme with "time" are more suggestive of a clock than a peal of bells or the music of the spheres. If the octave is a dreamy enigma, perhaps, with a degree of special pleading, the same might just be said of the sestet.

The eighth sonnet is an intriguing continuation in the same vein, but at the same time there is the option of a coherent narrative about a figure now explicitly referred to as "the dreamer":

> Time drags its heals on the dreamer who hears
> His body calling him like a discant
> Semaphore, a sign hung on a fruit shop
> Under the castle wall. The sheets are bright
> Anger the oxide of faith and he fears
> The fall into humanity, the slant
> Of honey and cream; those fair lids droop
> And he is solitary on the white
> Road across the heath, he is close to tears
> For the imperfected lives he couldn't want
> To bring to their moment of concord and float
> On further life. The swallows are in flight
> Over the russet fields crackling with fear
> As he enters the day's gate as is right.

Is *Ospita*, in fact, a generic "dream poem"? A parallel might be drawn with *Tracks and Mineshafts*, one of whose accompanying *Two Essays* is a treatise on geological formations and mining methods and the other a gnomic "Fragment" subtitled "Theses on Dream" (no more a fragment than Ashbery's poem of the same name in *The Double Dream of Spring*, a sequence of 50 ten-line constructions of impeccable formality and beauty). Not surprisingly, in the light of the poet's explicit intention to "elucidate some of the imagery of the poems," allegorical significance accretes like "fluorspar" in a "rake," culminating in an identification of mine and dream in a memorable neologism:

> In the dreamshaft it was faster: door in
> the whole, ore-body, world-image, sighted
> as a warehouse of the self from which
> we feed us a supply-line into time;
> but that copious garden (fire and ash
> crystallised in the night) is a globe
> of perception under great tension that
> at a touch flies open, bearing such
> strength and focus towards us at speed,
> faster than bone can ever withstand. (78)

Perhaps *Ospita* takes place "In the dreamward"? The lexical and symbolic parallelism between the worlds of the two poems is certainly remarkable: "door," "body," "world[-image]," "[ware]house," "time," "garden," "fire"/"flame," "ash" (in the ninth sonnet), "night," "globe," "tension"/"tenses," "open[s]," "bearing," "bone." *Ospita* would appear to be an extended treatment of this theme from *Tracks and Mineshafts*.

"Time drags its heals" is a variation on the proverb "Time heals all wounds," slyly inverted by Groucho Marx as "Time wounds all heels." Marx's poker-faced allusion to the legend of Achilles strengthens the association with the fate of Hector, whose "body" was dragged by the heels around the "wall[s]" of Troy. As contrasted with the consciousness of "the dreamer," "body" suggests a living person, but considered in relation to the series of opening images, it sounds like a corpse. There is a subliminal sense throughout the sonnet of heroic elegy. The opening phrase suggests unwillingness to wake up, but also some kind of infliction "on the dreamer." The synaesthetic "discant / Semaphore" (*OED* records "discant" as a variant of "descant") has a dreamy theatricality, reinforced by the "sign" in its enigmatic stage-setting, rather than any sense of urgency ("not waving but drowning"), and the "fruit shop" has some of the connotations of that "globe of health." Also, however, of "the fruit / Of that forbidden tree"; and "Under the castle wall" re-enacts the movement "Under" imposing or ominous "buildings" in the previous sonnet. "The sheets" belong to the dream-environment, in which, again, the synaesthetic faculty is at work: "bright / Anger the oxide of faith" mimes a simple phrase such as "bright red, the colour of desire." Anger considered as faith-oxide (perhaps the "russet" of ferrous-oxide) would be the compound resulting from the corrosion of faith, another link with the seventh sonnet, in which churches are "now / Empty and dark" and the "fall into humanity" has occurred. Perhaps "the slant / Of honey and cream" is a dream-trope of the loss of paradise, "the land of milk and honey," but there is also a suggestion of a fortunate "fall" into the compassion of the Wordsworthian "solitary."

The "heath" is Hardy's universal "Egdon," but also Macbeth's and Lear's, a setting for the endurance of "imperfected lives." The dreamer is "close to tears" on behalf of others; his "fair lids droop" in Pre-Raphaelite languor but also in sorrow. I associate the "moment of concord" with the "globe of health," "float" with "balance" and the "swallows" with the "metallic" lapwings, as though the eighth sonnet answers the two questions asked in the sixth: the dreamer is able to take "the white / Road" of dusty death as far as "further life" or immortality. Birds become emblems not of unearthly sexual glamour but of "fear"; and their "flight" is no longer an eager or predatory "dive" but an attempt to escape from a burning battlefield (not flying but fleeing). The migration of swallows has overtones of the transmigration of souls, as in the "swallow thronged loft" in "Fern Hill," but here the swallows strike me as emblems of chattering "humanity" in the mass, attractive and alive, but mortal men. The "day's gate" is the threshold of sleep but also that of death, which the dreamer crosses as of "right," despite his poignantly ambivalent relationship with the "swallows" or with those whose "imperfected lives he couldn't want / To bring to their moment of concord." The truly enigmatic phrase is "couldn't want": there is a strong suggestion of a Keatsian dreamer-poet to whom "the miseries of the world" are not "misery," whatever he might "want" to be able to feel; the "moment of concord" is unattainable by those whom misery "will not let…rest." The intention to "bring to bear" everything possible in order to find "a bearing point on hurt" culminates in an intimation of immortality.

In the ninth sonnet, however, the "body" becomes, unequivocally, a "corpse":

> They draw his body from the centre out,
> A decisive goodness. He lies flat out
> On the shore counting ills. The waves enter
> His total wealth into books of sand.
> It's enough. They are happy to inter
> His soul in lime and ash for the sake
> Of a comfortable end, the winter
> Of our success rebound in angel cake
> But winter is true numbers that blister
> From the corpse in a field, alternating
> Black and white name-tags that flitter
> Like sarcens in the treetops. Small birds sing
> His centre into holes in the snow and grey
> Doctors weeping envy send him on his way.

Little else is unequivocal. This is the most inscrutable of the ten sonnets. There is the shadow of a mythopoeic narrative of the interment of a "body," but who are "They"? None of the other sonnets begins with an indeterminate pronoun or implies a referent in the previous sonnet. To begin with, "They" sound benign, if not angelic, yet "to inter / His soul in lime and ash" is an image of ignominious oblivion. "Calcium" is the chemical basis of lime, suggesting an association between the institutions of the hospital and the prison, along the lines of Eliot's grim allegory ("The whole earth is our hospital…") or Rosencrantz's succinct rejoinder ("Then is the world one"). "But we knew the work they had been at / By the quicklime on their boots": in "The Ballad of Reading Gaol," Wilde describes the prison as the "House of Shame" in which "Grey figures" suffer and the "coarse-mouthed Doctor gloats" over the condemned man. If the "soul" is treated like the "body" of an executed criminal, what of the "body" itself? In context, "draw" might even suggest the traitor's fate of being drawn and quartered, but it also has connotations of magnetic attraction, as in Donne's first "Holy Sonnet": "And thou like adamant draw mine iron heart." The "centre" might be the heart, source of "decisive goodness"; but what are the "ills" in the next line? The metaphor of accountancy is extended by the "books of sand" in which "The waves enter / His total wealth," an image at once of inscription, an entry in an account book, and erasure, as in "writ on water," in compliance with tax legislation against taking it with you. The series of totalizing tropes including "chiming whole" and "globe of health" culminates in bankruptcy. Loss of "wealth" might be an allegorical blessing, but it's hard to see the interment of the soul as "a comfortable end." There is a suggestion of the Giant Albion and perhaps of Urizen's books of iron and brass, but even at their most mysterious Blake's epics retain a prophetic urgency that is missing here, that has indeed been calculatedly dispelled. Debits and credits cancel out in an oxymoronic charade in which "angel cake" is flavoured with "lime and ash" and the Shakespearean "winter of our discontent" becomes "the winter / Of our success." The Orphic conception of poetic immortality is scarified in the image of "true numbers that blister / From a corpse in a field." In one of *The Dunciad*'s most biting couplets, Pope allots Elkanah Settle a precise ephemerality:

> Now night descending, the proud scene was o'er
> But lived in Settle's numbers one day more.

Yet Pope's image is light-hearted in comparison. As an archaism for poetry, "numbers" has a sardonic ring in Prynne's "Numbers in Time of Trouble," in which immortality is envisaged as a modest economic reform: "That we could come off the time standard is / a first (and preliminary) proposal" (17). But what sort of poetic afterlife is denoted by "blister"? "Your name from hence immortal life shall have" (Shakespeare, Sonnet 81): the exalted sense of "name" is travestied in the image of "name-tags," perhaps those on body-bags in the aftermath of an Apocalyptic battle which lodges "sarcens in the treetops," otherwise about the last place one would expect to find a sandstone boulder deposited by glacial ice. There is an "alternating" current of meaning which switches between positive and negative implications but without generating illumination. It is hard to see how "sarcens" could "flitter": "name-tags that flitter / Like small birds" would make more sense, but the birds are engaged instead in a strange kind of singing. The "centre" is just as mystifying second time around and there is a suggestion of caricature about the "grey / Doctors weeping envy" who "send him on his way," as in the undignified image of the body lying "flat out / On the shore." My impression of the sonnet is of mockery of Donne's "sin of fear, that when I have spun / My last thread, I shall perish on the shore" ("A Hymn to God the Father").

With *Sea Watches* in mind, however, it is tempting to interpret the "dis[t]ant / Semaphore" of some of these images as "a kind of phonetic message running through the text, over above, or enmeshed with, the text's meanings": "the rhymes may follow their own logic towards a result: and if they do the fourth occurrence of each rhyme should be the result of its three antecedents" (*Sea Watches* 25). I find myself wondering if "sarcens" might be such a "fourth occurrence" in an analogous *lexical* sequence: "Calcium," "oxide," "lime," …? "Calcium night light" is a sentence consisting of three nouns, each of which recurs in various forms throughout the poem. "Sodium light" is a familiar piece of contemporary poetic diction, but the associations of calcium are primarily bio- and geological. As a constituent of all plant and animal life (specifically in bones and teeth) and of vitamin D, it is associated with healthy growth; and as a constituent of limestone (chiefly calcium carbonate) it is associated with the English landscape. The sculptural use and metaphorical properties of impure crystalline limestone, or marble, are also relevant (see Riley's reference to Hopton stone, favoured by Henry Moore, in "Spitewinter Provocations"). These connotations are countersuggestive at the point where they occur, but play freely around the "door" that "slams bone shut," the "globe of health" and the "great grey cliffs." If, as the chalky "white / Road across the heath" might imply, the "oxide" in the eighth sonnet is calcium oxide or "lime," the compound specifically named in the ninth sonnet, other wires become live. All are connected to the fourth term in the series. "Sarsdon stones," "sarsens" or less commonly "sarcens" are found on limestone, prehistoric deposits locally known as "grey-wethers," presumably as resembling sheep, though also proverbially hard. Flittering "Black and white name-tags" might look "grey," but the primary connotations of the sarcens" are of primeval age and perdurability, "aere perennius." The "books of sand" may be erased, but the "sarcens" endure like that "rock of ages, ecstatic finality." The unprepossessing "grey / Doctors" are cipher-opposites of the mythopoeic Orpheus, certificated NHS-officialdom or academia in all its pallor, frustration and dread of death, consumed by "weeping envy" for the "globe of health" that signifies the immortality of the poet.

The tenth sonnet completes the transition from summer through autumn and winter to blooming spring:

> I walked out on the morning of May 12th
> The blades were bright and coy and loud,
> Thick with languages I walked without stealth
> The fields of angry farmers, proud
> To be harmless and legal, half and half,
> No one could fathom my strong shoes,
> There is no paradise but tongue of love.
> I walked all day, I heard no news,
> When twilight filled the air with gravities
> I descended, heart full and slow,
> Down the dim fields dotted with stones and sheep
> To the house in its banks of trees
> The fire, the food, the Gurney piano,
> Having my wonderful labour to keep.

"Ac on a May morwenyng • on Maluerne hulles": the reprise of *Piers Plowman* clinches, for me at any rate, the generic status of *Ospita*, a contemporary dream-poem in which the poet walks "wyde in this world" encountering farmers who may no longer "putten hem to the plow" ("And never a ploughman under the Sun. / Never a ploughman. Never a one": Belloc again, in "Ha'nacker Mill"), but who certainly keep a jealous watch on potential trespassers. *Alstonefield* expresses it brilliantly:

> It would be specious to pretend
> that any bit of the British countryside is anything
> but an agricultural factory marked Piss Off. (28)

The awakened dreamer knows his rights of way, but wouldn't dream of trading insults whilst intent on arrival at a show-stopping pentameter: "There is no paradise but tongue of love." The sonnet is a lyrical expression of fulfillment, of a "heart full and slow"; in biblical terms, the sense that "my cup runneth over" (Psalm 23). "The bitter cup but true" of the first sonnet has its own biblical analogue in Christ's prayer for relief, but nothing could be farther from this Pentecostal joy. The "stones" are the "sarcens," "dotted" like the "sheep" they resemble across a limestone landscape, again reminiscent of Psalm 23 and the psalmodist's faith in a paradisal vision of the "Good Shepherd": "Yea, though I walk through the valley of the shadow of death, I will fear no evil." The "blades" are those of "scissors" or swords transfigured into leaves of grass, mercurial, biblical and democratic, "luminously peopled" as in Larkin's "Here" and suffused with the sexuality of the sixth sonnet or at any rate its daylight equivalent. The "languages" are those of the gift of tongues as well as the "words / Uttered on all sides by birds" discriminated by Auden ("Bird-Language"), "Thick" suggesting the richness and abundance of inspiration and desire. The "angry farmers" and "strong shoes" (unfathomable as they might be) provide a ballast of realism for the magnificent assertion of which Thomas would have been proud, as pregnant and ponderable as the conclusion of "A Refusal to Mourn...," itself reminiscent of the "Holy Sonnets": "After the first death, there is no other." A strong purple line in the grand metaphysical-modernist manner, this is the Apocalyptic climax of the poem.

Singer cites Thomas in his best-known poem, "Still and All": "There is no other. There is no other way." Not that incantation is his only mode: "Immortality is itself as plain / A hometruth though of heaven as the brain / Can recognise behind a metaphor" (Sonnet XXXVII). He regards immortality not as a portentous cliché but, in Sonnet IV, as the "least preposterous / Of the infinities that robe you round" ("robe" another, ironic allusion to "A Refusal to Mourn...," in which the child is "Robed in the long friends"). Riley's "paradise" is envisioned in the same homely and downright fashion. Hopkins's higher "cleave of being" is dated, localized and freighted with the "gravities" of life in time (Hopkins 337). If this is an epiphany, it is "not redeemed from time"; not one of Eliot's "timeless moments" but seamlessly part of it. There is a descent from "ecstatic finality" but not a decline. In this sonnet, "the house" is a complement, with its "fire," "food" and music, to the "fields" of fulfillment rather than an "escape / From harm" or a "source of new dolour." On the contrary, the "Gurney piano" associates it rather with the composer-poet Ivor Gurney, whose "harmonic style" (according to Michael Hurd) "is, in essence, rhapsodic" and whose "House of Joy" is "paradise":

> Out of my sorrow have I made these songs,
> 　　Out of my sorrow;
> Though somewhat of the making's eager pain
> 　　From joy did borrow.
>
> Some day, I trust, God's purpose of pain for me
> 　　Shall be complete,
> And then—to enter in the House of Joy...
> 　　Prepare, my feet.

In life, the body houses ("ospita") the soul like a guest, as in Hadrian's lyric, "Animula vagula blandula, / Hospes comesque corporis"; but after death, who knows? The nervous faith of "Song and Pain" is anything but Orphic, yet its meekness is deceptive and several of Gurney's own sonnets have a bearing on *Ospita*. "Pain" is an expression of anguish:

> Pain, pain continual; pain unending;
> Hard even to the roughest, but to those
> Hungry for beauty... Not the wisest knows...
> Men broken, shrieking even to hear a gun.
> Till pain grinds down, or lethargy numbs her,
> The amazed heart cries angrily out on God.

> 　　　　　　　　　(second ellipsis mine)

By contrast, "After-Glow" celebrates the pleasures of music, twilight and fire in the mood of Riley's sixth and tenth sonnets, whilst "Above Maisemore" envisions the Cotswold village as a "glorious City of the plain":

> O, lovely City! All the valley blue
> Covers thee like a garment of soft art,
> Harbour of peace, haven for contented and high heart,
> Desire is satisfied, sorrow finds salve in you...
> Distant is dim azure over pasture green
> And like the Promised Land your sight from far.

Gurney redeems the "blue remembered hills" of Housman's "land of lost content" ("Into my heart an air that kills..."). He stands above the distant village, but there is nothing to prevent him descending "the dim fields" to its "haven for contented and high heart." Gurney makes unabashed use of panegyrical bouquets such as "wonderful labour," by which he would mean, I imagine, much the same as Peter Riley. Music and poetry may involve "labour" but are unlikely to "keep" a poet, who will probably need to subsidize them out of income from other labours, such as teaching or bookselling. On the other hand, art needs to be "kept" like a promise, persisted in, and preserved like the gift that it is. Frost is homeward bound with "promises to keep" in "Stopping by Woods on a Snowy Evening," but there is a deep contrast between the deathwards drift of his imagination and Riley's rapture. Poetry is its own "Promised Land," not only a "dim azure...sight from far" but as tangible as "fire" and "food," as substantial (yet as fingertip-responsive) as a "piano" (or a word-processor). Frost's "promises to keep" are obligations, Riley's "labour" something not to be taken away. The "labour" of the poet might even be compared with the "eager pain" of giving birth, which brings us back, in a sense, to where we started...

Works Cited

Auden, W.H. *Collected Poems*. Ed. Edward Mendelson. 1976. New York: Vintage, 1991.

Belloc, Hilaire. *Collected Verse*. Harmondsworth: Penguin, 1958.

Forrest-Thomson, Veronica. *Poetic Artifice: A Theory of Twentieth-Century Poetry*. Manchester: Manchester University Press, 1978.

Gurney, Ivor. *Collected Poems of Ivor Gurney*. Ed. P.J. Kavanagh. Oxford: Oxford University Press, 1982.

Hardy, Thomas. *The Variorum Edition of the Complete Poems of Thomas Hardy*. Ed. James Gibson. London: Macmillan, 1976.

Haslam, Michael. *A Whole Bauble*. Manchester: Carcanet, 1995.

Hopkins, Gerard Manley. *The Note-Books and Papers of Gerard Manley Hopkins*. Ed. Humphry House. London: Oxford University Press, 1937.

Hurd, Michael. *The Ordeal of Ivor Gurney*. Oxford: Oxford University Press, 1978.

Larkin, Philip. *Collected Poems*. Ed. Anthony Thwaite. London: The Marvell Press and Faber, 1988.

————. "An Interview with *Paris Review*." In *Required Writing: Miscellaneous Pieces 1955–82*. London: Faber, 1983.

Morrison, Blake. *The Movement: English Poetry and Fiction of the 1950s*. Oxford: Oxford University Press, 1980.

Prynne, J.H. *Poems*. 2d ed. South Fremantle, Australia: Folio/Fremantle Arts Centre Press; Newcastle upon Tyne: Bloodaxe, 1999.

"Reality Studios Readers' Poll Results." *Reality Studios* 9 (1987): 106–10.

Riley, Peter. *Alstonefield*. London: Oasis; Plymouth: Shearsman, 1995.

————. Review of *Continual Song*, by Michael Haslam. *Reality Studios* 9 (1987): 93–95.

————. *Lines on the Liver.* London: Ferry, 1981.

————. *Noon Province.* Cambridge: Poetical Histories, 1989.

————. *Ospita.* Cambridge: Poetical Histories, 1987.

————. Promotional flyer for *Sea Watches.*

————. *Sea Watches.* Kenilworth: Prest Roots, 1991.

————. "Spitewinter Provocations: An Interview [by Kelvin Corcoran] on the Condition of Poetry with Peter Riley." *Reality Studios* 8 (1986): 1–17.

————. *Tracks and Mineshafts.* Matlock: Grosseteste, 1983.

————. *Two Essays.* Matlock: Grosseteste, 1983.

Singer, Burns. *The Collected Poems of Burns Singer.* Ed. W.A.S. Keir. London: Secker and Warburg, 1970.

SEA WATCHES, SET VII:
EIGHT SEASIDE CHAPELS

Peter Riley

1   *St Beuno's at Pistyll*

A place where people can shelter from one dream
In another, the finished dream, the walls hung
With medicinal herbs, the light dim and opaque.
Here you could silence the press and begin to address
Directly the separation of desires. Through thick
Stone walls the fruit trees rattle like the sea.

2   *Llangwnnadl*

Where travellers rest. I sit in the silence,
Doing and thinking nothing for as long
As I can bear it. Triple aisled light in which
I lose my name. But my stomach hurts, my nose
Bleeds, isn't that enough self for today or
Anyone? The lark turns, rest your shadow and belief.

3   *St Merin's Church*

Grassy humps in a clifftop field. A sunset beam
From the sea spreads through the stalks, among
Nettles and cow-parsley faint turf lines, dim shape
Of nave and apse. Here I lay my self crest
To rest, I hope, and crowned commoner O quick-
ly, turn north where distance makes three.

4   *Bryn Celli Ddu*

Gentle Orpheus, son of light. You are the sense
At the centre, the mechanism through which the long
Beam passes at morning and evening, the bridge
Across the heart in the darkness that grows
Daily finer as the body ages and at the core
Of which a line of light writes final relief.

5   *Llandudwen*

What is that relief? O wait and see, the cream
Of liberty is not to know, the cream is the sung
Response echoing in a stone room the shape
Of a person built over a grave. Cornered. So dress
Your anxious head proudly in the thick
Brightness. Be that engine which learns to be.

6   *Capel Anelog*

And this site of which nothing at all remains
Was where the final question was asked on the long
Pilgrimage to Bardsey. "Did you remember to bring
The tin-opener?" or "Did you really expect the rose
To be an inner answer to unwelcome law, or,
If now is almost time isn't it far too brief?"

7   *Ffynnon Fair*

Now is over, over the hill. The waves scream,
The waves crash. Here on the brown rocks hung
Over nothing, here at the impossible landing, cape
And hood gathered close, distance is set to our best
Sight—for we saw people prepared to stick
To their truth. The island lies before us on the sea.

8

The salt raging within, the ravenous remains
Of the earth running in the vein, reaching the tongue
And bursting into courtesy. An everyday thing,
Far removed from the sickness and errors that bring
Every day of self to a weary and troubled repose.
Far away on the night shore the salt wings close.

SEA WATCHES:
LITTLE MORE THAN ARRIVAL

Peter Larkin

Sea Watches is among Peter Riley's most highly wrought, topographically venturing texts, and is also one of his most expansive, despite its bed of compositional intricacy. It ranges across the horizons and seasons of a place, in times of crowd, family or solitude, at headland or cove, beside shore, port or island, while enrolling them in a watching brief which notates brisk reflexes of contemplation over a slower but more multifarious ground. The poem consists of eight sets of six-line stanzas, apparently unrhymed but in fact rhymed or half-rhymed two stanzas apart, with the *same* rhymes mutating through an entire set. The sets are themselves set in North Wales, on the Llŷn Peninsula (adjacent to Anglesey), and are built up from notes in the form of rhyme-exercises taken on a number of visits at different times of the year between 1978 and 1989. The horizon or principal "watch" of the poem is Bardsey Island, a destination for medieval pilgrimage (also a coffin route) off the blunt foreshore of the peninsula (where holiness or sanctified burial seemed conferred "by little more than arrival" as Riley's notes neatly have it). It's a site which attracts all the routes and relics scoring the peninsula towards itself, but is never visited as such.

John Hall has written that much of Riley's work links back to "an earlier (Christian) tradition of spiritual exercises and battles with meaning" (40). Hall correctly implies that it is the Christian element which generates the agonism of meaning, and my own reading will acknowledge this as a struggle *inherited* by the poem's post-Christian moment, one initiated by that moment. The most concentrated notational episodes occur at Set VII, invoking eight seaside pilgrimage chapels of rest now ruins or less than ruins, but even before this encounter with a wealth of Christian archaeology it has become clear *Sea Watches* consists of a linked vigil, a contemporary profile of the

115

residues and disappearances of a spirituality in excess of its own past whose trails still appoint the peninsula as a set of watch-sites, threaded through the "unoriented buzz" of a present lacking any outposts of its own (*Sea Watches* 21). The business of the poem is to ferret a line of dedication towards an horizon, a line along which an unprivileged set of days can nonetheless watch. The dedication, one can say, is "in the ordinary of itself," post-Christian and doctrinally reticent, but only archaeological in terms of orientation and passage. The "ordinary" bears with it the trace of a latter-day, sensed through its small-scale admission of sacral desire, a desire which can't be fully accommodated or naturalized because its prior acceptances were rituals, outposts, islands, watches. As such the poem's "now" must relearn the rites of distance, convention, even obstruction, which make up the fabric of a sustainable discourse of desire: not a global eroticism but a placeable passion burdened by the muddled textures of sites not just sightings, but themselves thresholds to be watched *from*.

Since Wordsworth's "light of common day" and the tradition of Emerson and Thoreau, the ordinary has been the bearer of a sense of diurnal watching, an outlier or aftereffect of a sublime whose extraordinary revelations had partly timed out, or were in search of a domestic moment by which to extend time. The American philosopher Stanley Cavell (echoing Thoreau) has characterized the natural relation to existence as our being next to the laws of nature by neighbouring the world (*Cavell Reader* 257). The ordinary, which alone has the power to negotiate with our basic conditions, is in essence the condition of being drawn to things, remaining on the watch for them where they cannot be grasped but where there is a presencing which cannot be secured as an absolute ground. "All our words," writes Cavell, "are words of grief [if we] forget the rightful draw of our attraction, our capacity to receive the world" (*This New Yet Unapproachable America* 88). The fact that we can't get it any nearer than this is the "handsome part" of our condition, nothing less than the direction of reception, or of being approached (109). The appointment of the ordinary is to watch for that direction. As a philosopher, Cavell sees the ordinary as a stand against world-erasure, but one which can't refute the absolute negativity of skepticism, and so it is an ordinary which bears within itself the scarce limits of what can be connected; this is a lean sufficiency nevertheless able to take the "next step" of finding a way to and through the world. But the ordinary is before anything a poetic idea, an alternative metaphysics which is a faith in what will suffice, one picking up its radiant horizon at that scarce point, rather than a nihilism which seeks to open out an orgiastic abyssal purity of knowing-not. The diurnal is not so much the commonplace, as the common put to a place which can be figured, made a source of giving onto, by watching. The ordinary is commonly available to what it is *can* draw it. Receiving the world is not a triumph but a matter of being drawn to what is scarce (or partly withdrawn under the burden of limits).[1] That world congregates as both horizon and inaccessible morass, a world which in every diurnal move poetically attended to shifts slightly from excess to rarity.

The eight sets have their own varying points of watch (as Riley's helpful notes are generous enough to clarify), together with implied meditative stations (at times wholly overt) which also partake of the thinning or padding of the compositional weave. Set I approaches the peninsula from outside and above, from a mountain-pass which lays out the "soft / Edge of Britain," a geography of convergence which is a peninsula in direction though one lacking a tapered profile, a coming together where there is "after all a focus, an intellectual love" (5). Images of hardness take over around Porth Or, a "Grey concrete road," or a "marble boulder" at Porth Witlin which is "so hard and clear a thing that / We are put to guess what harm we could be in." After the soft opening prospect the poetry puts us to a guess: not knowing if we may lament, we are more simply hard put to. Is it to guess a harm which might kick-start the poetry's "watches," emerging through a scarce but necessarily overlooked harmlessness? Set II gives us resonances between crowd and solitude, each discrete and sufficiently located, but nonetheless juxtaposed as more than one crowd and one solitude. Distance itself comes to feel like a stereophonic effect of divergent crowds chiming by means of a solitary headland. Set III is at, or offshore from, the peninsula's south coast, at Porth Neigwl (Hell's Mouth), or on board a small fishing boat which the notes call the "Pilgrim." The land finally encrusts with detritus, and the soul of the poet is called out to sea in a thirst for rebirth. The fallen ordinary ("the wasteful and gaudy shops / Of this life") on the "untruthful land" is wryly troped as a "dark divided church" (10). Any church not in ruins is a secular parody, any soul not already summoned to sea stares at "a lost horizon" (10). Set IV takes us out of the peninsula and back by a different approach route, and suggests a time of guilt or expiation ("At a bad cliff corner the family leaps in my throat") or a season of "razor-sharp days" (11). The set ends with the poet's mind again miles away "in the still slow / Garden at the roots of the wind the voicing maze" (12). Eliot's "still point" here supervises a self-adjourning world, one which lets in the daylight of the ordinary but which doesn't conceal the basic remoteness of the common. What is within ordinary distance is a garden at the roots, but the available light can't penetrate the nonscarcity or sublime interminability of a "voicing maze."

Set V deploys yet wilder solitudes, and at Porth y Nant brings in the handled desert of industrial remains. A return to the crowded strand brings a half-descent into hell ("The same old tale with its ropes and its dogs") and half a hell is the hell of a half-life: "God save us from half-life, it is also necessary / To note" (13, 14). Again a garden, "richly flawed, flowered, brief," creates a respite amid an ordinarily profuse hell. Set VI touches degree zero of the everyday, where habitual activity (a man prepares a barbecue to which no one comes), lacking any answering object, transcends its own functionlessness and is able to wait upon the scarcity of a supervening world. What it comes to know is an "empty cardboard plate across the table," where the emptiness seems at the same time the condition of its appearing (15). Set VII is the most topographically Piperesque of all and the most directly beautiful, each stanza evoking a single pilgrim chapel along either the northern or southern routes of the peninsula. Among these is Ffynnon Fair, the final embarkation point to the island. The poem watches before an arrival it doesn't record, speaks before what it speaks about can be ascertained, but speaks in the way of it (as direction and obstruction). Perhaps it is Bardsey Island itself which appears as a "tongue…bursting into courtesy" out of the "ravenous remains / Of the earth," a place where the corroding aspects of life and its arrests at the very moment of achieved orientation are the "salt raging within," though at this found and halted watch-point "the salt wings close" (18). The final set records an all-night, solitary vigil near the poet's caravan in a "grave green chair," a sunk hollow in the cliffside which half-recalls the "stone room the shape / Of a person built over a grave" of the preceding set (19, 18). This concluding watch affirms its postreligious attentiveness at a nonsecular station, an invented chapel for the passing of time in a cleft, a self-imposed rite (or Walkman-packaged personal ritual) which is burdened by the afterlives of poetic words which live on (as did the medieval chapels themselves) within a fore-expected disappearance which is not a retraction.

Riley's two-stanza-remote rhyme scheme, a sort of ars nova of the overheard by God, traverses spans of meaning across a meniscus cusped for polar attraction, offering the ordinary nonlinear darts of access which overtake or undertruss a surface of linear narration from across equally charged tips of chiming lineation. It is this, however much a "completely extrinsic control factor," which allows the poetry to play across itself without crude self-jamming, reaching outward to what is fully "circumscribed, as any being is, by a dark line" ("Creative Moment" 108–9). So, a guard dog's barking emerges into narrative account out of a "sea barking / Up both sides of the peninsula" two stanzas before (5). And if there are episodes of parodic imagism which seem to rejoice in the arbitrary notational strain, as when a "noisily munching ocean… / Thrusts behind our ears like a jewelled hatpin" and the "sky stamps its foot and raises its hat / And charges out to sea rattling its tin" two stanzas later, these moments remain compositionally ligatured, their freakish naturalism distanced and lightened by being first parodied beyond the terms of a usable description (6). Other remote rhymes slap at the ordinary: when "car and lunch" are essential ingredients of a visit to old manganese mine-workings at Porth Ysgo, they are acknowledged with a "Thank you, Mr Punch." It's a banality of response pre-reinforced by the echo of working at stone in "Punch" and in the more sweeping phrase "From here management decides hurt" (9). Later, "a truly human fix" matches a "sky curtain" which "stirs and leaks," where a fix leaches out as part of a local distance in relief (10). In VII "shadow and belief" are linked to "writes final relief," which neither the one nor the other does, but the connection is traced at a remoteness across which it is possible to watch for analogy or dissonance within a commonality of what *are* the relatable meanings (17). In VIII "adoring stead" is chimed with "later dead," which neatly illustrates the scope of the ordinary, but when the beautiful "if we are one we are met" jangles with "Swathed in shade I let it go for sixpence net," the reader is inclined to cry out against a forcing, even if it's one which minimally bends the ear (19). A forcing is perhaps what it is; certainly something inconveniently found and needing to be coped with. Lyric reconciliation doesn't sublimate the procrustean, but is a letting be at the price of a letting pass or stand. It may celebrate what the next stanza will as soon call "a notion / To validate with truth this brittle / Spending" (20).

Sea Watches is frequently explicit about the ordinary, though threading it about with entails and obstructions which textualize the drawing of the ordinary towards its world, a world lightly dedicated but heavily owed (though neither attribute is a scandal to the other). The ordinary involves burden, but one which recognizes the weight of where it is given to be: "we carry what we conceive. / We carry carrying, being carried, fear and fatigue, we carry it all" (8). The ordinary is also a matter of scarce relief: "No unit of life's pain will be eased this day / Or by being out here" (9). Being at sea equally prolongs burden in its wake, only watching towards the sea enables dedication. A life unwatching on the land (where a field can be addressed as "you") is an enclosure in time unventilated by horizon or the (scarce) vertical: "I walk you this morning / End to end wondering how a new day won't reach more / Than an inch or two forwards or raise its head above shame" (13).

This flatness of the everyday can only get fresher and more pointed through a lack which is also a nonabsolute, a cultivation and a dedication shareable with what partakes of the order of plenitude and the unconditional: "And some spin quietly and miss / Reward, but turn an acre of inhospitable land / Into a terraced garden, richly flawed, flowered, brief" (14). Spinning quietly connotes an empty prayer-wheel but also the idling of a repose sufficiently regarded in a garden as the work of staying put. The elegiac justification for what is a lived and performable reward *missed* is that it is also a fall into the scarcity of the ordinary, an ordinary which lends ample perspective to a garden's brevity. The sixth stanza of Set VII, commemorating the site of Capel Anelog, superbly enacts the pilgrimage of the ordinary and elects it with comic analogue:

> "Did you remember to bring
> The tin-opener?" or "Did you really expect the rose
> To be an inner answer to unwelcome law, or,
> If now is almost time isn't it far too brief?" (18)

Bathos is watching for pathos, though here rose and fire are not one, and the world of spirit has no standing as an alternative realm, given the harsh law of temporality. Should there be any occasion for watching from this site it is painfully scarce and too thin for dignity. The rose has to contend with an abundance of downward connotations, the immediate neighbour of a tin-opener, though a rose is also an opener. But not only is it only "almost time" (echoing Wordsworth's "deep almost as life"), but the rose's moment hardly realizes any significant interval before a pursuing question which might as easily intend metonymically "Where did you leave the watering-can?" The ordinary is turning elegiac at its star of scarcity which *does* cover the distance, but as such is hardly noticeable. A Wordsworthian world of the unremarkable is overlain with too many other produced layers and surfaces to be sure of its visitors: "Spots / Of rain on my coat, are you with me yet?" (20).

What responds to the commonly shared and entrammelled spaces of the near and far is love, not as erotic specialism but as the vigil and context of the everyday. The word "love" closes the first stanza of the opening set and mutates through remote rhyme to "proven," "power" and "hour." What is "after all a focus, an intellectual love" is what is "called together" in "a life's coming *and* going" (5, my emphasis). Arrivals and departures enter into the community of their passage, not time as such, but a force of love which mediates juxtapositions of the near and far. One of Riley's characteristic strengths is that he is never quibbling while evoking love as primary value. The *placing* of love may be approached wryly, as in Set VI when a deserted barbecue finds its place among the "things / Of residual time worn lightly because / A long past means a sure future"; past and future give "extent" to a sense of love: "Where centres meet and agree to become unstable" (15). Meeting and agreement dedetermine instability, accept it by referring it to the shareable and unprivileged, a turn to the ordinary of con-fusion rather than to the sublime of diffusion. This meeting of domains is the occasion of cherishing, not a mathetical space as such, but more like Winnicott's "non-order" which is not instability as defiance, but sheer ease, unambitious for disorder. The very next stanza cashes in the agreement: "And the Centre of Anything is a Hell of Lack" (16). Here a parodic corporative "Centre of Anything" with its titled product "Hell of Lack" parades its own necessity to be one version of amplified instability, admitted as much as the earlier gentled drift towards non-order. As Cavell reminds us, the ordinary possesses no power of refutation, only the local skill of another step. Love as centre is a visitant and site of visitation rather than a permanent possession or defensible estate. It is more akin to the chapel's silence in which "I sit in silence, / Doing and thinking nothing for as long / As I can bear it" (17). This is the "Triple aisled light" where the poet hopes to "lose [his] name" before the ordinary supervenes in the shape of aching stomach and bleeding nose. What speaks enough nonself for one day with the reminder of bodily cares both rests from the silence of horizon and rests in it as in the scarce and rare, but these have granted permission to leave: "Here I lay my self crest / To rest, I hope, and crowned commoner O quick- / ly, turn north…" (17). What comes home amid a ruined chapel is the love-register of a self which doesn't own itself in a way to command absences from itself either positively or negatively, and so bides with itself, by being on the watch from itself. This watch ordinarily arises among the distances of for and from, as part of a too-little within which the whole of a concern has not been left out.

The fiercest trope of the ordinary is the machine, the "Engine behind the shop chugging away" which can amount to an invocation: "Be that engine which learns to be" (15, 18). As Cavell might remark, it's perfectly possible to see human beings from the perspective of the machine, but that doesn't mean humans *are* mechanical. The repetition implicit in the machine, its being always with us, is also the repeated comings and goings through its own ordinary terrain, an ordinary whose self-burdening excesses (including machine production) come and go across the range of scarce horizons. Also implied in the machine trope is the apparatus of a journey or pilgrimage, with its baggage prepared for alighting at a distance, for disappearing at the watch for journey's end: "Almost asleep in the thin walls, undeliberately / I send my soul out like a night bird" (8). The thin walls of the caravan, the technical way into the peninsula, are also the thin walls of the body, a body which is the way out, the horizon of the trodden way outside. The small nucleus of the caravan is site for a similar moment where "I send my consciousness out like a gull / Over the sea," a matter of mental pilgrimage in terms of the scarce and not a technique of mind expansion (10). The body is a machine entrusted to the limits of itself and able to rest there occasionally, at the nonprogressive point of dedication. As such it underwrites the final sea watch of Set VIII. The "grave green chair" is less an enclosure than a lightsome roaming which casts off from the saturated temporality of the in-finite towards the numinous sparings of a more exactly finite infinity (19). It is a roaming over distance from a moment of attention, that attention and dedication being the bodily placing; it is not a self-launching which aims to project its own machinery of being with the design of swallowing distance in progressive arrival. Travel is towards a watch-point, not absorbing distance but towards a point at which distance can begin where the sublimity of travel ends:

> Why do we roam the land as if finding and lose
> Everyone's time?...
> The slightest construct of care would cast
> It all behind us like salt as we turn to face
> A clearing sky to landward and a truly human fix. (10)

That "slightest construct," the burden of sociality and political answerability which lies landward, must share its own excesses, its ubiquity, with what is slight and locally dependent, a land which watches for the scarcity of its horizons. The nightly "focus" which "climbs / To the caravan skylight" kisses the "ghost of distance" in order to "watch the sea, and stick there, weathered leaf" (14). Across such spaces a leaf hardly joined to life but stuck with it is nonetheless weathered rather than withered by the ligature. It is placed outside its immediate area of functional vitality, a particle not of the expansion of thought to its horizons, not an object or even a limit, but the "weathered" texture of the spaces which coast this range of dedication, one not home to leaf, body or mind as such. The "separation of desires" which the writer longs to address at St Beuno's chapel is the desire to offer desire, to allow dedication to be the further neighbouring of the ordinary (17). The space of dedication casts the body in relief as what will highlight the illumination of a positive scarcity within the ordinary. Or as Set VIII will have it, "Stuck in the middle of life" (where we all have to find ourselves, a mockery which prepares the ordinary for its designated horizon), "the sea is a knife thrown / Across the earth" (19). It is a knife which severs the text of the self from in-finite immersion, but figures as lean edge, contiguity, a beam of unconditional relation, a distance sharing its path with the untransformed. And transpiring at the point of watch (the most persistent and least calculable turning of the ordinary) whose "line of light writes final relief" (17).

Notes

1. The term "scarcity" doesn't feature in Cavell, but I add it here as the quality which permits a "turn" in the ordinary, one which Cavell might not want to follow all the way. "Scarcity" evokes a mediation between the ordinary as bounded and the ordinary as a drawing towards the horizons of the mysteriously given.

Works Cited

Cavell, Stanley. *The Cavell Reader*. Ed. Stephen Mulhall. Cambridge, Mass.: Blackwell, 1996.

———. *This New Yet Unapproachable America*. Albuquerque: Living Batch, 1989.

Hall, John. "On *Lines on the Liver* and *Tracks and Mineshafts*." See pp. 35–42 of this journal. Reprinted from *The Many Review* 2 (Spring 1984): 12–18.

Riley, Peter. "The Creative Moment of the Poem." In *Poets on Writing*, ed. Denise Riley. Houndmills and London: Macmillan, 1992.

———. *Sea Watches*. Kenilworth: Prest Roots, 1991.

FIVE POEMS

Peter Riley

THREE RURAL POEMS

Corkerbeg (2)

The goats eat everything, have you seen
the goats today could you tell me
which field they're in?

They have stripped the lower branches
of the trees outside my house

The cuckoo on the corner tree my alarm clock
the beating of the snipe my evening bell

Alone and melancholy for many weeks
especially in the long winters

Neither winning nor losing
attaches a cup at the spring.

CINQ POÈMES

Peter Riley
(Traduit par Lorand Gaspar et Sarah Clair)

TROIS POÈMES RUSTIQUES

Corkerbeg (2)

Les chèvres mangent tout, avez-vous vu
les chèvres aujourd'hui pourriez-vous me dire
dans quel champs elles sont?

Elles ont arraché les branches basses
des arbres devant ma maison

Le coucou dans l'arbre du coin mon réveil
le battement d'ailes de la bécasse ma cloche du soir

Seul et mélancolie pour des semaines
surtout durant les longs hivers

Ni gagnant ni perdant
il laisse une tasse près de la source.

Nancy's

"I was a soldier in Belfast for four years"
and suddenly the bar was empty

We also
tire ourselves

and tired of proof, tired
of acknowledgement

move out
even of the short song

and the beautiful quiet talk.
Galleon starfield.

Corkerbeg (1)

Air courses down from the mountain   across the lightly
constructed space   left to right   tired but adamant
to teach adequacy   light from dark things

Cold in the walls the wine of age
the lost masquer settles for good
bends forward to feed the small fire

Waterlogged ground   cross slabs on back field knolls
far from advancement or delay
women and young children hitch-hike without fear.

Nancy's

"J'ai été soldat quatre ans à Belfast"
et soudain le bar était vide

Nous aussi
nous nous fatiguons

et fatigués de preuves, fatigués
de reconnaissance

nous sortons
même du chant bref

et de la belle conversation tranquille.
Le ciel: un galion chargé d'étoiles.

Corkerbeg (1)

L'air descend de la montagne à travers l'espace
construit avec légèreté   de gauche à droite   fatigué mais inflexible
pour enseigner la justesse   lumière de choses sombres

Froid dans les murs le vin de l'âge
le comédien errant s'installe enfin
se penche pour nourrir le petit feu

Sol détrempé   croix gravées dans la pierre sur des tertres
loin de toute promotion ou retard
femmes et enfants jeunes font du stop sans crainte.

Bar Carol

for Schubert

There are worse deaths than singing,
worse singings than death's.
Gently over black ever

Shifting water the wooden craft
moves out. The newspaper
soaked in itself, sinks.

And the city, there, the circles floating
on the sea articulating growth we
adore by rote and touched in the

Tainted fall of socialistic promises
like petals of death sign out
with a blown shrug. The city divides

And sheds but the world waits for ever
the great curve of thought we
slowly sail round towards singing.

Bar Carol

pour Schubert

Il y a pires morts que chanter,
des chants pires que celui de la mort.
Doucement sur des eaux noires

Toujours mouvantes le bateau en bois
quitte le port. Le journal
noyé en lui-même, coule.

Et la ville, là-bas, des cercles flottants
sur la mer: croissance qui articule
que nous aimons par habitude, émus

Dans la chute fanée des promesses socialistes
comme des pétales de la mort et partons
avec un haussement d'épaule. La ville divise

Et disperse, mais le monde attend
à jamais le grand virage de la pensée que
lentement nous promenons sur les eaux vers le chant.

The Little Watercolour at Sligo

The point of pain
at which the voice either
cracks or cruises. The little fat man

Makes it, whoever he is, drunk but
not too drunk on his way home in
village night, mouth like a typographical

O he stops to sing. His head rises, his
arms fall, and it works: he
cruises, out across time

Nameless and small, he
sails a stranger's psyche, saying
Cast your (care) crown. This

Is success, this is being, this
is where love nails us to earth
and time sets all things right.

La Petite Aquarelle à Sligo

Ce degré de douleur
où la voix craque ou s'élance.
Le petit homme gros —

Peu importe qui — y arrive, ivre,
mais pas trop, sur le chemin de chez lui
dans la nuit villageoise, la bouche telle un grand

O il s'arrête pour chanter. Sa tête se lève, ses
bras tombent, et ça marche: il prend son essor,
loin à travers le temps

Petit et sans nom, il
navigue au bord d'un esprit étranger, disant
Jetez (soucis) couronne. Voilà

Le succès, voilà l'existence, voilà
où l'amour nous cloue à la terre
et le temps remet tout en ordre.

New from Wild Honey Press

Blackwards   Rosmarie Waldrop
24 pp, 14 x 21 cm, £3.50 / $5.00 US, ISBN 1 903090 15 6

A set of nine linked prose poems in which an elegant and sinuous syntax embraces an extraordinary range of reference while maintaining a deceptively smooth narrative flow.

Faint Optimism   Keith Waldrop
20 pp, 10 x 15 cm, £2.00 / $3.00 US, ISBN 1 903090 14 8

A set of fifteen linked poems, written in a spare and minimalist style. The degree of formal invention achieved with this reduced palette is striking.

The Pillar   Mairéad Byrne
12 pp, 14 x 21 cm, £3.50 / $5.00 US, ISBN 1 903090 21 0

Nelson's pillar, one of Dublin's best loved monuments, was blown up by the I.R.A. in 1966. This poem explores the rich layers of associations that it accumulated.

Untitled Sequence   Peter Riley
16 pp, 14 x 21 cm, £3.50 / $5.00 US, ISBN 1 903090 16 4

A sequence of ten poems, first published in 1977 in Peter Robinson's *Perfect Bound*. A narrative concerning a touring production of Macbeth by a college dramatic society is the pretext for a series of wonderful flights of philosophy, wit and lyricism.

All chapbooks are hand sewn and have a card cover with a colour illustration. Visa or Mastercard accepted. P&p free in Ireland and Britain. Overseas orders please indicate if you'd like to be charged economy or priority rate.

WILD HONEY PRESS
16a Ballyman Road, Bray, County Wicklow, Ireland
e-mail: suantrai@iol.ie

THE ACCOMPLISHMENT OF KNOWING ONE'S PLACE

Keston Sutherland

Plato's Ion never thought to respond to Socrates by suggesting that a familiarity with the emotional responses of auditors, like a knowledge of charioteering or military leadership, might be exploited in a manner distinctly useful to the *polis*. Could he have claimed this successfully, he might then have argued that poetry is in fact a species of cognition rather than mere giddiness. Any materialist of a good cynical bent must allow that Ion should have been correct. Choosing for a moment to side with them—without, however, contradicting Socrates—we might say that the efficient uses (within a functioning State apparatus) of any insight are the grounds for its status as knowledge: insights without efficient uses are not knowledge but affection, albeit a kind of affection which people tend to feel ought to be articulated comprehensibly, or even logically. When critics and poets complain that (e.g.) marketing executives have appropriated the resources of poetry and somehow made them unfit for daintier craft, this is an accurate and earnest complaint; yet critics and poets might also see how the defiler proves thereby that poesis is cognition, that words made well to cohere are overtly useful. Sometimes preferable to this dialectic is the quite different view, espoused almost tacitly in most of Peter Riley's poems, that poetry need not be called cognition—need not really be called anything in particular—merely to satisfy some pedant remote from the primary satisfactions of writing, or merely to add to the available jargons on poetry which in any case can never be more or less than what it is. What is it? Perhaps the question is, in its halting way, for Riley a kind of answer.

If poetry certainly is or certainly is not cognition, this is often because it is considered as a product or process within a State. Trotsky considered it this way, and so could argue for its value as a labour of cognition the precise status of which must always be dependent on State exigencies. In asking what use poets might have during "the default of God," Heidegger ran rings round the same idea differently obscured. If poetry happens within and constitutes (or might constitute) part of a State, as Pound thought his *Cantos* did, then it can also happen *among places* only when those places are also the *locations* of facts or of events implicated cognizably in State history. This is not because there must be some chronicle or anecdote pertaining to any place a poet might choose; the reason is more abstract-seeming. Yet really it is not at all abstract: since the poet accepts voluntarily that poetry does happen within a State, he accepts also (and apprehends while writing) the corollary that each particular, local reference in his poem constitutes an act not merely of description, but of historiography. The flurry of literary-critical speculation over the real location of Gray's *Elegy* is quite wrongheaded: whether or not it was in fact Stoke Poges that inspired him, Gray wrote the poem without accepting voluntarily that it might help constitute the State in which it appeared. For this reason, his Churchyard is simply a place; it is not a place at which we feel something ought (in either the active or the passive sense of the verb) to be *located*. Places, in poetry that happens within and as part of a State, are by their own necessary accountability the locations of things at least potentially consequential to the State, or to the poet's expressible conception of it. They need not be real places, or ever stand a chance of becoming so: Churchill was indifferent as to whether his Gotham should be "a real country, or one made in jest," but adamant that it ought to be a monument which might, in Prynne's early words, help to "revise governance, / of the *local* disposing" ("The Numbers"; emphasis mine).

There may be no place like home, but surely there could never be any *location* like home; home is too much the proper ambience of the individual to be thought of as a location. Things are located because finally they remain particular and not only general things. General things have their places: there is a time and a place for everything (since "everything" is a generality), but not necessarily a location. Poetry which happens among locations happens among particular things whose more general importance is conceivable only in terms of, or as an expression of, the general inclusion of people within a State. Poetry which happens among places and not locations is marked frequently by the tendency to conceive hypostases, to discover aspects of experience which might be common to all or many people, without, however, any subtended insistence that the very experience of commonness should inevitably connote the experience of a State administration.

Peter Riley's book *Reader* (1992) includes poems the titles of which are particular places: Macclesfield, Denmark, Egbert Street, etc. As a variation it includes also a seemingly unparticular place: Somewhere. This is not a contradiction of the other titles, but rather a repetition at the titular level of an argument maintained fluently throughout the poems: that it is the proper device of poetic attention to resolve particular instances of experience into moments of sympathy, or of intelligence, whose content is essential and not exclusive or provisional. The device is just about guaranteed, *provided* we are generous and that we desire it without obscuring our sense of humility (we might recall that Olson brandished the word contemptuously: "that horror and practice of western man, humility"). This provision is not a paradox, but is simply anterior to the unprovisionality of what is hypostasized: we ourselves must provide for our ability to be sympathetic, but the sympathy we achieve is itself unprovisional. It is the determined content of a poetry that happens among places.

Somewhere

Listening to Schubert's songs
sung by Robert Holl

It becomes obvious
anywhere

The hunter's call in the forest
is the tenderest thing we know

Is the thing that tells us
What does it tell us?

We are an always,
like it or not, that

Is what we are. We
nourish our hunger.

What we are is for Riley very much distinct from where we are located. The distinctness of our *quid* from our *qua*: eventually "anywhere" will do, as for the lyricist who wishes to write descriptive ontology it surely must. Specific things in Riley's poetry, such as "Schubert's songs / sung by Robert Holl," are necessary insofar as they are objects from which we can become morally diverted. Particular things, when in their places, divert us away from themselves and into speculation less tied to anything in particular (Beckett made some good jokes about this, particularly in *Malone Dies* and *How It Is*). We begin this poem with a head-start, already diverted (this time forcibly, or I should say, insistently) from the specific place-name which by this point in the book we have come to anticipate. The poem has this slight hortatory instinct, that we ought not to wish to have the particular name we lack, since after all we have not been given it, "like it or not." Where in other poems we do have this name ("Hastings"), it is implied that we should have it only if we are prepared to understand how unnecessary it is that we do; the name is not quite superfluous, since it does urge upon us this attitude of presumptive independence, but a sort of gratuity, given over by someone for whom it does evidently have a special significance, but who prefers that we should not apprehend particularly what that significance is. The movement characteristic of Riley's poems is from privacy to descriptive ontology, from particular but unnecessary instance to common and necessary intelligence (that is also to say, they do have a characteristic movement). A good definition of what I mean by "common" is Wordsworth's in his *Preface*: the knowledge of the poet (as opposed to that of the scientist) is "a necessary part of our existence, our natural and unalienable inheritance." *What we are.* And what we poets are able to communicate is therefore "not individual and local, but general and operative."

"Public" is never so much a stage, in this movement of poetic insight, as an opportunity for contention which the poem can eschew, morally, by advancing immediately to the *essences* of public life, the "what we are." It might seem equally valid to say that Riley's conception of the "public" is of something from which we must divert our attention if we are to see its essence. What we divert our attention towards is, in the first instance, the "private."

This would seem paradoxical: how is it that Riley's poetry could be so little preoccupied with questions of public (rather than common) significance, while at the same time its syntax, prosody and diction are very markedly different from those of other poets in the Cambridge area with whom Riley is often associated, precisely on account of their great lucidity and immediate comprehensibility? That is, their quality of being accessible to a hypothesized "public," in the sense perhaps that Habermas uses the term *Öffentlichkeit*? Riley has often claimed that he dislikes how some writers have become wilfully hermetic, closing off their work from all but the most recondite clutches of initiates, and certainly from the public at large. This might lead us to think that his own work is written in the opposite spirit, intended to be accessible without punctilious, theoretically derived obscurities at any level of language; that is, written not only so that the public might read it, but indeed *for* the public, in favour of their opportunity as readers who are without esoteric expectations of difficulty. Yet he does not write about public things. Instead he reflects on memories, experiences and desires; it is characteristic of this reflection that it tends to validate an insight of common appeal that seems as if it always ought to have been obvious. This kind of writing does include a tacit criticism of contrary types: they do not understand how and when to be diverted, when to encounter the present limit of any particular fact and to meditate upon some issue which transcends this (such as *who we are*), and so they are themselves in danger of becoming mere, intransitive diversions and hence not effective upon a "public" at all. I would suggest that Riley might see much "Cambridge" poetry in this way.

Is this a paradox? Is Riley's desire to be comprehensible by means other than presumptuous default a commitment to the "public," even though he does not write about public things (or *res publica*) so much as commonly impressive insights?

Riley's poetry happens among places and not among locations. Or rather, its most characteristic compulsion is to divert the resources of insight away from any located fact: it is a perceptible aspect of oneself which that diversion suggests we ought to value, and not the dynamics of diversion per se or any consequent, dialectical *reversion* to located fact. It is a poetry not of processes but of results. These may be fleeting, precarious, variously perishable; yet they have nonetheless the value of summary delight, they are conclusive with respect to that through which they emerged; the gasp of recognition is not the mere sequitur of beguilement, but at once its negation and its apogee. We might say also that places (where finally we are) are for Riley the sentimental fruition of locations. As such, they need not really be the objects of cognitive fuss or oblique procrastination about the status of what we mean by "knowledge" when we say that we know them: this would be a kind of reversion, an unwelcome negative.

Since we in fact are something, it seems fair that we should wish to know what we are. Peter Riley can assist even those readers least inclined to ontological hypostasization and wonderment, in finding out just what that something might be. His prosody is often delicate and precise, often scrupulous, never showily fucked-up in the arrogant expectation that mere syntactic derangement is a reference to some rancour of a *political* ilk. His diction is likewise quite exact; it is not laden with semantic sediment visible only to the philologist, but settled into its place both casually and with patient discrimination. Riley's poetry knows its *place*, and knows it well.

Its place is not a public place, though members of the public might take great pleasure in being led there. It is not a public place, because the public is conceivable only within and exceeding a State structure; Riley's poetry neither wishes nor attempts to understand itself as the kind of intellectual labour which happens as something included ineluctably within a State. It does not focus on any of the State's locations, but diverts insight from them. In fact, I would go so far as to say that Riley doesn't really believe that States are anything more than the aggregates of economic and financial management, together with the bodies of divided sovereignty whose principal purpose is to keep that management competitive. That is to say, he excludes from the concept "State" the population subject to organized authority. For this reason (I cannot verify it by reference to any statement of Riley's), the poetry is not troubled by having to deliberate upon the possibility of being itself utilized. In fact, the accomplishment of its prosody is itself the conspicuous aspect of that freedom.

It is a freedom not enjoyed by violent political outsiders like Pound, who didn't want generalizations, but wanted particulars; it is the freedom of a committed, thoughtful democrat. Principally on account of this freedom, which less overtly democratic writers (or writers who refuse the liberal-democratic concept of State) sometimes enjoy with almost opposite results, Riley's is also a poetry hostile to prosodic novelty. As Thomas Mann orated on his tour of the United States in 1938, novelty is the great charm of the antidemocratic impulse; the true democrat is finally unimpressed by this. Instead, he will have "the humanly timeless aspect of democracy"—an aspect which Mann, contemning an impressionable generation of *unzeitgemässe* fascists, calls "inexhaustible" and "absolute." Riley's poetry celebrates the idea that, given the right diversion, we can know this aspect anywhere.

PETER RILEY'S *AUTHOR*: MUSICAL ALLUSION AND THE "CLIMATE OF POSSIBILITY"

Mark Morrisson

In "The Creative Moment of the Poem" (1992), Peter Riley carefully disentangles the written language of poetry from physical, vocal communication: "Seen messages must in a sense come from nowhere, since they are not caught in the act of dispersing and fanning out from a vibrating node towards which you can turn for direct transmission, but are themselves focused to an eye-point from an elsewhere known or unknown" (93). Moreover, for Riley, the poem is a self-contained and impersonal object, neither a direct revelation of the voice, mind or heart of the poet, nor a direct transmission of mere information. He writes: "The poem can be conceived as an object between poet and reader which is both a means of communication and a barrier to communication. It is neither opaque nor transparent. Things are seen through it only by being seen in it" (93).[1] Yet, in spite of his emphasis on the "structure of the written language" (93), and on visual metaphors for how poems communicate with readers, much of Riley's poetry, and indeed almost all of his recent volume, *Author* (1998)—the concluding volume of a trilogy that also includes *Reader* (1992) and *Lecture* (1993)—bears an important relationship to music. Riley notes in "The Creative Moment" that music serves as a metaphor for the particular ontological nature of poetry and our experience of it as a distinct form of writing: "The raising of the voice from speaking to singing could be seen as a…direct transmission in favour of a postponed and circumscribed message, the music itself a retardation of transmissive time-sense, sent floating into the world rather than directed, bomb-like, to the target at which it expires. 'Song' informs all poetry with a sense of vocal attenuation and isolation" (95). Clearly, Riley's thinking about poetry and his poetry itself have been informed in varying degrees by his abiding interest in music.

And that interest in music leads to much larger questions about the function of the cultural past, and the relationship we have to that past. For Riley, poetry and music have the ability to exist both in material acoustic transmission in time and in a kind of extratemporal state of isolation, to facilitate communication and to challenge and even obstruct it, to produce continuity and affirm ritual meanings, but also to prompt renewal and experiment (or, in the worst outcome, to enable a stultifying cultural nostalgia). Back in the heady atmosphere of "free" or improvisational music during the 1970s, Riley wrote for the major journal of improvisational music, *Musics*, and even guest-edited a special issue (*Musics* 10, November 1976). In a *Musics* article, "Old European Music (an essay)," Riley explained that improvisational music is not a music of "idea," of "*note* (abstracted, sectionalized, mathematical, conventional)," but rather of "*sound* (direct, total, instinctive, actual)" (3). The new musical avant-garde, for Riley, challenges the nostalgia that one sees rippling through post-World War II British poetry as well as music.[2] Riley's almost Futurist-sounding critique of "old European music" accuses it of having been "taken over by the commercial/academic sector where it serves as a staple second-hand product of middle-class culture," and Riley aligns it with "the State," nostalgia for "a societal condition that no longer obtains," "decadence" ("Mr. Heath at the organ," Riley jibes), and ossified bourgeois taste (3–4). In contrast, he describes improvisational music using those other mantras of the continental avant-garde in the early twentieth century: "energy," "individuality," and "innovation" (4). The polemical tone of the essay was certainly necessary in the '70s, when, as *Musics* documents, improvisational musicians were fighting hard for legitimacy (and for small Arts Council grants)[3]—and when British poets were simultaneously attacking the orthodoxy of the Movement.[4]

But reading this brief account of Riley's interest in improvisational music, one might be puzzled at the eclectic list of musicians to whom Riley dedicates various poems in *Author*: John Sheppard, Syd Barrett, Hans Leo Hassler, Leoš Janáček, Amédé Ardoin and Franz Schubert (allusions to a Monteverdi madrigal and a Beach Boys tune also make their way into the volume). Indeed, I have only represented one side of Riley's thinking about "old European music," even in the '70s. In the same article, he also lists "disadvantages" of improvisational music's attack on the structures and musics of the past. He argues that this kind of individualism and freedom, and its break with the past, carries with it a kind of danger. Noting that "the past of a culture bears an experiential relationship to the individual past of the person," Riley argues that

An over-stress…on achievement as some kind of epiphanic, instantaneous rebirth which cancels all previous acts, not only bears a potential of total egocentricity, but renders virtually impossible a whole set of virtues under such headings as consistency, coherence, extended development—in fact I don't see how any sense of purpose can operate under the constant threat of instant cancellation. The whole "freedom" thing becomes a meaningless fetish. What I'm suggesting is that it can be rendered impossibly difficult to conduct a life, or produce something worth knowing about, with some purpose and coherence, when the entire context of activity is insistently seen as discontinuous, fragmented, alien and superseded. That a sense of the continuity of the culture you stand in relates intimately to the continuity of your own acts. (4)

This kind of argument sounds closer to the Anglo-American modernism of Pound, Eliot, H.D., Bunting and others, in which to "make it new" also meant to use and to reshape the cultural resources of the past, rather than simply to make the radical and total break with the past advocated by, for instance, the Italian Futurists. This kind of conflict between innovation and a cultural inheritance—both sides of which Riley represents in his article—has emerged in several forms throughout the twentieth century, and more than two decades after his writings for *Musics*, Riley's work in *Author* seems to have followed his exploration of the resources of the past. This is not to say that Riley's is a poetry of nostalgia for some golden premodern past— rather, it explores what kinds of dialogues the forms and creativity of the cultural past can have with our own search for the meaning of the present as it remains always poised upon the edge of the future.

I want to turn to the first four poems of *Author*—"In Manus Tuas" and the three untitled poems that follow it—to examine how specific musical works become involved in Riley's poetry. These first four poems, I would argue, function as a block, moving with a coherence of tone, imagery, and theme toward a climactic vision before *Author* shifts tone in "E Questa Vita Un Lampo." And this group of four poems sets in motion many of the themes and images that will recur in the later poems in *Author*. For example, their probing of the relationship of natural processes to our lived experience, of decay to life (and even their specific chalk and lime imagery), re-emerges in the fifth poem, "E Questa Vita Un Lampo": "The beneficial worms bite the white rock / to a soil, that holds the stem / of a marriage cup, future price of // Written flesh." And the initial poems' meditations upon the nature of loss and desire in love are refigured in "Do It Again," which adapts much of the Beach Boys' 1969 hit about yearning for the pleasures of youth and love, stripping it of its explicit surfer imagery and re-"authoring" its defiance of the passing of youth to consider the shadow of death even in the hair of young women and the froth of breakers: "Girls we knew when their / Hair was soft and // whiter than star / heavier than sea // death white as glass / pass over me."[5] "Bar Carol" picks up the initial poems' critique of a government and society that have lost their empathy: punning on Schubert's fondness for the barcarolle, Riley transforms the lilting songs inspired by the Venetian gondoliers into a poem describing a boat drifting down the polluted river ("Shifting water the wooden craft / moves out. The newspaper / soaked in itself, sinks") through a city in which "we" are "touched in the / Tainted fall of socialistic promises."[6] And the hopes for voice and song as ways of expressing desire and loss and meaning that unfold in the first four poems re-emerge as the "barcarolle" becomes a "bar carol," an emblem for the consolation not just of drink, but above all, of song: "The city divides // And sheds but the world waits for ever / the great curve of thought we / slowly sail round towards singing." So, the first four poems—"In Manus Tuas" and the three untitled poems—offer a significant entrée into the thematic and imagistic concerns of *Author* as a whole, and they also demonstrate the range and use of musical allusion that Riley employs throughout *Author* in a practice that might be seen as a kind of "excavation," to borrow a word from the poetic project that began in 1995 with *Distant Points: Excavations Part One Books One and Two*.

Riley dedicates three of these initial poems to very different composers: John Sheppard, the sixteenth-century English composer of liturgical music; Syd Barrett, founding member of one of the earliest psychedelic bands in Britain during the '60s (a band whose hour-long live performances of songs like "Interstellar Overdrive" were following paths similar to those of the improvisational groups *Musics* lauded in the '70s); and Hans Leo Hassler, the sixteenth-century German Lutheran composer of masses, motets and madrigals. Riley himself has said of *Author*, "My hints at music in titles, dedications, notes, etc. are usually oblique. I mean the way any particular music gets into the text, if it does, varies a lot, and may not be known to me."[7] Indeed, there isn't a single systematic way in which Riley uses musical allusion in these works, though this isn't to say that the musical echoes aren't tightly woven into the poems—they are more than just grace notes. But when Riley speaks of the poem as "an object between poet and reader," he emphasizes the linguistic resources through which the poet filters his or her experiences, and, I think I might safely add, the resources which the reader brings to his or her commerce with that poetic "object":

As the poet sits there focusing into the poem, the face on the back of his head, the one that scans the world for its materials, is also a language-working faculty. It scans for events which have meaning, for images which combine together and force a focus through the mind's eyes, but it finds these things also as nouns and verbs and adjectives. Anything which cannot be named does not yet exist. A vocabulary is thus brought to bear on reality and fed and vitalised by it, and not just words: syntaxes, combinations, rhythms of extent and summation.... And where would these tools or vessels come from if not from other texts? I do not speak of memorising poems; most poets are too involved in their own work for that—but again of inhabiting a climate of possibility brought about by the work of others. ("Creative Moment" 112)

Though Riley uses visual and tactile metaphors here—"mind's eyes," "tools," "vessels"—the reader who picks up *Author* must necessarily also confront the mind's *ear*—an ear for both language and music. Choosing to call his volume *Author*, rather than, say, *Composer*, suggests that these poems will not be short vignettes about the composers invoked, but rather will speak to the broader resources of word, voice and tone available to poets as they seek to reveal and create meaning.

The "climate of possibility" created by the poetry and music of others produces a set of tensions or oppositions in Riley's poems, tensions Riley explores through both the *elusive* and the *allusive* qualities of his musical references, and through his choices of transitional composers who used the turmoil of their cultural moments and their lives to produce enduring works. He considers, too, how poetry and music structure our relationship to reality—to death, loss, desire, embodiment, natural processes—but also acknowledges that reality, in the form of extralinguistic, extracultural forces, feeds and vitalizes our language. The resources of language and music with which Riley grapples in his poetry certainly include the verbal texts used by the three composers invoked in these poems: the title of "In Manus Tuas" comes from a respond in the Compline service, and the poems also work in snippets of Syd Barrett lyrics and lines from Psalm 120 as set to music by Hassler. These texts serve as semantic components of the poems, but the reader must also consider Riley's attempts to capture musical form and effect in words—a difficult and abstract task, and a cross-genre move that must here, regrettably, be reduced to a discussion of semantics and language more appropriate to the discussion of poetry than to the appreciation of music on its own grounds.[8]

The four initial poems survey aspects of "need" and "care," and, I will argue, they explore the ways in which the voice helps to situate us; to protect and comfort us against loss, hostility and death; to provide meanings, even ritualized meanings, that allow us to live in our modern world and that connect us to the natural world upon which are built the cityscape of "pavement," "arcade" and "foiled traffic." And these uses of musical allusion, rather than inviting the kind of "cultural nostalgia" that Riley has always wished to avoid, help advance what might be seen as a central theme of the poems— the invocation of the cultural past to help us meditate on our attempts, as Riley puts it in "Old European Musics," "to conduct a life, or produce something worth knowing about, with some purpose and coherence" (4).

"In Manus Tuas" begins with a musical allusion that has a strong extramusical semantic component: its title invokes the Latin respond "In manus tuas, Domine, / commendo spiritum meum. / Redemisti me, / Domine Deus veritatis" ("Into your hands, Lord, / I commend my spirit. / You have redeemed me, / Lord God of truth"), from the Compline service. It is followed by the antiphon "Salve nos, Domine, vigilantes, custodi nos dormientes…" ("O Lord, keep us waking, guard us sleeping…") before the "Nunc Dimittis," and these prayers have an obvious importance in Compline, the last prayer of the evening in monastic orders.[9] They are supplications for protection and salvation while we are at our most vulnerable: we sleep; will we wake up? The words take on a meaning not simply from the semantic content of the phrases, but also from their ritualized repetition—more than simply "existing," the words are spoken aloud or sung regularly. The same words are said each night, in the same context, and this repetition is part of the fabric of a monastic community, a Compline service and, indeed, an entire religious world-view.

But Riley hasn't merely invoked a line from the Compline service; he has invoked John Sheppard's mid-sixteenth-century settings in particular.[10] Sheppard's three settings of "In manus tuas, Domine" were composed for Compline from Passion Sunday to Maundy Thursday (Chadd 250), and thus would certainly bring its supplication into line with the story of a human and vulnerable Jesus in one of the most important weeks in the Catholic year. Indeed, if the reader is familiar with Sheppard's beautiful and tender settings, the first few stanzas of Riley's "In Manus Tuas" seem to complement both the music and the words themselves, their supplication for care and redemption from gentle hands. Riley begins the poem:

> Gendering touch that gathers
> and cups like a boat on the
> rotting sea because I tendered
>
> All I am to your safety. Then we are eye
> to eye, heart to purpose, bent
> forward in the western wind
>
> That blows over the hard and
> blanched ground towards an idea
> of work as shelter.

The soft vowels, the flowing dactyls, the neat encapsulation of the first tercet in the rhyming "Gendering…tendered," the confluence of words like "gendering," "gathers," "cups," "boat," "tendered" and "safety"—these all work to give the same image of care and trust that seems at the heart of Sheppard's "In manus tuas, Domine." So the musical allusion helps to set a tone for the beginning of the poem and introduces the hand as a symbol that will recur with varying meanings throughout the group of poems. Moreover, the allusion reinforces a theme of importance to the sequence as a whole, that of the ritually spoken or ritually sung word as an invocation of protection and redemption.

But I want to examine this "neither opaque nor transparent" poem a little farther, to see what else the dedication to John Sheppard might do to a reading of the poem. Other aspects of Sheppard's career and music seem significant. Like Syd Barrett and Hans Leo Hassler, invoked in the third and fourth poems, Sheppard was something of a transitional figure. His work flourished between the Catholic Latin mass that was still a feature of Henry VIII's reign and the coming Protestant reformation of church music, between older "florid ornamental" styles and recent continental innovations (see Chadd 249–50), between plainsong-dominated composition and powerful contrapuntal polyphony in England, and between the midcentury Tudor style and the Elizabethan manner that eventually eclipsed his work (see Wulstan 273). He was a key figure in the last decade of Latin liturgical composition in Tudor England, yet he, John Taverner and Christopher Tye each set a mass to a popular tune, "Western Wind," thus creating the only English cantus firmus masses from the period to be set to a secular tune, one involving sexual love:

> Westron wynde when wyll thou blow
> The smalle rayne down can rayne
> Cryst yf my love were in my armys
> And I yn my bed agayne. (qtd. in Wulstan 275)

Sheppard's ability to synthesize seemingly disparate religious and cultural demands, and even sexual and spiritual experiences, makes him an important figure for the kind of synthesis Riley's poem attempts to effect.[11] Out of a moment of turbulent change, Sheppard created an enduring setting of a supplication for care, protection, stability.

And, indeed, the presence of Sheppard, whom Wulstan calls "an Olympian figure of mid sixteenth-century polyphony" (274), serves to suggest something of Riley's poetic procedures here.[12] There are first-person pronouns in "In Manus Tuas," but there is not a strong sense of a single unified poetic voice. Instead, the poem hints at a polyphony of voices, which function not quite like those of *The Waste Land* or *The Cantos*, where a vast array of identifiable dramatic voices speaks in a kind of verbal collage, but rather as a set of implied resources of language and music from the past. Riley's polyphony gestures outward to the "extra-musical semantics" that connect his poetry to the forms and words of a broader cultural field.[13]

The gentle feeling of support of the opening is followed in stanza two by a sense of mutual agreement, resolve, direction: "Then we are eye / to eye, heart to purpose, bent / forward in the western wind." Two humans are in agreement but this is figured in terms of the body—eyes, hearts, the body bent forward (as if looking positively to the future) in the wind. The "western wind" in such a context might draw us to Shelley's Romantic "Ode to the West Wind," in which the poet explores the effects of the wind and the changing season on the land, and draws some hope that, as a poet, he can help create changes in humanity like those the west wind creates in the seasons and on the land: "O Wind, / If Winter comes, can Spring be far behind?" And, indeed, the western wind in Riley's poem "blows over the hard and / blanched ground towards an idea / of work as shelter." The effect of the wind on the ground parallels a move in the speaker's mind toward an idea, as in the first two stanzas, of "shelter"—

but the idea of shelter here is found in work, not in religion, just as the "Western Wind" song that Sheppard used for a mass setting pulls against the religious purpose of the music with its much more embodied invocation of rest and sexuality. So though to begin with "In Manus Tuas" evokes religion, it does not explicitly continue as a religious poem. Even the title leaves out "Domine"—into whose hands are we to commend our spirit? The poem quickly turns to more secular concerns, examining that world in which we work (is it possible for a Carlylean or Ruskinian sense of work to redeem us still, or is work now just work?) and raise children who give themselves up to television, "hand / themselves to aerials" and become the heirs to the world we make: "with one / mutual cry—of succession // Dying to a rich suture of the future. / Deep then in the oily mulch a / smouldering hope."

By the time it reaches these stanzas, the fifth and sixth, the poem has turned from a musical and linguistic evocation of shelter and support created during a turbulent time of change to the question of what hope can be preserved in our current day for the future. If our use of the past is to be anything more than a decadent cultural nostalgia, it must be able to point toward the future. The terms in Riley's poem become ambiguous and begin to unravel themselves as their implications become more complex: ideas like "succession" and "future" are undercut by "dying" and by words like "suture" and "patient" (which is used as an adjective but brings the noun to mind), words which suggest a different and darker kind of care altogether—the medical profession. "Mulch" protects plants, enriches the soil and keeps it from drying out, and keeps roots from freezing, but "oily mulch" suggests a kind of polluted ground that cannot nourish more than "smouldering hope." Yet the poem concludes with some hope: the lines "a patient ear // To another's woe and a door behind the snow" evoke sympathy, communication and shelter from the winter, while the final lines, "How it seals the film of spring, / where we ride forth in company," call to mind the beginning of *The Canterbury Tales* and of *The Waste Land*, and introduce the theme of a pilgrimage or journey leading to rebirth and renewal.

But if "In Manus Tuas" ends on a suggestion of renewal in both nature and pilgrimage, the next poem, the only one of the first four without a musical dedication, suggests darker themes—death, unfulfilled hopes, the need for love, the failures of contemporary society, and even the draining away of the fertility of nature. This untitled poem begins with evocations of death and burial (many moments of this group of poems resonate with *The Waste Land,* as different as the poems and poets are):

> Pure need scores the pavement,
> sweet advert to sliced face.
> I know the mind is a final place
>
> And a stone violently peaceful
> to lie on, hidden under the grass
> as I would for the shadow of her arm.

"Pure need" might, in fact, be the generator of a thought like "in manus tuas, Domine…," but here it is given a more sinister context. The syntax and multivalency of the words and images evoke numerous dark possibilities. "Pure need" could be understood to rack up a "score," to take a toll that leaves a mark—the city's pavement is marked by "pure need," or even, to keep up the musical metaphors, composed by or of need. Riley has argued that "the whole course of western notated/composed music derives from vocal music (whether actual song or ritual music) and in the instrumental sphere has never fully removed itself from that condition" ("Slow Music" 12), and one might imagine here a kind of polyphonic "scoring" of the many voices of need in our culture. The second line continues the multivalency, with a disturbing image of a "sliced face"—both that of a human and that of the pavement—that also (jarringly) suggests sliced sweet fruit: "sweet advert to sliced face." But does "advert to sliced face" imply care, "sweet" attention being paid to the wounded face, or does "advert" signify "advertisement," the omnipresent marker of the urban landscape that plays upon our "pure need"? The mind is indeed a "final place," a refuge, but here "final place" immediately evokes burial and death, so that the mind is a kind of oxymoronic disturbed rest, "a stone violently peaceful / to lie on, hidden under the grass"—a disturbance also figured in another form of "need," unfulfilled love ("as I would for the shadow of her arm").

We move further from the musical supplication that began *Author* as the "suture of the future" in "In Manus Tuas" is replaced by an intensified sense of the present not as a significant reality in itself, but as merely a momentary step before something else occurs: "The present becomes an interlude / to fearful chance, alder / and birch, hawk over the closed hill." The signs of vital nature—alder, birch and hawk— merely preside over another evocation of the grave, a "closed hill." The present's "interlude" is described in terms of the tentative hopes and failures of postwar society, and seems particularly urban:

> Lights sign the arcade
> to a zero offer, begging
> in the streets for sacrifice. I know
>
> The tired are a fine people,
> hands almost touch almost turn
> hearts almost tread.

Following the emptiness and numbness of the tired workers, who can't quite make the meaningful gesture, the sixth stanza seems to offer what might be a positive moment in the urban grind:

> O memoria felice! Nights at the
> star loft, days in advance of reason,
> good measure at the trading station...

But it becomes difficult to read this evocation of the business world, of "good measure at the trading station" (musical pun aside) and the imagined "work as shelter" of "In Manus Tuas," as spurring anything more than an ironic "O memoria felice!" given the somber recycling of images and tropes that follows:

> Slowly failure became an honourable nation
> in which I wait for someone's arm, specific
> hopes wind-borne on rendzina,
>
> Counting the miles to home
> while quieter waters leech the soil
> and closer minds bow to the pavement
>
> Tracing the future of mineral solutions
> under the meadows, and meadows
> of desire.

Hope is undercut by "failure," which becomes "an honourable nation." The rhyme ironically connects "trading station" (itself evoking the outposts of failed and morally suspect empire) and "honourable nation"; even the earlier stanza's "hearts almost tread" is etymologically metamorphosed into the "trading station," the word "trade" deriving from the Old English *tredan*, "to tread."

This fraught sequence quickly becomes more directly personal: the speaker waits "for someone's arm, specific" (to help him up? to give him the absent "hand" evoked by "In Manus Tuas"?) and imagines his "hopes wind-borne on rendzina." Moreover, though one might construe the enjambed lines as saying that the "specific / hopes" are "wind-borne," the lines also look back to an older medical vocabulary: "specific" was used in the seventeenth and eighteenth centuries as a noun, meaning "remedy." The unfulfilled (lover's?) hopes in stanza two for even the "shadow of her arm" as a "specific" and the imagined refuge of the mind as a final place, a rest, now give way, as hopes are blown in the wind on chalky soil. Nature continues, but only to "leech the soil," and the "meadows / of desire" are losing their fertility. But, as with "specific," to "leech the soil" suggests multiple meanings. To "leech" can carry both a negative sense (to attach oneself to someone like a leech, draining away vitality) and a positive: to heal by leeching (another oblique invocation of the medical profession, here in a medievalized form). But "leech" in the context of soil also suggests "leach": such a leaching of minerals and oxygen is the way bogs are made, and bogs, of course, preserve. Just as "minds" were earlier said to "bow to the pavement" in exhaustion and defeat or in respect for the culture of modernity, these stanzas preserve the tensions between the senses of healing, preservation and the draining away of vitality. Bogs can serve as a metaphor for cultural memory, for the preservation of the past: our modern interest in the mummified remains of bog-people speaks to the power of this idea (see Heaney's bog poems).

But what is at stake here is not the remembered past, or the buried and mummified past, but rather the future—the future of "desire" (a term which itself always implies direction toward the future)—and this second poem ends with a moment of extreme alienation and displacement, "Counting the miles to home," as the poem introduces the metaphor of "the dark road" for this search or pilgrimage:

> So set in the foiled traffic my vocation turns
> as the tired turn, downwards, dark road to a
> chip sandwich, weeping prisoner almost touched.

The density of Riley's phrasing and imagery intensifies as the poem draws to its conclusion. The "foiled traffic" in which the anxious and tired "vocation" is "set" evokes an image of street traffic made brilliant against the background of the road, as "foiled" and "set" suggest the setting of a gemstone onto a thin layer of metal to make it more brilliant. (This sense of the word was common in the sixteenth and seventeenth centuries, making its way into the dramas of Marlowe and Shakespeare, for instance.) But "traffic" also resonates with the themes of "commerce" and "exchange" (in terms of both finance and communication) that run through *Author*; this might suggest a kind of backlighting of "traffic" in its monetary and its communicative sense. Yet "foiled" might also be read as a pun on "failed." Hence the failure, the thwarting, of "traffic" (in both senses of the word) is high-lighted as the speaker's "vocation" turns away from the brilliance of a gemstone down the "dark road" to the banality of "a chip sandwich" (perhaps itself wrapped in foil, thus further undermining the lustre of "foiled"), and finally to the pathetic: "weeping prisoner almost touched."

The third poem returns us explicitly to meditation upon language and music, and their ability to negotiate the sense of loss and unmet needs that the second poem developed. For this poem's musical emblem, Riley turns to Syd Barrett, founding member of Pink Floyd and one of the key figures of the nascent psychedelic music scenes of Cambridge and London in 1966 and 1967. Barrett's imaginative lyrics and his increasingly loose and improvisational experiments with echo box and the outer limits of electric guitar (even playing above the nut) fueled a lively scene in London clubs like the UFO Club and at events like the Fourteen Hour Technicolor Dream. But psycho-logical pressures and an emotional breakdown—that must in part be attributed to his regularly taking several hits of acid a day (so the story goes)—made Barrett incapable of continuing to perform live, and finally precipitated his ouster from Pink Floyd after just one album. He made two solo albums in 1969 and 1970 that showed much of the verbal and musical creativity of his earlier work, but his drift into isolation and mental troubles, evident even in the most imaginative lyrics on the albums, brought his musical career to an end. Since 1967, many of Barrett's fans have conceived of him as a crazed visionary, a heroic acid prophet of the psychedelic scene—a romantic glorification that has always ignored the cold facts of his troubled and lonely life. He has become a Cambridge fixture in the memories of many (unfortunately for him, those who have found his address sometimes make his house a stop on a kind of pilgrimage), but the reality is far bleaker: he has lived as a virtual recluse since the early 1970s.

As with "In Manus Tuas," dedicated to Sheppard, Riley clearly doesn't intend the third poem to be an explicit portrait of the dedicatee. But Barrett's music and life lend images, words and tonality to the exploration of need and care in poem. Carrying on the themes of death, the need for love and solitary wandering that were figured in the "dark road" of the second poem, Riley begins the third with images of wandering and darkening days, images that recur in Barrett's lyrics:

> Voiced consonants buzzing through Suffolk
> to a dark road white houses when I
> knew the cost I had no language,
>
> My death spread over the fens, love
> predicates a real future or
> burns to nothing like a white leaf.
>
> My hands felt like two balloons. Did you
> yes you did, see the great flocks
> of Scandinavian wood pigeons and
>
> Plovers on the ploughed fields, hundreds, in
> slowly dimming winter light wearing
> a question to be proud of, bending
>
> To the day's end calling where is the
> river where is the course of us
> where is the bridge of flesh?

Riley skillfully interweaves two separate themes, in a kind of counterpoint: the dark road theme of searching and needing, and the rhythms and constancy of the natural world, of bodies and seasons and migrations. The lines "Voiced consonants buzzing through Suffolk / to a dark road white houses when I / knew the cost I had no language" evoke Barrett's wandering and reclusive existence, when he had essentially given up his musical voice, his ability to express his inner life; yet they also bring the buzzing of music over airwaves into alignment with the migrations of shore birds—of plovers moving over the fertile farm lands—and of abundant wood pigeons flying across Suffolk skies (perhaps even to neighbouring Cambridge where both Barrett and Riley live). The syntax of the second stanza leaves a certain degree of ambiguity: is it the speaker's death, "spread over the fens" (like a flock of birds?), that "predicates a real future"—in which case "love" is a noun of address—or does love itself predicate "a real future," now that his death has "spread over the fens"? Or are love and death in apposition? And does the subject, whether love or death, burn itself to nothingness, "like a white leaf"—a leaf without the chlorophyll it needs to gain energy from the sun—or does it burn into nothing that resembles a white leaf? To have no language is to have no way of grasping and arbitrating among these collapsing relations among love, death and the future, and it is at this point that the poem raises the issue of Barrett's own language.

"My hands felt like two balloons" invokes a line from a later Pink

Floyd song, "Comfortably Numb" (1979), written by David Gilmour and Roger Waters eleven years after Barrett's ouster from the band. The full lyric complements the previous stanza's image of burning: "When I was a child, I had a fever; my hands felt just like two balloons"; and, though the lyric isn't by Barrett himself, many of the bleak, inward and disturbed visions of *The Wall* certainly recall Barrett's life and Roger Waters' childhood (both had lost fathers early in childhood, and they came together in school through their musical interests). The contrasting images of "dark road white houses" (which encapsulate the conflict between the bright promise and the murky reality of the modern suburb) come together with this evocation of numbing fevered alienation, but Riley adds another element. He continues the line, "Did you / yes you did, see the great flocks / of Scandinavian wood pigeons," invoking Barrett's fascination in later life with ornithology,[14] and also the verbal formula used in so many of Barrett's songs: "Yes we do—yes, yes we do!" ("Waving My Arms in the Air"), "Yes I'm thinking of this, yes I am" ("If It's In You"), "Wondering and dreaming, the words have different meaning. Yes they did" ("Matilda Mother"), and so forth. These stock phrases in Barrett's music have always seemed to me not so much an accusation ("yes, you did it") as rather a kind of willed assurance, a confirmation, a sense of bringing to truth by telling and asserting. In Riley's poem, the fact of a "great flock of Scandinavian wood pigeons" is something: something whose importance is worth asserting, something worth seeing ("yes you did"), and something to "be proud of." The questions "where is the / river where is the course of us / where is the bridge of flesh?" are thus somehow elemental, are questions to be proud of. To ask "where is the course of the river?" is in some way a tantamount to asking "where is the course of *us*?" The "bridge of flesh" connects all the emotional and psychological themes the poems have been exploring in forms of language—the nature of our experience of need, of loss, of death—to the natural world, of reality "out there," that keeps emerging into the poems.

But the poem returns from such meditations to our social world, and, rather than suggesting, as in "Old European Musics," that it might "produce something worth knowing about" (4), the poem answers these questions bleakly:

> Not here, or worth knowing
> in a society that reckons care
> by tenths. The sheen of their wings

> Makes a sea of the field
> and a person's age is a grateful fact
> sailing out in it with you
>
> Sitting in the car in a dark road white
> houses bookshop open answer closed
> fruitful company in a closing world.

I can't help but read here Barrett's sad and reclusive life and his thwarted significant talents as a songwriter and musician—his period of ineffectual institutionalization ("a society that reckons / care by tenths"), his lonely haunting of Cambridge bookshops, his slipping into "a closing world," his wandering "dark road[s]" past "white houses"—as setting the tone for this poem. But it ends in a gesture perhaps tender in some way to Barrett, but also urging us back to that "bridge of flesh," that connection of final things to the earth:

> I have to believe what the earth so
> distinctly says. Settle noisily honourable birds
> onto everyone's food.

There is something redeeming, and perhaps a little funny, about "noisily honourable birds" settling "onto everyone's food." Perhaps they are spoiling the picnic or eating the crops—but perhaps it is into nature's hands that we ultimately commend our spirits.

The fourth and final poem of this initial grouping is dedicated to Hans Leo Hassler (1564–1612), another figure who like Sheppard represents a transition in styles, a new synthesis of influences. He and Heinrich Schütz, as Grace O'Brien puts it, "mark a new era in German music," and Hassler's Venetian training opened up new possibilities in German music in the late sixteenth and early seventeenth centuries (83). Like Sheppard, Hassler composed at a moment of great change. In musical style, his career marked the gradual metamorphosis of the dominant Franco-Flemish polyphony into the Italian proto-Baroque style (Langlois 8). Like Sheppard, he composed in the intersections between Catholic liturgy and Protestant services: though a Lutheran, he composed Catholic masses and motets, secular madrigals and love songs, and Lutheran motets and psalms, tempering the earlier counterpoint style with newer monody and vertical harmonies (O'Brien 83–85). He studied in Venice with Andrea Gabrieli, from whom he learned much about colour and harmony, bringing Gabrieli's interest in chromatic experiment back with him to Germany (85).

And it is one of Hassler's strongly chromatic compositions, his motet "Ad Dominum cum tribularer," that Riley works into this poem in complex ways. This poem moves away from the "dark road" and "closing world" of the Barrett poem, to images of light and dawn, and to an echo of the tender image of safety and deliverance Riley took from Sheppard's "In manus tuas, Domine" settings at the beginning of *Author* ("Gendering touch that gathers / and cups like a boat on the / rotting sea…"). The Hassler poem begins:

> Set to a hyaline edge the dawn
> light heavy with milk. Over the
> rim it spills as it is bound to,
>
> Creeps among the grass stalks like a silent snake
> as the rusty tank yells the lads back to plunder
> that they surely will at the chime of ten.

With the clarity and transparency of glass, the "hyaline edge" of dawn overflows as if it were a glass of milk spilling over—the "cup" and "boat" of "In Manus Tuas" become an inevitable restoration of daylight, as "Over the / rim it spills as it is bound to." The seemingly oxymoronic phrase "light heavy with milk" at once suggests both the sunlight's provision of a kind of nourishment, and the cheery emotional "lightness" of abundance; and the poem even hints, dare I say it, at Housman in the image of "lads" at play on the grass.

Yet Riley is no neo-Georgian pastoral poet portraying the failure of a corrupt modernity when measured against the golden dawns and larks of days gone by. And he has something other than Housman in mind here, and that is the highly chromatic Hassler motet setting of Psalm 120's recounting of supplication for deliverance: "Ad Dominum cum tribularer, clamavi et exaudivit me. / Domine, libera animam meam a labiis iniquis et a lingua dolosa" ("In my distress I cried unto the Lord and he heard me. / Deliver my soul, O Lord, from lying lips, and from a deceitful tongue").[15] Riley again turns to an ancient text, a ritually repeated song, that cries out for protection and care, that tries to forge a communicative link through language against isolation, and he tries to capture the musical quality of Hassler's motet in the words of his poem:

> Yet it continues slowly and chromatically
> mounting a reasonable despair
> that finds an answer in its own folds
>
> In the crests and commerce of
> the shadowed fields its own voice
> reaching to the upper tonic or

> Scooping light to the soul's mouth the body's
> lack while the city clocks its advantages
> turned back to back with hatred, hand in pocket.
>
> Hand in blame.

Hassler's motet does indeed unfold "slowly and chromatically": it begins with a simple ascending ("mounting") chromatic melody, and gradually increases in complexity, in a growing agglomeration of voices that "folds" back on itself as each new voice begins the ascent during the singing of "Ad Dominum cum tribularer." The blending of these ascending chromatic lines creates a rich vertical harmony, finding "an answer in its own folds" and clearly "reaching to the upper tonic." The musical setting and the semantic content of the lines from the psalm have the effect of bringing "light" and "dawn" to bear upon the lack, the neediness that the poems have elaborated, and again ties this need for hope to the city, to modernity: "Scooping light to the soul's mouth the body's / lack while the city clocks its advantages / turned back to back with hatred, hand in pocket. // Hand in blame." The insistent multivalent play with "hand" that began with the title of "In Manus Tuas" (hands as protecting) and carried through the Pink Floyd line about childhood, emotional numbness and loss ("my hands felt just like two balloons") now holds out the promise of an almost erotic embodying of the spiritual, in the "Scooping [of] light to the soul's mouth the body's / lack," that complements the experience of Hassler's sensual motet. Yet the poem again moves toward another failed moment of relationship: "hand in pocket. // Hand in blame." The poem figures the alienated culture of the city as a hand that, rather than caressing or protecting, refuses human connection as it is held distrustfully in pocket, in blame.

But the speaker can't extricate himself from the hatreds he enumerates, from "lying lips, and from a deceitful tongue," as the psalm puts it. The last three tercets bring back many of the themes of the four poems:

> Hand in blame. I can't exactly
> unregister myself from harm as the first sugar truck
> cuts across the fens one September dawn
>
> Cold and faint cuts purpose from self
> and state in all innocence. But the light
> spreads, green and brown folded in water.

> Chalk under foot. Domine libera
> animam meam a labiis iniquis et
> a lingua dolosa. Chalk under bone.

Does the speaker have his own "hand" in the "blame"? The phrase "I can't exactly / unregister myself from harm" recalls the second poem's "good measure at the trading station," and the commerce and clockwork of the city in the second and fourth poems; the road that "cuts across the fens" bringing sugar reminds one of the lines in the second—"Pure need scores the pavement, / sweet advert to sliced face"—and, again, of the "trading station." Similarly, the truck that "cuts purpose from self / and state in all innocence" reminds one bleakly of the "heart to purpose, bent / forward in the western wind" that seemed so much more positive in the first poem, leading toward some oblique vision of "work as shelter." Indeed, the "hatred" in the city is the very "deceitful tongue" from which Psalm 120 begs deliverance. Like Hassler's motet, the poems unfold in continuous succession, each line echoing previous unfoldings.

The final tercet—"Chalk under foot. Domine libera / animam meam a labiis iniquis et / a lingua dolosa. Chalk under bone"—is a remarkable confluence of musical and literary resources, whose repetitions invoke renewal and deliverance. Psalm 120, from which the Latin text comes (via Hassler's motet), is the first of the psalms (120–34) labeled as "A Song of Ascents" in the Book of Psalms. This group was probably a set of songs used by pilgrims on their way to Jerusalem, and they reflect the spiritual concerns about everyday life that preoccupied the pilgrims on their journey (see Mays 385–86; Rogerson and McKay 114). The pilgrimage theme that ends "In Manus Tuas" ("How it seals the film of spring, / where we ride forth in company") thus repeats at the end of the group, and Psalm 120 introduces the declaration "I am for peace" that appears in other "Songs of Ascent." Psalm 120, in its entirety, reads (in Rogerson and McKay's translation):

> I called to the Lord in my distress, and he answered me.
> "O Lord," I cried, "save me from lying lips and from the tongue of
>   slander."
> What has he in store for you, slanderous tongue? What more has
>   he for you?
> Nothing but a warrior's sharp arrows or red-hot charcoal [or "live
>   coals of desert broom"].
> Hard is my lot, exiled in Meshech, dwelling by the tents of Kedar.
> All the time that I dwelt among men who hated peace,
> I sought peace; but whenever I spoke of it, they were for war. (113)

The lines used in Hassler's motet are a ritual prayer for deliverance, but the Psalm goes on to invoke a kind of curse upon neighbours—those who, like the distant (and metaphorically invoked) peoples of Meshech and Kedar, promote war and hatred and not peace—asking God to rain burning coals down on those with deceitful tongues (see Mays 387–89 for this reading of Psalm 120). Deceitful tongues, then, are explicitly thematized at the end of Riley's poem, and the punishment of burning also neatly brings back to mind the epigraph Riley chooses for *Author*.

The epigraph comes from Zimbabwean author Chenjerai Hove's novel *Bones*: "I eat fire sometimes. But I have to control myself because my father taught me that even a chief's son is a commoner in other lands." The novel tells through a series of voices (in itself a kind of polyphony) the story of a woman, Marita, who lives on a farm run by a dictatorial and capricious white man and wants to find out if her only son has survived the revolution he has left her to fight. Much of the book is about forceful language, which expresses anger but often reveals truth: as one character says, "Did our people not say the tongue is a little flame which burns forests?" (29); and the phrases "words of fire" and "tongue of fire" recur through the novel. Words have a certain power that can, as one character warns, be destructive: "Tongues are bad things, Marita, bad things. They burn the small logs of the heart into big fires which nobody can put out" (107); "words are little flames that are thrown around carelessly by all those who own them" (108). But the epigraph Riley has chosen emphasizes the ability to show restraint, to have a tongue of fire but one used for truth, not for simple destruction—a direct contrast to the "lying lips" and "deceitful tongue" of Hassler's motet.

The exploration of need in this group of poems begins and ends by invoking language and song from the past. And deliverance from false language is shown to be deliverance into more language—into the ritual repetition of "In manus tuas, Domine" in the Compline, of Psalm 120, and even the refrain of a Syd Barrett song. In one of Barrett's calmer solo efforts, "Wined and Dined," the verse repeats several times: "Wined and dined, oh it seems just like a dream. / Girl was so kind, / kind of love I'd never seen. / Only last summer, it's not so long ago / just last summer, now musk wind blows." Between repetitions of this wistful evocation of a fulfilling moment of love appears the refrain: "Chalk under foot, life I should prove / dancing in heat, our love and you." And Riley adds, "Chalk under bone." Lime is used to fertilize fields, but it is also used for burial, for a "final place." But even here, death seems to have lost some of the darkness it had earlier in the poem. Love and death: chalk under foot, chalk under bone—both coexist in the last line of the poem, the line that breaks from the insistent tercet structure: "Spreads and means, turning home."

The poems thus conclude on a marvellously rich resolution: chalk, soil, love and death are all part of natural processes like the creation of soil from limestone, from chalk (the "rendzina" of the second poem), the return of bone to soil, or the creation of love from communication in Barrett's song. Like the physical "spreading" of chalk, soil and bone as life ends and begets new life, such human concepts as love, desire, communication and loss also "spread" through time and among humans, and in our human interpretation, they all "mean" something. Human meanings ultimately derive from the natural world to which we are connected by a "bridge of flesh," but language and its voicing in music give a structure for meaning throughout these poems, and it is ultimately into the hands of language itself, in all of its ability to explore these final things, that the poem commends us. Poetry and song, and the way Riley has interwoven these resources of the past and brought them to bear on the present, participate in the "climate of possibility" of which Riley has written. Their cultural and tonal structure permits the enunciation of meanings that they, in their iteration, also help create—but, as the poems suggest, there are also meanings "out there" in the facts of biological existence. And all of these meanings, at the end of a group of poems that has been a kind of pilgrimage itself, resolve into a "turning home," a sense of the musical and literary resources of the past providing deliverance and redemption by giving a "home" to our meditations on contemporary experience.

Notes

1. Keith Tuma sees Riley's poetics as "late modernist—if categories are required," and explains that "Riley understands that this view of poetry is explicitly at odds not only with a shriveled neo-Augustan 'mainstream' poetry of 'anecdote and self-distancing, wry observation of conditioned reflexes, wistful delineations of trappings of the heart' ['Creative Moment' 96] but also with various process-based, procedural, and aleatory poetries which often appeal to heightened reader engagement but which in his view abnegate 'the poet's duty to truth,' leaving 'the reader helplessly alone' ['Creative Moment' 103]" (Tuma 221).

2. Riley sees improvisational music as representing "Automatic deliverance from one form of cultural nostalgia, which is valuable in a society which specializes in living culturally in its own past" (3).

3. See Colin Wood's "Account" of a meeting between improvising musicians and the Arts Council (*Musics* 6 [February–March 1976], 25–27).

4. Contributors to *Musics* made connections between experimental music and the new directions being forged by avant-garde British poets as they turned away from the Movement, looking instead to such American inspirations as Charles Olson, Jack Spicer and the other poets of Donald Allen's 1960 anthology *The New American Poetry* (see Tuma 48). Bob Cobbing's "On Sound Poetry" (*Musics* 6 [February–March 1976], 8–9), for example, draws together statements of aesthetic ideals from the continental music avant-garde of the Dada and Futurist generation with more recent writings on concrete poetry. Glyn Pursglove, whom Cobbing quotes, invokes Olson's statement in "Projective Verse" about the source of poetry being "down through the workings of [the poet's] own throat to that place where breath comes from" (8). Cobbing's assertion of the relevance to poetry of the materiality of the voice and the body tie the poet's craft to the larger interests of the journal in improvisational music.

5. Similarly, Riley's "Delphine" captures the tensions and uncertainties about love and risk in Schubert's demanding and rarely performed *Lied* of that name, adapting its imagery of fading flowers and its final concern about the loss implicit in love: "What indeed is the good / of planting rows of flowers / and watering them if / what it all is is precisely not / but what could hurt / and pleasure more?" Schubert's Delphine ends her monologue asking, "Why plant rows of flowers and water them? / They are stripped of their leaves! / Thus he sees / How love weakens me / The rose's cheek will fade. / And so, too, will mine. / Her lustre is ruined, as clothes / Grow threadbare. / Ah, young man, if you bring me joy / With your devotion, / How can that joy fill me / With such pain?" (Translation from the liner notes to *The Hyperion Schubert Edition*, vol. 9, Arleen Augér and Graham Johnson, Hyperion compact disc CDJ33009.)

6. One wonders if the newspaper "soaked in itself" is meant to recall F.S. Flint's poem "Easter" (*The Egoist*, May 1915, 75). Flint uses not gondoliers, but rather the swan imagery of Baudelaire's "Le Cygne" and Mallarmé's "Le vierge, le vivace et le bel aujourd'hui," to explore failed hopes of escape from a society that cheats beauty (taunting the swan with food that is withheld). Urban mass society is represented by a soaked newspaper in the path of the swan: "its breast urges before it / a sheet of sodden newspaper / that, drifting away, / reveals beneath the immaculate white splendour / of its neck and wings / a breast black with scum."

7. Riley, e-mail to author, 4 May 1999.

8. Riley has complained of the "attempt to reduce music to something the semantics of which are knowable; listen to the BBC apologists, note how the more 'profound' Anthony Hopkins or Hans Keller get about the music

the more they talk about it as something which *isn't music* (but is poetry, philosophy, etc. as they understand those terms). But surely the whole point of the semantics of music is that we don't know them, because if we did it wouldn't be music any more" ("Slow Music" 12).

9. I'm using the English translation of "In manus tuas, Domine" from the liner notes of the Tallis Scholars compact disc *John Sheppard: Media Vita* (Gimell CDGIM 016), and the translation of the "Salva nos" antiphon from *The Catholic Encyclopedia* (1913), electronic edition (http:// www.newadvent.org/cathen/). A brief history of Compline and of the Roman Divine Office can be found in *The New Catholic Encyclopedia,* vol. 4.

10. Little is known about Sheppard's life. He was born between 1512 and 1520 (dates vary with different accounts), and died between 1560 and 1563. He served as an organist and Fellow at Magdalen College, Oxford (where Compline was held to be particularly important, and was written into the college statutes [Wulstan 273]) in the 1540s until around 1551, and then became a member of the Chapel Royal during the reign of Queen Mary. He attended Queen Elizabeth's coronation on 17 January 1559, and probably died shortly afterwards. For two of the many sketchy accounts of Sheppard's life, see Reese 784 and Chadd 249–50.

11. And Sheppard also pushed the boundaries of liturgical composition in other ways during this turbulent and confusing time for liturgical composers. Between Henry VIII's break with the papacy in 1534 and Elizabeth's ascent in 1558, English was not yet the official language for the mass, and Henry VIII continued a form of Catholicism (simply without a pope), but there was pressure for the service to be understandable, and a chapter from the English Bible of 1536 was ordered to be read during the mass in 1542 (Reese 781). Yet Tallis and Sheppard effected an important change right at the end of the Tudor period: as Paul Doe notes, "Earlier Responsory settings had been limited to a very small number of texts, mostly for Compline or certain ceremonies, in which only the solo parts of the plainsong were set in polyphony. These new festal Responsories, however, are fundamentally different in that they set the choral part of the chant" (93–94). Sheppard was able to take full of advantage of the possibilities presented to him by his position at the Chapel Royal, writing compositions scored "regularly in six-part combinations that included five adult voices, usually extending to alto, two full-range tenors, tenor and bass. His patterns of vocal scoring, therefore, were exceptional, and do not constitute a standard against which the usages of other composers (especially his successors, composing to the vernacular texts of the Protestant Church) can be compared—except, of course, for those of his Chapel Royal colleagues" (Bowers 42–43). Roger Bowers describes the Chapel Royal as "uniquely the largest, finest, and last, of the pre-Reformation choirs in England"; Bowers explains that "following the depredations of the Edwardian Reformation no other choir in the land could match the potential for richness of scoring offered by its staff of 32 gentlemen and twelve boys" (42).

12. Riley proclaimed his respect for polyphony long before the writing of *Author*: he has described polyphonic vocal music as "the most exalted and ambitious music possible" ("Slow Musics" 12).

13. Riley argues that polyphonic vocal music "was not song, and only remotely song-derived, but [can be] sharply distinguished from 'pure' (instrumental/improvised) musics," in part, by "vitally important extra-musical semantics of the most serious and wide-reaching kind" ("Slow Music" 12).

14. In an e-mail to me of 30 March 1999 Riley noted Barrett's interest in collecting books on ornithology.

15. The Latin text and translation are from the liner notes to the compact disc *H.L. Hassler. Missa super Dixit Maria, Motets* (Harmonia Mundi HMC 901401).

Works Cited

Bowers, Roger. "To Chorus from Quartet: The Performing Resource for English Church Polyphony, c. 1390–1559." In *English Choral Practice 1400–1650*, ed. John Morehen. New York: Cambridge University Press, 1995.

Chadd, David. "John Sheppard." In *The New Grove Dictionary of Music and Musicians*, ed. Stanley Sadie. London: Macmillan, 1980.

Doe, Paul. "Latin Polyphony under Henry VIII." *Proceedings of the Royal Musical Association* 95 (1968–69): 81–96.

Hove, Chenjerai. *Bones*. London: Heinemann, 1990.

Langlois, Frank. Liner notes, trans. Derek Yeld, to the compact disc *H.L. Hassler: Missa Super Dixit Maria, Motets*. Ensemble Vocal Européen de la Chapelle Royale. Philippe Herreweghe. Harmonia Mundi, HMC 901401.

Mays, James Luther. *Psalms*. Louisville: John Knox, 1994.

O'Brien, Grace. *The Golden Age of German Music and Its Origins*. London: Jarrolds, 1953.

Reese, Gustave. *Music in the Renaissance*. New York: Norton, 1954.

Riley, Peter. "Old European Music (an essay)." *Musics* 1 (1975): 3–7, 26.

———. "Slow Music: A Thesis with Instances and Some Pictures." *Musics* 17 (1978): 12–15.

———. "The Creative Moment of the Poem." In *Poets on Writing*, ed. Denise Riley. Houndmills and London: Macmillan, 1992.

———. *Author*. Cambridge: Folio (Salt), 1998.

Rogerson, J.W., and J.W. McKay. *Psalms 101–150*. New York: Cambridge University Press, 1977.

Tuma, Keith. *Fishing by Obstinate Isles: Modern and Postmodern British Poetry and American Readers*. Evanston, Ill.: Northwestern University Press, 1998.

Wulstan, David. *Tudor Music*. Iowa City: University of Iowa Press, 1986.

SOME THOUGHTS ON
SNOW HAS SETTLED [….] BURY ME HERE

Peter Hughes

The first poem in *Snow Has Settled [….] Bury Me Here* (Shearsman, 1996) has a title with musical associations—"Prelude"—and I find myself while reading it developing an image of the landscape as a great stave. The score is partly the traces of power and history, partly the response of "the calm baby in the self" which, however inexpert and unqualified, "suddenly says outright / The entire brochure of love and all. / Stay here before you fall." Your fall (into the "gently sloping dark" which hovers through the poem in spite of the enjambment of lines 3 to 4) is the final individual decay, but also a lapse from a kind of inclusive attention to the present.

Whilst it is entirely natural that poetry refer to, or evoke, music, Peter Riley's work does so with unusual persistence. He sometimes deals with music explicitly, as in *Company Week* and its associated sequence *The Musicians The Instruments*. In the former he writes: "you don't make notes at the time. You either hear the music or you don't…. You've only got this once; you have to put yourself out." There is an urgent tact here: don't muddy the waters you intend to drink from. Check the current before you stick your oar in. "Putting yourself out" suggests both inconveniencing merely private agendas, and extinguishing or marginalizing egoistic promptings. This emphasis on an alert and unselfish receptiveness to the world's diverse and complex musics seems to me to lie at the heart of Peter Riley's poetry, and this book.

Music and poetry are both made of sounds and silences. The silence is at the same time threatening and fecund: the antithesis of the art—as unbroken silence—yet also its site and essential ingredient. "We continue…" says "Wirksworth [2]," "resisting the arts of silence" (11). Yet in "Wirksworth [1]," it is a gap, or silence, that enables and resonates with the second half of the poem.

> ...wait
> For that pause in the business and shopping
> When a spark of world falls and locks
> Itself behind the ear, a sky-connected fate
> Capsule, small as a bee's sting, groping
> Down the spine in search of a heart, down the throat
> In search of a voice to say you make an art
> Of these days among people, your prime state. (10)

(The way "art" helps to form "heart," as well as vice versa, will not have escaped your attention either, because it is part of the business of the poem to make sure it doesn't. A whole book could be written on Riley's use of and investigations into rhyme.)

That potentially fecund silence, associated with a darkness not of absence but of germination, is given a local habitation throughout this book in the form of an arc, or dome. It is like a watermark through the text, a spectral presence, a vault in which the echoes never quite die away. Sometimes this is the dome of visible stars (most of the book has a nocturnal setting); sometimes a hill; sometimes the cupola of a church; sometimes it's the skull. These images accumulate as a kind of key signature: a form which variously traces human imaginative, moral and spiritual potential and the inter-relatedness thereof. And the delineation of this arc is associated with writing, as in "Djebel Bou Dabbous [1]":

> The only God place I know is made in script
> As a rich hollow at the heart of meaning
> That can't be finished (43)

The following poem, also entitled "Djebel Bou Dabbous," concludes with the line: "The God hollow throbs and hurts." Many of the poems powerfully register a precariousness in which "The day is held upright on the edge of nothing" (12). Yet the nothing is repeatedly plied back into the script as that

> rich hollow at the heart of meaning
> That can't be finished
>
> And finishes us (43)

A paranoid interpretation would be to read "finishes us" as "destroys us." An entirely optimistic reading might paraphrase it as "completes us." The poem, of course, simply manifests the continual tension between the two.

The picture which remains most strongly for me as an afterimage of the whole book is that of the dome as experienced from the inside. It suggests a large receptiveness, a certain inwardness, and a simple curve which could picture an aspired-to sufficiency. The concave curve has nothing to do with withdrawal, however. Its shape is one of embracing the perceived; of gathering in the available signs. The self as satellite dish. "Gathering" as both verb and noun, each as precondition of the other.

"Gathering" reminds me that the collective, political dimensions of Peter Riley's poetry are sometimes underestimated. Early in the book, in "Wirksworth [1]," he says unequivocally:

> you make an art
> Of these days among people, your prime state. (10)

And in the final poem, the superb "Grand Hôtel du Square," the informing purpose of the whole text and life are given as "fullness" and "justice," the one dependent on the other. The poetry's ethical and aesthetic urgencies come from a fear of absence, and a fear and distrust of political and economic systems which pervert our residual human goodwill and desire in the name of abstractions and capitalist concepts of "profit."

> Questions live like lit windows in the city night
> Because they are needed because a death early or late
> Is what the modern state delivers us to without a thought
> Without a question asked or a truth known and carries itself
> Through us from nothing to nowhere on a cheap ticket, a theatre
> Of mutual hatred dressed in everything money can buy. As if
> The vastness we inhabit spoke a single word of explanation
> Or comfort, as we ease ourselves into its mouth.
> A distant industrial murmur consigns hope to parallax
> As the river runs massively out of sight.
>   It would be easy
> To settle here and now these unresolved endings by warm
> And reaching image defiant rhythm or domesticating token. (52)

Peter Riley's poetry does not pretend to replace traditions. Rather, it takes its place in the traditions it inevitably inhabits. He draws upon classical, medieval, romantic, modernist and postmodern presences. (In the last quotation there are vast associations which include Shakespeare and Dante. It's a big poem.) This book is perhaps unusually open to the voices and tones of English Romanticism, and to images from the Christian tradition. I think, for example, of the Keatsian last line of "Little Bolehill" with its "real and final thing as true as leaves" (22), or the end of "S. Cecilia in Trastevere" where "a centre to the wasted life" is "finally standing / Whole and obvious, like an orchard in the rain" (34). To exemplify the use of Christian art and its icons we might quote the stunning opening quatrain from "S. Maria in Trastevere":

> Final beings in a golden field, ravenous concavity,
> Glowing up there in the darkness, impossible promise
> Sucking our very breath to their eyes, every single thing
> That's worth a thought burning away and there it is. (35)

Peter Riley is not an exclusive writer. He is willing, perhaps anxious, to include many philosophies and poetries within his own. This unusually receptive celebration of the world and its various human arts through the distinctively varied forms, metres, rhythms, rhymes and disjunctions of his work is the central purpose and achievement of Peter Riley's formidable body of poetry over these last thirty years. I look forward to watching it continue to grow, and glow.

A DÉMARRAGE, A LETTER AND A POSTSCRIPT, CONCERNING (MOSTLY) PETER RILEY'S *ALSTONEFIELD*

Tony Baker

Draw a line on the map of Britain roughly along the route of Hadrian's Wall, and the landmass prescribed to the south—including Wales with its own language, a portion of the Borders with its Lallans, Cornwall whose language is lost, and a host of other regions with distinctive local speeches—would have, as the *convocal* point of all its linguism, an approximate geographical centre among the Derbyshire moors and limestones. In this talk-defined heartland, north south east and west seem like equal extensions: *starting from everything we could possibly be doing a line tends out* and no one direction lays a greater claim to it than any other.

Try to cross this upland region by car and you fall into a mesh of narrow roads that traverse the plateau, drop into unexpected valleys, and aim towards no more distant destination than the next village. It's un-toward country, full of distances certainly, but distances inhabited *not from-to: the distance at*; a hub that receives voices from all sides and has nothing to do with any of them except to let them meet; a dome of calcareous rock enclosed in a horseshoe of gritstone, where the local accent is prone to sound like proof that you come from somewhere else.

Of the two major east–west routes that do head out straight across the region like they mean it, one collapsed in a landslip two decades ago and only a neglected sign as you approach retains an option on "road open." The nineteenth-century railway routes, blasted from the rock with linear precision, have evolved by natural selection into cycle tracks. Transport systems mostly skirt the region, or improvise; no one imagines there are connections to be made. Signposts on the national motorway network can conceptualize "the North" and "the South," but this mid-land place doesn't merit an indefinite article. Even "the Midlands" are somewhere else, portioned out between a belt of industrial towns around the region's southern limits. The centre is missing, the very notion of it is absent. *So you delve the labyrinth, and…it should have a centre.… And what is that core?… There simply isn't. The notional centre evaporates.… All that remains is a warren of its own making but with signs of hope…which…seem to inhabit the persistence and continuity of the long journey to here. Signs in the walls.*

"Labyrinth" is no casual metaphor, for this absent core, this *voicing maze,* is nonetheless crisscrossed by people and their tracks. Nor is the "spectral / city" phantasmic (15); it sits on the region's rim and diffuses a low orange glow into the night sky, from Derby and Nottingham, Sheffield and Manchester, that mars the highest stars. People encircle the region; they occupy it in transit. So that the landscape — from its geological bed, through its "usual water tank at the back of a / farm in the mud" (28), to its pub-talk — sustains human presence as a huge ambiguity: that presence is evident everywhere, invoking none of the in-spite-of-the-place struggle that runs off the moors further north, but it never really seems to have determined tenure. This is an intermittently populous heartland, of which no "version of cultural modernity" has the sort of impelling need that will lay any resolute claim to it (7).

Alstonefield, the site of Riley's poem, is a village on the limestone toward the south of the region. We have his word for it that the necessity for the poem was first felt during an overnight stop when "in the evening I suddenly had the distinct sensation that it mattered, this place, its very existence mattered" (7). Taken aback, he was prompted to make repeated pilgrimages to the village in the following months and years with the more or less conscious intent of writing sense out of (into?) the experience. The motivation shouldn't be underestimated: these trips aren't useful excuses for weekend breaks from bookselling, but acts of urgent obligation — "a writing was needed"; "it would be necessary to enter this scene again and again" (7). Since so much of Riley's writing is concerned with what it means to be present fully in the world — his world — and the difficulty of relating this to a truly human continuity or communality, the absolute necessity to the poem that he be present in Alstonefield ought to be read as an authenticating gesture. One can't easily mistrust a need for presence in a place when the engagement entails these terms:

"I keep going back. It's still there, every time.... I'm just making sure...for which there's no alternative but to be there, there's no channel of information in the world I could trust" (9).

No channel whatsoever? Can this really true? How can the landscape justify this intensity of attention; and how can the poet expect his readers to find common ground if his determination to witness is partly fuelled by a readiness to trust nothing and nobody but the perceptual self? If only actual witness is likely to lend integrity to a poem's evidence, how are we to judge what place there is for trust? Indeed, what trust can any place, thus imagined, hold; and how can we place trust *in any event*, in any imaginative *community of act*? Is the only possible verification of *the enduring imagination bearing on particulars / as loving care* the fact that we get the evidence on the author's say-so?

These are surely misleading questions, for *Alstonefield* is, to my ears, amongst many other things, actually a manifest and hymn to trust, and the meaning of this I think is embedded in the meaning of presence in a landscape and the ability of such an unlikely place as Alstonefield to sustain such a poetic project. An "unvalued space... Void of us" becomes the locus for "the only true thing we are, a record / of love" (11); and this record is made to happen, is truly registered in the detail of the text. How come?

For a start it should be said, though Riley confesses to have been taken by surprise by the "manifestly necessary" evidence of the landscape in the vicinity of Alstonefield (7), the poem's location isn't really very unlikely. When Defoe travelled through the region at the beginning of the eighteenth century he reckoned it "a waste and howling wilderness" which not even the putative "Wonders of the Peak," a fixture in every Gentleperson's Tour Calendar, could redeem for him. A century or so later and "Estimate" Brown, as the first of *Alstonefield*'s prefatory letters explains, equally "hated the place," but for the opposite reason: it lacked wilderness (8). Whilst this difference may to some extent be attributed to the increasing enclosure of land in the eighteenth century which partially domesticated and privatized it (a process of which contemporary tourism is the appropriative descendant, hence the undercurrent to the imagery, ostensibly referring to the poem itself, of *Alstonefield*'s opening stanza—"Thus a slight and special enclosure is set, / slight as the dark spaces I fill tonight"), to a much greater extent the difference between Defoe's and Brown's responses reflects a shift in sensibility. To Defoe the Peak is a wilderness because remote from "society"—his journalistic instinct even led him to search out an impoverished family of local cavedwellers to prove the point. Whereas for Brown, "society" remained too near at hand for the self to dramatize itself completely in the luxury of the landscape. It was inadequate because, as Riley indicates, it was only partway to what Brown sought: "the horror without the beauty or the immensity.... It wasn't simple and it wasn't enough—it was half way there, it was untidy" (8).

Which is what suits Riley—the place is a "messy," "running-failed" compromise, a slap-happy, happen-to-be-there ground of overlap (8). Alstonefield's landscape proposes nothing "that any version of cultural modernity needs for half a second" and yet finally seems "the very literature of what people actually are" (7, 8). It's a point of intersection between absence (the missing core, ambiguous goal of the labyrinth) and occupation by the cohorts of contemporary presence (car boot sales, England Now, television shopping, farm machinery rusting in a logo-scripted virtual reality). It's precisely a fulcrum between modalities. If lines can tend away in all directions equally from this pole of human geography, they can also converge, so that Riley's presence in Alstonefield might actually be a *likely* conduit for the particular intensity of lived script that he intends. Only Alstonefield's landscape is sufficient to satisfy this phase of the human cartography he first proposed three decades ago—*to make it at least feasible / that the lines should intersect the way they do / on the map / of it all.*

Nor should it be forgotten, as Riley himself admits temporarily to having done in the first prefatory letter, that Alstonefield is actually a likely location for the simplest of reasons: having lived nearby for four years, he knows the region intimately. It's his Gloucester and Paterson. From prolonged meditative scrutiny of its landscapes he has quarried two books, *Lines on the Liver* and *Tracks and Mineshafts*, that resist any Olsonian quotation from other sources: presence in the place is his entire resource. Many other of Riley's books (perhaps most) work writings out of this same ground. The earliest published work I have, *Love-Strife Machine*, tends lines towards the **Derbyshire moors**; almost the most recent, *Distant Points*, is part of a continuing project whose next section will derive its essential material from Riley's readings in Peak archaeology.

If, because of what the writing itself verifies, we can accept Riley's insistence on the need to be present in Alstonefield, I think we should also acknowledge both that for him landscape appears to be a lived thing in proportion to the degree of presence words instill, and that presence doesn't have to imply any undifferentiated version of the self as witness. Indeed, the self may be read as a fiction of presence that allows the not-self to walk as freely on the poem's stage;[1] for *Alstonefield* in this sense is a deliberately plupersonal construct. Even a narrowly literal reading implies this for, as Riley notes, his pilgrimages to the village are often undertaken in the company of others with the explicit intention that their "different living and divergent vocabularies" should push him against "the limits of personal poetry" (9). Any act of witness can't be "*settled* by anything I know" (emphasis mine), so the writing is entrusted to a transpersonal condition which is similar to that which Riley himself finds commonplace in Japanese renga, *where you can go from spring to winter from one unit to the next, turn a corner and change from a man to a woman*, though in practice the shifts in *Alstonefield* are rarely this dramatic. Presence implies a manifest of the many—"I and I" (23), "we," "you and I" (26), "gods and goddesses" (16)—in whom the script of the landscape becomes legible the way the quality of a musical chord becomes audible in the detail of its voicing. *As time fills out*, as the reader reads, the writing develops into *a polyphony / involving more and more people.*

Neither Defoe nor Brown read the landscape this way for they were content to report what they found. Just as Messiaen needed to hear birdsong in the flesh, so Riley in *Alstonefield* needs to write directly onto the stave of being the notes that he finds pertinent. I don't mean the writing is invented on the spot (Riley specifically denies this) but that it requires his presence in Alstonefield because its purpose is mediate, not, as was sufficient for Defoe and Brown, inter-mediate.

So how is this version of a temporal, conditional landscape apparent in the poem? There are in fact enough more or less conventional versions of "landscape"—"Limestone hills, sheep pasturage, meandering river dales" etc. (7)—that the word might slip through customs unnoticed were it not that the writing constantly chooses to veer off down the red channel and quite deliberately declare its more than conventional load.

> Hanging on Thor's lip, the whirlpool cave
> hung over the valley… (17)

might almost have been lifted from an eighteenth-century topography if you happen to know that Thor's Cave is a hollow scooped out by river currents millennia ago, and that the cave now overlooks a valley not much more than a mile from Alstonefield. Even what immediately follows—

> …and the miner's hammer
> sounding traces of enriched water far under
> the floor to a palace shining with conditionals

—has a quasi-conventional tone fortified with less metaphor than might at first appear. For the river that carved Thor's Cave carved also the valley whose deposits of lead were worked by miners until the middle of the nineteenth century (see Riley's *Two Essays*), and now runs several hundred feet below the cave on a limestone bed so fissured that in the drier summer months the river disappears altogether into underground gulleys and grottoes. One might question "conditionals" as if the word veered towards an uncalled-for textuality, though I think to do so you would need to overlook the nature of the river, of the precariousness of the miners' lives, and the leitmotif of the person as conditional which recurs in Riley's work.

But what in heaven's name does one make of the rest of this stanza?

> To take what's offered, a gentlemanly mode
> in the bed of state. I don't blame you
> for running love against profit, O
> lubric self; but I know the victim well.
> I know the unsexed epitaph, graven serif,
> sore throat. I know the passing bell.

What is this rhetoric in which something approaching contempt for the imagery and false gods of a seductive politics lies barely masked beneath a crafted music whose knowing cadence seems ironically disposed towards the very idea of graveyard elegy, one of *Alstonefield*'s quite conscious points of departure? I have no better answer than the question, but I do respond to a coherence in these lines which is more than the deliberation with which they're constructed, and which I'm sure has something to do with Riley's version of landscape.

Here, in pursuit of that "coherence," I'd like to make a brief excursion back into a personal topography. For, if Riley shares J.H. Prynne's *aspiration*, cited as epigraph to Riley's own *Reader*, ***to establish relations not personally with the reader, but with the world and its layers of shifted but recognisable usage; and thereby with the reader's own position within this world***, then the meaning of landscape as I read *Alstonefield* has surely something to do with my own relation to the place, recognized afresh in the light of the poem. (If this is sidetracking, bear with it. "Am I rambling? I hope so" [8]. Why hammer away at geological folds if you can insinuate?)

The valley overseen from Thor's Cave works such a serpentine route through the bellies of hills that it has gathered, as human sediment, the name "Manifold," a detail which alone might have fixed an imaginative attention like Riley's. Its script, as read in its rocks and vegetation and Vibram-soled bootprints, is illegible under any banner of "nature," however well-suited to English Tourist Board brochures, for it's a script, like every inch of the nation's soil, of interventions. The riverside track, managed for walkers, is the gravelled remnant of a narrow-gauge railway dating from the heyday of the lead-mining. The trees that clothe the valley-sides are largely a record of plantation and introduction. Those species likely to be native have naturally been subject to exploitation: you'll find few better surviving examples of a former hollin (groups of holly trees once cut to supply winter fodder) than that in this valley, though "hollin" is common still in local placenames. Clefts in the limestone that look like archaic geological features are likely to be rubbish-scattered vents hacked out by miners in order to aerate the mines. On the plateau that extends from the valley-tops, the tracts of *Lolium perenne*, a grass that shines green like the folds of some vast plastic macintosh, are grant-aided, chemically-treated deserts of silage-stuff that merit industrial awards for their success in appropriating Defoe's "wilderness." No one goes public with shares in this:

> It would be specious to pretend
> that any bit of the British countryside is anything
> but an agricultural factory marked Piss Off. (28)

Yet this landscape *is* a script: it's vivid documentation. You can trace the sites of former villages in the grassed-over outlines of foundations in certain fields (often these, or the sites of isolated habitations, are discoverable even if invisible, by reading the plants growing round about); you can chance upon prehistoric workings — tumuli, barrows, standing stones — woven into the fabric of thoroughly farmed land; you can read ancient seas in the fossil encrustations of almost any coping stone of the limestone wall-systems; you can earwig into doorstep **groans and blamings** and...and sooner or later you recognize that the landscape is, like any, a palimpsest. Look at it as if it falteringly belonged to a vision of landscape derived from an eighteenth-century painterly genre, and it goes belly up and lies dead on the page. It tells you nothing that you didn't think you knew. It has, in the perfectly accurate sense of the French phrase, *rien à voir avec*, nothing to do (see) with, an external reality which graces by counterbalance an unreconciled inscape of individual or social discomforts. But as layered text, as human palimpsest,[2] it's a seamless imprint, for we're in it up to our necks, one more inclusion in its multiple strata, poised across the fulcrum of its possible readings. We're read into by the landscape as much as we read into it, so that the script of it is also the script of ourselves.

Landscape, then, as interlocution, intercalation, interaction. And the poem as "interlinear commentary" (7), born out of a nurturing attention, out of nursed presence... And lines in the poem as newly opened veins in a world of stratifications. "For it is a sedimentary landscape however contorted in details of the disrupted surface; the horizontal successions of settling fundamentals underpin everything you see and hear"...(10).

For "landscape" in that sentence read "poem" and you have something like literary criticism: the poem really does seem to work this way—as a detailed, disrupted surface underpinned by an awareness of fundamentals that have the primary force of plate tectonics. It's one of the striking qualities of Riley's writing that the authority of his words as individual instances, fine-tuned to history and the tones of intelligence, should remain such bright instances even though subject to so much qualification through echo, pun, rhyme, realignment etc. that finally you have to read them like the exposed geologies of a cliff, as embedded in buckled, often discontinuous layers that you can only make provisional sense of by reading the entire, revealed assemblage.

Let me give an example of the kind of thing I mean. Consider three stanzas from near the beginning of the second section of *Alstonefield*. The first ends with these lines:

> Making clear what I thought I knew, that truth
> is always at the rim and rings back cash. (14)

What is "rim" doing here (leave aside "truth" and "rings back cash" which belong to tropes worked throughout *Alstonefield*)? Are these lines a marginal lament, of a kind that's rarely far from the poem's surface, which insinuates that truth is vulnerable to commercialization in some way even on the perimeter to which it irreducibly clings? You could actually read "truth" here as either embattled profundity or ironically invoked superficial product, but neither seem entirely satisfactory.

Is "rim" a detail of observation then glancing back to the "hill crests" in the preceding lines? To walk in the vicinity of Alstonefield, "at evening when…the light bows and / turns its back on the receding uplands," would indeed offer a range of both literal, twilight-enhanced rims (contours of the limestone dome) and figurative perimeters (that keep, for instance, the lid on an "earth full of locked spirits"). Given that the stanza following begins, "At the rim of land is a return of knowledge, / spilling from the lip," you might think that, sitting in the stalls, this is one "masquer" whose guise you've more or less recognized (7).

But then the fabric of these words seems also to be cut from a cloth woven elsewhere, particularly in *Tracks and Mineshafts*, one of the two earlier books that meditate on this landscape, in which there's a consistent, redemptive imagery sourced in cups, rims and lips. So the first poem in that book offers "life carving itself out / of its knowledge and the earth / is like a cup, to which the lip fits." There are plenty of examples. Doesn't this imagery have some common ancestry with the lines in *Alstonefield*?

So "rim" has a relation to other texts? Look on to the next stanza again, which this time opens with a direct refusal of any personal claim on things envisioned—"A sight not mine I mean"—and then continues

> The fields are dark
> and the sheep with their long ears are alert
> in the night, where we purchased the wine,
> of separation and took it at the rim where
> the bubbles winked.

There's surely some allusion to, or illusion arising from, the crepuscule in Keats' "Ode to a Nightingale" here, the Hippocrene wine sitting in a glass "with beaded bubbles winking at the brim," so this third use of "rim" leaves an echo of some broader literary ancestry haunting the ears without ever becoming citation—an intrusion in the strata. In the end "rim," in the way it recurs, gets to be all of these things at the same time, without ever lifting free of the mesh of alternatives.

This is all laborious detail but I need to give some idea of how the texture of the writing works on me, in order to illustrate what I mean by "coherence" in the previously quoted stanza that heads off from Thor's Cave. For it's the inclusive concept of landscape, manifest in the detail of the way that words like "rim" work, which creates *Alstonefield*'s authenticity, even when the details actually seem unclear to me; the poet, his companions and all the poem's various plu-personal embodiments are incorporated as layers in the manifold strata—"rims" if you will—that the writing sifts, so that reading becomes a kind of geological attention in which you have to scrape away at modes of perception, at tones and voicings, and attempt to make sense of their continuities and fractures.

We are faced, like the poet, with "the slightness of the piecing mind" (11), purposefully laying itself open to what the midwifery of the landscape, in the labour of the moment, delivers into the hands as articulation. And that, depending on the quality of attention, is likely to move fluidly between the mundane, oracular, rhetorical, impersonal, allusive, opaque. If we don't get many signposts to these shifts (and it's worth noting that Riley himself has wished that "difficult" poets would more often offer genesis as clue in any commentaries they might make—hence the prefatory letters to *Alstonefield*), it's because the particular attentiveness which imbues the poem, purged of sustaining theologies, pre-empts the gesture. If we're in it together, we *have* to make do. The poem isn't a trail carefully waymarked for visitors: it's the site where the words *live*. So while we might expect landscape in the form of "the whirlpool cave," as played by itself in Defoe-ish costume, to appear in "this theatre of outrageously manipulated light," we should also accept that alongside the self's "lost masquer" will be other lantern-bearing figures, as played by companions, passing walkers, half-forgotten authors, mumbling Presences and Intelligences, the obscure forms of bushes in the darkness etc.; otherwise we should leave before the house-lights come up… (17, 7).

Landscape as sufficient sustenance, brought to definition (or not) in our various acts of sustained (or not) attention. ***The linear drift, of what it is you are***, bound into the fretwork of circumstance in absolute continuity…

The poet finally convinces me perhaps because he offers no false dichotomy between opacity and coherence: he makes me trust the thoroughness of his research because he resists facile interpretations where the evidence is resistant, because he himself is utterly committed to the geology of his imagination…

Dear Peter

thanks for the package. I hope you're not right about the French *Noon Province* though I fear you might be. I do sort of remember having it… Everybody here has colds again & we had the heating turned off on the assumption that cherry blossom & April meant some sort of exit from winter. Wrong, wrong…

But I should come clean: this is my "prosodic gesture" since, like you say, "everyone needs help getting started." Recently I've been accumulating material towards a piece on *Alstonefield* & I reckon I need to change tack—alter the form somehow. I seem to have been trying to argue something when actually I don't think I have any argument at all. I just want to ramble on & see if all my readings over the years can provide some half-interesting responses…

Actually I blame Michel Petrucciani. You surely knew of him—jazz pianist with enormous hands who played with monstrous attack though he had some bone disease that meant he never grew much taller than the average adult's waistline. Not that his playing engaged me deeply, maître though he was—his solo concerts were a technical treasury; maybe I should have heard him live, to see his diminutive figure tackling a Bösendorfer, to understand fully. But I saw an obituary in which he was quoted as having said "music is like a god you must not cheat. You must keep a clear soul, be sure that what you do is what you really want to do." If you could strip away the public address from its tone & place the voice by a fireside with a glass of Coteaux du Layon (our local vin traite), then it would be the admonition I was lining up for myself. For I've started to believe that what I'm writing is becoming something other than what I want to do.

And surely, if it's true that *the world returns us to ourselves in the end by the formats of our acts* (which I think I'd choose to revise to "*in* the formats") then, if I cheat by my format—in it—I'll end up with a reading of a world made false by conformity to my preconceptions. It's a hackneyed truism I suppose, but the format into which the language is cast really is the cast of the language: a true solution, not a mixture. Which must be why what we say lines up alongside what we do—language *is* an action, a deed, co-extensive with breathing and putting the kettle on. I don't think I ever did understand how it could describe anything if that meant putting the lineaments on some yonder thing; by the act of giving voice to it, it weren't yonder no more…

So hey-ho for the format I (think I) was chasing, & see if it looks right(er) under this shake-up. The format is in any case the result of the language one chooses, so I'm only saying that I want to choose the right words and am looking for a method. When I first got hold of *Tracks and Mineshafts* I'm pretty sure I was battered into bewilderment by what I read as a torsioned exegesis of stuff my poor head was never going to get itself around. I'm not sure I even took proper note of your afterword which doesn't so much dis-own the prose as redistribute it amongst its shareholders. I think now I read that book's densities as if they were lifted from a Rosicrucian alchemical text: the labyrinthine intensity of detail asks a kind of lostness as prerequisite before you can hope to find your way around its forest of signs. Your text looks like something similar, without the recourse to allegory (though maybe all those sources referred to as part-forgotten are your equivalent of allegory). Without that lostness the text has meagre meaning, not because meaning is in a Buddhist way illusory, but because the writing is formatted so closely to the moment that its meanings necessarily leach away into the landscape and can only be invoked by threading questions and metaphors afresh into the prose-labyrinth. Which is all meant to illustrate the point where this paragraph began: because the language of, say, *T&M* summons such presence, the moment I try to write anything about your words, mine, like Mary's lamb, seem to be constantly trending after them. For God's sake, if I have a choice I'd rather sound like Ron Padgett...

But it isn't a choice of course. I simply want to get the soundings right for what, for who, I am. And in the case of reading *Alstonefield*, this reduces, at least as a point of departure, to getting the address right. I mean the physical and mental address—the attentions—as much as any sense of an addressee. If your persistence with the themes proposed by the vicinities of that village mean that nothing but being in that landscape can authenticate the writing, surely any reading of the landscape that the poem is can fairly ask a similar presence of the reader before the text (though the author would need to earn it constantly in the words which are committed—yes!—to paper). So I think finally I've come to realize that I can only address the poem as invited companion, unable to be sure whether what you write is "a term of the meditation in my entire acquaintance" with you, it (the place), or even—by some circularity which arises out of detours like this letter—it (the poem). Sure only, in fact, of an engagement with the text that seems to operate like your pilgrimages to the village, as a repeated entry into a kind of conversation with circumstance that's concerned less with elucidation and more about the precision, or not, of the exchange (on which elucidation depends). The formats of our words—I hope that inclusion is justified—are the trace, the lived evidence, of the exchange.

And now this occurs to me as unlikely addendum:

I don't know whether on your trips to France you've been to

Lascaux. We did last year and for a pennyworth of birdsong I'd have gone for a walk rather than visit the cave. I was certain that a visit would end up as shopping-for-sights. I hate that. And at Lascaux of course the cave itself is anyway a reproduction, the original being sealed off to prevent the decay brought by people actually breathing on it. So I went there fully equipped with tetchy rhetorics to keep the place at bay. Wrong again.

How the place circumvents, partly by accident, some elements of tourism, don't matter here (though the meticulous, passionate care of the reproduction, and the fact that there can only ever be a handful of people at the site at one time, are relevant, and the former is more than a palliative). Nor am I wanting to tangle with the meaning of the place as "fake" right now. I'd have chosen to visit some other local cave—a more modest "original"—but it wasn't an option at the time; besides, like the best theatre, the reproduction at Lascaux invited enough suspension of disbelief to persuade the most fastidiously critical mind yearning for alienation. Go with the fiction and what was there? Utter contemporaneity… nothing prepared me for that. Of course, a whole shelf-full of books would have told me it, but their mediated testimony permits an assimilation so much more easily than the instant of witness, those powder paints traced on the cave-wall, its leprously calcined surface right before the eyes.

And I *could* argue that the images are con-temporary with *Alstonefield* not least because in spirit the two seem to share so much: both are in a way ritualistic and result from repeated pilgrimage; like *Alstonefield*, Lascaux traverses the limits of the personal (a category comically impertinent & noted only because we happen to have it) with a fluid sort of animism (the only human figure cast on the whole screen is actually a kind of hangman pin-figure, colourless & emptied, with a stubby fingerlike penis, the outline shown flat on its back like it's just been stampeded over, and in my ignorance I can enjoy that as joke as much as ceremony: at Pêche-Merle I think the human is directly represented by a single handprint only); Lascaux, like *Alstonefield*, is palimpsestic, image drawn on image, the ensemble so well embedded in the cave-wall that the compilation looks to emerge from the chemistry of the rock (which might actually be a product of the chemistry working over eons?); it roots its meaning in the contours of the surface on which all that imagery is scripted—I mean it takes its format from its ground, working through the curves and bumps of the wall (the antithesis of the flat surface of a canvas, which I suppose was invented to accommodate perspective better?). All of this underlies the tone and texture of *Alstonefield* for me…landscape (artifact) made out of landscape (the field of beasts) understood as extension of the spirit, not by transcendental means but by the intensity of the engagement conferred in inquiry. Which is surely as much transfiguration as the theologyless body can want.

But what really flung out all my misgivings—really flung out as in a centrifuge—was that all those lines tracing bulls & deer & horses & bison, so assuredly, have such proportions that you don't begin to register the obvious perspectival distortions; to invoke perspective is strictly impertinent. You simply see an irrefutable formal truth—frescoes made with such devotion to presence, rather than re-presence, that the lines plunge straight through history into now. I can't imagine those images enduring through millennia: they seem to have existed rather through an accretion of nows whose sum is what we call history. It's a matter of utter witness, bearing in mind the etymology that takes "witness" back into notions of knowledge and further towards Latin *videre*, to see. At Lascaux, you almost inevitably *see* what the frescoes mean.

And I say all that knowing the reproduction bears the kind of relation to the original that theatre does to reality…

Which all has to do with *Alstonefield*, or at least my attempt to get the format of my words right.

Maybe this is my attempt to get that walk in, which at the moment looks more likely in our Loire vineyards than Derbyshire. Some day…

love Tony

Postscript

Amongst the various notes I made while rereading Riley's work are the following paragraphs concerning the form of *Alstonefield*. I had the sense that the passages towards the end of the poem, where instead of text the page has several rows of dots, were what prompted my questions about the sort of "trust" a reader has to put in the author, and how reasonable that requirement is. In so closely argued a text those absences might seem like a failure to resolve—only they operate on me in exactly the opposite fashion: they seem an appropriate cadence because of the consideration the poem shows in trying to find itself on speaking terms with its readers.

But I wasn't sure how this actually happened. I thought maybe something in the form justified the ellipses. So I made this outline, completely missing the obvious possibility, which the author himself later pointed out, that the ellipses are there because the lines, at the time of publication, simply hadn't been written! *Alstonefield*'s subtitle, "stanzas unfinished," which I had read as meaning "this poem is completed with some unfinished stanzas," reflects merely that the project in its published form is incomplete.

Subsequent to publication it has developed considerably, as the author himself recently described: "It may be pertinent... to note that the published section (I–IV) turned out to be Preludial — Part V is in itself some 75 pages long and is a much faster-flowing, spoken ramble with narrative incidents (at one point I meet the ghost of Shostakovitch) in a night-long circular walk. So the comparatively tight, meditational writing of I–IV represents a kind of delay at getting started — Preface and all is a sort of 'what am I going to do with this place?' and very much a static consideration of the stratification. When I really get walking a lot of society and politics comes in, and at *night* which to some extent cloaks the place or makes another place of it."

I don't think however this makes any difference to the formal outline I made, for the reader can only respond to the text as received, and nothing in *Alstonefield* asks that the poem should be read as preludial. So I've included the sketch here because, though based on a misconception, I think it nonetheless does have something to say about the relation between reader and writer, the extent of trust that has to exist between them, and offers at least another plausible account of why the published poem sounds satisfyingly resolved.

$$\bullet \quad \bullet \quad \bullet$$

Alstonefield is comprised of 47 stanzas of ten lines each, grouped in five sections. Two of the stanzas are broken so as to end one section and open another. Three of the last five stanzas have lines missing: the last ends

....

in immense varieties of light.

You could say, as Riley does in his review of Langley, *if there are inexplicable hiatus[es] between items, we don't have to think in terms of connectivity submerging into a subconscious where an alternative logic speaks itself in silence. The connectives where absent, seem to me to be simply absent,* and this seems true of the ellipses at the end of *Alstonefield* too. But Riley also remarks that the units from which a typical Langley poem is built are completions, and that too seems true of *Alstonefield*'s aerated cadence.

This isn't contradiction. The integrity of *Alstonefield*'s structure is such that the final respiration emerges from control rather than any reluctance to resolve. Of the poem's stanzas, 23 (i.e., almost half) refer to "light"; 15 invoke "dark"; and fully 29 sustain an assonance with "light" through words such as "night" or "delight," or others semantically remote which nonetheless form complete rhymes — "sight," "slight," "might" etc. This vocabulary is worked into the texture with such care that only half a dozen stanzas don't contain one or other of these word-types, yet the variety of usage is such that you might not really register the motif on first reading. As formal arabesque written on a landscape of "light," the final line could hardly be more precisely earned or more complete summation.

Or look it on another scale. *Alstonefield*'s form might be very crudely sketched:

I: graveyard pastoral (undoing Gray) — twilight — tense rheto-ric — solitary (companionship implied only in a tenderly in-voked Madonna-ish figure who visits from the realms of medieval lyric)

II: larger landscape of Alstonefield — tense rhetoric — solitary, but alluding to company — evening, passing into night, with sec-tion broken in broad daylight

III: excursion into Beresford Dale — daylight — inquiries threaded into the labyrinth of place — tensest rhetoric, nearly over-wrought, most clear in four stanzas that repeat and vary one another without advancing the excursion (poem's midpoint) — solitary, but precisely invoking company ("I grasp an absent hand") and redefining solitude, "an abandoned centre" (23) — section broken by a morning of "blinding light" (24)

IV: wider-ranging excursion — daytime (mostly) — companions specifically named — inquiry eroded (partly) before a much less tense rhetoric: "Look how the bones of the / landscape trellis the darkness, how nothing / intervenes between the eye and its home" (27) — final stanzas abandon tensions to ellipsis — evening

V: coda — beginning of an orientation beyond rim of the region — daylight/any time — tone pretty much that of relaxed chatter —

Travelling Man and His Discontents—more ellipsis—final line, infused with, diffused from, whole poem.

Under this scheme the easy breathing of the poem's end is earned, the way chicken and chips at the end of the day in The George is earned; the ellipses are pauses, if you like, in a conversation with the reader which has resolved to the point that no one's fighting for connectives any more because the terms seem to emerge as sufficient already. Taste the beer, watch the light.

Which is all said in the light of the sketch's approximateness (it's fully contradicted at times), and the entirely different formal strategy which often appears to treat each new stanza as a grid for improvisation whose substance looks for a point of departure in the immediately preceding stanza (e.g. the play around the word "rim"). If *Alstonefield* has some sort of overarching form, it also has form in its small-scale ramifications which arch (lurch?) in quite unpredictable directions by variation.

But I don't think this is actually what I primarily respond to in the poem's elliptical end. I recognize rather a sense of achieved community, provisional, "messy and running-failed as it is" (8), which circumscribes the need to write more because it reconciles, as so much of Riley's writing seems to want to do, his speech to a world stuffed full of vivid, alternative chatter; and since speech—language on the tongue—is how a poet knows the world, his world, her world, this reconciliation embraces the pauses in which the "alterior" voice might speak for itself (20). Which is a gesture of immense, measured and necessary trust—"each in performance integral, are we. I trust so" (18).

Notes

1. This is made explicit in the recently published sections of *Alstonefield*. A note to stanzas that appeared in *Gare du Nord* 2.2 (1999), for instance, reads: "The person speaking the poem (or actually about half of that person) is nearing the end of a night-long circular walk in the hills of central England during which he (if it is he) constantly talks to himself...."

2. Much of Riley's oeuvre could be read as palimpsest, if by palimpsest is meant writing that is written over, or out of, some pre-existing work or occasion. There are obvious examples—*Distant Points* (written over a collage of archaeological researches, Tudor lyrics, and much else), *Strange Family* (over Prynne's *day light songs*) or *Royal Signals* ("From the War Diary of Arthur Riley"); equally the early books concerned with improvised music—*The Whole Band, The Musicians The Instruments*—are palimpsestic in that they

are written over the "residue" left by music; both *The Linear Journal* and *Lines on the Liver* are palimpsests as implied by the titles (the former, like *Alstonefield, Sea Watches* or much of *Snow Has Fallen [....] Bury Me Here* being lines written over places visited); *Tracks and Mineshafts* contains prose that is perhaps more truly collage but its originals are so thoroughly assimilated—forgotten even by the author—that the effect is palimpsestic. I think you could argue too that the technique of many other pieces is akin, though I'm not sure it wouldn't be more accurate to say that they appear palimpsestic simply because Riley is so continually aware of history not just as a matter of scholarly detail but principally as an informing energy whose detail may not always be recoverable. His lines often read like the transformed evidence of other evidence whose history is so thoroughly embedded in the text that you wouldn't recognize it even if you tried to exhume it. We get instead a sense of pre-existence revised into re-existence in order to pursue an inquiry re: existence—a survey into a continuing present.

Works Cited

Quotations in regular typeface are from *Alstonefield* (London: Oasis; Plymouth: Shearsman, 1995); quotations in bold italics come from elsewhere, as follows:

convocal: *Distant Points* (London: Reality Street Editions, 1995), p. 9.

starting from everything...: *The Musicians The Instruments* (London: The Many Press, 1978). "Derek Bailey, An Essay."

not from-to...: *The Musicians The Instruments,* "Lol Coxhill, An Essay."

So you delve...: *Manchester* (Cambridge, 1992), p. 4.

voicing maze: *Sea Watches* (Kenilworth: Prest Roots, 1991), p. 12.

in any event: *Preparations* (London: Curiously Strong, 1979), section 14.

community of act: *Preparations,* section 4.

the enduring imagination...: *Tracks and Mineshafts* (Matlock: Grosseteste, 1983), p. 79.

For Defoe, see *A Tour through the Whole Island of Great Britain,* especially the section concerned with Wirksworth.

to make it at least feasible...: *Love-Strife Machine* (London: Ferry, 1969), p. 9.

Derbyshire moors: *Love-Strife Machine,* p. 19.

can go from...: *A Poetry in Favour of the World* [a review of R.F. Langley's *Twelve Poems*] (London: Form, 1997), p. [5].

as time fills out...: *The Linear Journal* (Lincoln: Grosseteste, 1973), p. 17.

aspiration...: epigraph to *Reader* (London, 1992).

groans and blamings: *Two Essays* (Matlock: Grosseteste, 1983), p. 12.

the linear drift: *Love-Strife Machine,* p. 24.

the world returns: *Tracks and Mineshafts,* p. 24.

if there are inexplicable hiatus[es]...: *A Poetry in Favour of the World,* p. [4].

EXCAVATION
AND CONTEMPLATION:
PETER RILEY'S *DISTANT POINTS*

Tom Lowenstein

On the front cover of *Distant Points* is a reproduction of a page of William Blake variously credited: in *Distant Points* as "Elisha in the Chamber on the Wall" and by the Tate Gallery as "A Vision." It is a monochrome composition, in sepia wash over pencil. One former owner of the drawing, W. Graham Robertson, wrote on the back: "A Vision. Probably representing the Poet, in the innermost shrine of the Imagination, writing from angelic dictation." Whether prophet or poet—and for "fairly obvious reasons," he has said, Peter Riley modestly suppressed the Tate Gallery title—this inspired figure at the centre of the page sits at a table beneath the circular glow of a lamp, presumably writing to the dictation of his spirit helper, who shines beside him with an inner light. The two forms are situated in a classically proportioned shrine, which is recessed in a series of frames whose severe perspective draws the eye uncomfortably towards the centre of a chilly, somewhat repellent composition.

More cheerfully, and in apparent if not intentional counterpoint to Blake's drawing, the back cover of *Distant Points* shows a photo of the author—on holiday somewhere in northern Europe—propped against the sunlit wall of a small house. The vegetation, variously battered and springing up in pots round the white pebbledash of the house exterior, suggests that the season is late winter or early spring. The sun strikes the poet from the left, creating a reduced diagrammatic shadow leading from his right leg. The sun is low and misses Riley's head, so the shadow is truncated, extending downward from shoulder level, rendering only the arms, leg and open jacket in a shape which, somewhat in the Vorticist manner, is cleanly angled and irregular.

While Riley's figure leans intently toward the camera, his shadow moves away into the house, sloping purposively into the recess of a doorway, which is one of two cut into the façade. The shadow's long neck, wrinkled by the moulding of the door jamb, is already halfway in. What will the shadow encounter in the dark house interior? Will it, like Blake's prophet, sit at the writing table—"drown'd in shady woe, and visionary joy," as in the Preludium to Blake's *Europe*—while the poet himself is off in a landscape of neolithic burials or the relics of nineteenth-century industrial workings? It is landscapes such as these that have inspired much of Riley's poetic excavation of the last two decades.

If the figure in Blake's shrine suggests a visionary poetic project, the half-rhyming coincidence of its twentieth-century shadow is perhaps just as close to the issue. Many of Peter Riley's volumes of the 1980s and 1990s have evoked this process of entry and descent into solemn, frequently dark, almost always stony places. The strata of the locations can be geological and industrial, as in *Tracks and Mineshafts* (1983), which excavates the counterpoint of local habitation and exploitative economic invasion; while in *Alstonefield* (1995), the impulse is instead to explore or reconstruct a midlands pastoral. The downward spiral of *Ospita* (1987) takes the reader into a more subjective *nekuia* with a grim symbolic trajectory. *Sea Watches* (1991), a work in gestes of more happily manoeuvred consciousness, takes the opposite direction. If one impulse is to descend, another is to travel through light and the marine breezes. The one direction demands its contrary, without which, to paraphrase Blake, there would be no progession.

Riley's work is comparable to Blake's in one further respect. Blake's later poems were designed and self-published as books, just as much of Riley's work is conceived in terms of integral poetic volumes. Even *Ospita* and *Sea Watches* (the latter's writing magnificently extended over twelve years) are *works* which, despite their relative brevity, are comparable in scope and complexity of texture to the longer poems.

Distant Points is also a "work" in a different sense. Like *Alstonefield*, whose parts are likewise in continuous, parallel composition, *Distant Points* is ongoing. Comprising Part One, Books One and Two of *Excavations*, it runs to about a hundred prose paragraphs, and is followed in typescript by *Vacated Thrones*, which is *Excavations* Part One Book Three, a text of roughly the same length as the pages so far published.

If *Distant Points* is, in the modernist tradition, a work in progress moving gradually into print with independent presses, it is also "work" in a more traditional sense, that of focused research and fieldwork. Like any work of scholarly habit, *Distant Points* concludes with its appropriate—albeit disconcertingly abstruse—bibliography, the central items of which are two distinct kinds of writing which accompany, counterpoint, contradict and coincide with each other throughout the text. One idiom, to which I shall return later, consists of brief quotations from English madrigal verse of the sixteenth and seventeenth centuries. But the other, lying at the core of the work (as acknowledged by Riley's title page), is that of "the researches of J R Mortimer in the Yorkshire Wolds." Riley's poetry is excavated from Mortimer's *Forty Years' Researches in British and Saxon Burial Mounds in East Yorkshire* (1905), his commentaries continuing or insinuating themselves into the syntax of passages from Mortimer's treatise. The second, unpublished installment of *Excavations* is based on the similar but slightly earlier archaeological researches of Canon William Greenwell. Part Two—which I haven't seen—apparently develops a similarly montaged idiom from records of excavations in the Derbyshire and Staffordshire Peak District.

Mortimer's work is "concerned with the human burial deposits of the so-called Neolithic/Bronze Age culture" (Riley's endnote), unearthed round the turn of the century from tumuli in the Yorkshire Wolds. Riley's numbered paragraphs follow the somewhat confusing numbering-system with which Mortimer identified individual burials. Each paragraph—the longest is about twenty lines—dwells on an individual burial. "Excavation" thus takes place on two related levels and in two senses. First, on the level of poetic structure, there are the lines excavated, quoted, transferred from Mortimer (often in altered form). Second, and more important to the argument of the poem, is Riley's excavation of a particular and previously submerged life. Anonymous as it remains, this life is unearthed, brought to our view and warmed by the imaginative counterinhumation of the poet's regard—even though this regard remains incommunicable to the anonymous dead, and the poet can only be, to the dead, reciprocally anonymous.

Riley opens *Distant Points* by focusing our attention on the word "commerce," a word which he has for some years pursued and reviled, but for which he now suggests a new connotation. The book opens in this way: "the body in its final commerce : love and despair for a completed memory or spoken heart." Politically and economically anathema to Riley in its transactional, nonmetaphoric sense, the word here evokes human interaction with earth, with world. It is in death and burial that the body, previously an inhabitant of earth's surface and an escapee from its embrace, becomes a component of the earth, at last absorbed completely into the "commerce" or inter-relationship that until now has sustained it. Riley's four final nouns, "love," "despair," "memory," "heart," with their strangely elevated naïveté, are forced at once to cohabit with the nineteenth-century writer's impassive mortuary record (quotations from Mortimer throughout the volume are in italics): *"enclosed in a small inner dome of grey/drab-coloured* [river-bed] *clay, brought from some distance…* and folded in." This archaeological fragment spliced into Riley's opening gesture is paradoxically more alive than the disingenuously general-ised love–despair–memory–heart quartet of the twentieth-century poet. Next comes the first of the bold-type madrigal fragments—**"So my journey ended"**—followed by a more tightly entwined pas-sage of archaeology, madrigal and commentary that extends to the end of the first paragraph, the language serially acquiring tension, releasing it, and again intensifying, in a movement of phrases bewil-dering in tonal variety. Once more the reverberant words rumble into the prose-poem: "heart," "death," "life," "pain"; this second heavy nominal quartet, reminiscent of Tudor song or Blake's "The Divine Image" ("To Mercy, Pity, Peace and Love…"), is closed with a loosely thrown-off "signed and delivered," while the final eight words, fol-lowing a raised W.C. Williams period in bold, read: "tensed wing / spread fan / drumming over the hill."

I have followed the first paragraph closely so as to indicate some-thing of how Riley has constructed all hundred or so meditations in *Distant Points*, and to suggest that his method is one that goes a step further than the more familiar process of montage or collage. The weave and movement here rather suggest a continuous unpicking and intertwining. Just as persons and the stuff that supported their iden-tities have been buried and their elements semi-dispersed, so their remains, once exhumed, are both further dismembered and, in the process of archaeological classification, reintegrated. This double process of unpicking and convergence, disintegration and consolida-tion is re-enacted in the collaborating yet mutually discordant elements of the poem.

But while Riley controls the developing process of this movement, there is nothing that resembles a conclusion in any of the poems or the book-as-poem. Units of Riley's own language are offset with frag-ments of archaeology and piercingly disruptive song, but however imbricated or polyphonically scored the poems are, they remain an opaque netherworld jumble. Amongst the bric-a-brac—the bricolage of the end-product of so many lives—the poem elaborates the bric-a-brac of possible ways of evoking that complication and confusion: this is its compulsive motif, and perhaps its most compelling interest.

I have described the writing in *Distant Points* merely as paragraphs, but as Riley points out in his endnotes, the paragraphs are "poems or meditations"—similar in certain constructional ways to seventeenth-century devotional writing, in which discourse is hung around scriptural citations with which a reader is assumed to be familiar. The nearest thing in Riley's bibliography to Traherne's *Centuries* or anything like it is a work of 1658 by Sir Thomas Browne (Tudor madrigal is a far cry from the detached or even semi-impersonal conscious thought I have in mind), but it is important to consider Riley's longer works as, among other things, meditative structures. It is meditation, the uninhibited movement of thought arising from the contemplation of places, landscape and encounters, of the passage, strata and character of time, human and nonhuman—the *imbrication* of all these things in the developing process of registration—that lies at the heart of his contemplative process. Meditation, a term that Riley uses in *Distant Points* and with more frequency in *Noon Province*, is a condition of receptivity and observation: a mode suspended between mental activity and a quasi-passive repose, as thought moves in and around its object and then sometimes reflexively back to the contemplative moment itself.

In *Noon Province*, for example, the poet is in Provence (sometimes, as in *Sea Watches*, listening to music on headphones), meditating on the juxtaposition of the present moment with some ancient habitation:

> Anywhere in the world the
> Mind wakes while I
> Contemplate a field corner...
> and I
> Harvest exclusive result. (46)

> Stretched in the stone chamber
> Awake and listening
> To the dark stone silence that
> Grew from nothing. (74)

Riley's humanistic meditation, or "Walking the mind, walking the prosody" (56), works on the assumption that all experience may be incorporated within poetic apprehension, and that prosody, the spontaneous product of the exercised, learned and practised mind, follows as a natural reflex. That experience is heterogeneous and transient, yet unified and inclusive; the phenomena that go into it issue from multiple strata of time. The poet is a continuous and, as far as possible, impersonal observer; he struggles to track the continuum without either succumbing to its welter or letting his work fragment into "occasional" poems which ignore it. Though *Noon Province* is apparently a collection of short, discrete poems, they in fact hang together as topographically dispersed elements of a single, semivisionary process.

What is the nature of Riley's meditation in *Distant Points?* It is helpful to look first at a few passages from *Alstonefield*, a volume chronologically parallel to *Distant Points*. I have used the word "imbrication" to describe at least one element of Riley's method. In *Alstonefield*, this process of woven interfoliation of multiple preoccupations is suggested in several places. For example:

> I retire to a distance…
> keeping to the edge of the necessary plot:
> trade, marriage, maintenance, the sacred cast
> of continuance always at risk, fixed with loss,
> moon marks on stone, trenching the calendar. (12)

The speaker is involved yet at a distance; free but conscripted; balanced between the quotidian present and celestial contemplation. Tangled in necessary trade balances (cf. Riley's oxymoronic self-description as an "unemployed book dealer" in the unpublished *Excavations* Part One, Book Three), he yet views them as elements of a "sacred cast" whose ostensible banality is nonetheless part of a unifying visionary enterprise, just as the banal lives of ancient people were calendrically sanctified. These tensions, depersonalized in Riley's characteristically offhand phraseology, are the stuff of a meditation not on any single experiential element or sacred project, but on the texture of human experience, where such contradictions may occur both serially and more or less all at once.

Another *Alstonefield* sentence: "Poor / accidental thing, she said, poor rabbit" (13). This line-and-a-half is the conclusion of a scene in which a woman anticipates the closure of her child's innocence, while "the cruel captains of earth" stand waiting in heavy poise. Whether or not the lines are parodic sentimentality or another daring geste of feeling, they are relevant to *Distant Points* in their unsentimental truth.

Our origins and destinies are accidental; we hop around like rabbits grazing where we happen to have cropped up. Pity and love (we are close again to Blake) offer no protection: but neither is despair in the face of that knowledge serviceable or morally interesting.

Finally, a yet closer figure from *Alstonefield*, in which the grave is an "unvalued space,"

> where we didn't take any
> advantage but sailed away, leaving
> old bones kicked around the churchyard
> and carried off by dogs and wrote out
> the only true thing we are, a record
> of love. (11)

The dogs in the churchyard are making off with yesterday's bones, but what of the more deeply unknowable encrustations, the ruins that fill every surface metre which is not ostensibly a burial site? We coexist with countless dead, whose individual, family, tribal, national assocations are beyond statistical classification. The chain of historical process that leads from the Bronze Age through Mortimer in the nineteenth century and down to the late-twentieth-century poet is in retrospect an unlikely one. Riley's preoccupation with such concerns emerges elsewhere and everywhere: in *Tracks and Mineshafts* where "thousands of deaths [scar] the walls of the tunnels and shafts" (37), or in *Noon Province* where "we think we hear faint voices // In the ground and between the stones, / Dealing and deciding in a lost tongue / A far and fragile history" (20).

Distant Points draws all these concerns into deeper, more extreme, if more obliquely expressed, contemplation. If the victims of industrial workings in eighteenth- and nineteenth-century Derbyshire cannot be known, they may analogically through other historical sources be imagined. Neolithic people may likewise be imagined in various ways—most convincingly, sometimes, in the children's historical romances of Rosemary Sutcliffe, or in the patient empathetic scientific writings of P.V. Glob (*The Mound People, The Bog People*, etc.). But neither of these writers is primarily engaged with the condition of unknowability. The one reconstructs retrospectively into narrative. The other seeks to shed humane agnostic light on what had been deliberately consigned to the netherworld of a peculiar and by now impenetrable cosmos. Riley's project is, by contrast, to muse unknowingly on the inchoate. His paragraphs and the language from which they are built collect, converge, into simulacra of the opaque objects which they make no reasonable attempt to describe. Yet the present, he would suggest, is no less jumbled and complex.

Of course the suspicion arises that such collocations may be just too easy. Perhaps anything with pretense to some sort of majestic expression ripped out of context is liable, on account of the more hygienic air through which it is transported, to accrue meaning (cf. what Tom Phillips extrapolated from *A Human Document*). The love/death commonplaces Riley has dismembered (and sometimes rewritten!) from Renaissance lute songs and madrigal books become almost suffocatingly intense in their new setting, traces as enigmatic as those in the depths of Bronze Age burials, or as brutally truncated as the humanoid bits of supper Alstonefield's dogs run round with.

Phrases such as "**Making all the shadowes flie**" (18), "**you cruell cares,**" "**that was you, and not you**" (19), "**Come, come, while I have a heart**" (24), enjambed with Riley's similarly dismembered passages from the archaeological record and the cement of his own lyrical philosophizing, combine to create suggestions, and powerful ones, of what it is, having enjoyed a present that was once passionately contemporary but is now distant, to have no reality. To the unknowable Bronze Age individual both the madrigal performer who sings "**that was you, and not you**" and the twentieth-century poet who writes equally of "bilberry dust" and "A plastic bag rustling in an aspen" are distant points (18, 38). It is not just the dead who dwell at the extreme point, or "those who, like Ilyich, suddenly pass at death into adulthood" (38): the present too is no more or less a portion of the continuing historical and posthistorical movement into the air and into earth. The poet is himself defined by history, generated from divergent points, like the jumble of earth, stones and bones that shoots up from neolithic strata. He may attempt to imagine what an ancient body might have been: "massed shadows behind the head, where if the neck were touched it would be sexual" (19). But the spade stops bluntly on what remains opaque: "*burnt matter: charcoal, with earth, lumps of chalk, human bone fragments and probably flesh, in a dish-shaped hole behind the head.*" "The person," he concludes, "becomes an object…cut into its own ground" (52).

The dead want no books, for their underworld knowledge and/or post hoc nescience is already more complete than the living can imagine. The living, on the other hand, must be grateful to a scribe courageous enough to explore, as in *Distant Points*, a vantage from which the contrary states—being/nonbeing, person/nonentity—find balance or at least some mutually informative commerce. If *Distant*

Points is in some quasi-ceremonial way a book of the dead—a guidance text for the recent dead or a map of their territory—it is also a record of contemplation of the dead. If *Distant Points* shows Riley at his most uncompromisingly modernist, it is also a book which harks back to models—from Egypt, Tibet or seventeenth-century England—that are recognizably archaic.

Poets and shamans in traditional societies often have the task of raking through the boneyards on which humanity improvises its present. It is a risky business, for the ghosts will, likely, take a snap at sacrilegious divagations. But if this book has ancient, escatological formulae somewhere within its framework, its energy lies in the agnostic freedom of Riley's imagination. There is in *Distant Points* nonetheless a recognizable trace of a shamanistic process that has informed several of Riley's later writings. Shamanism can be unpleasant. If, in tribal situ, the system offers harmony, it can also displace nonpractitioners to the sidelines. Shamanism may provide communal theatre but, looked at another way, it may inflate the lead psychic ego at the expense of the ensemble. Neoshamanism in the West can take on these negatives as well as many new ones of its own.

Nonetheless, shamanism like other systems of thought can move sideways over previously tight borders. And it has its place in Western poetics so long as the practitioner, as in Riley's case, makes no claims to actual shamanistic practice; the poetic authenticity of the shamanistic element depends on the presence of Blake's "shady woe, and visionary joy." I have mentioned the painful *nekuia* of *Ospita*, a work of bleak personal negativity. At the opposite extreme are the happy lines in *Sea Watches*:

> Almost asleep in the thin walls, undeliberately
> I send my soul out like a night bird or a witch
> To fly over the dark roads (8)

Here the writer's consciousness achieves a rarefied uplift which is as pure an exaltation as the spiritual dereliction of *Ospita* is deep in netherworld subjectivity. Suspended between these opposites, perhaps less visibly, is the skein of meditational experiences which informs *Noon Province*. Here the poet moves both along the surface of the landscape and down into historical shades which over the centuries have given the landscape its surface character. Provençal heat, colour and stone, the rhythms of darkness and light, and of the connective thought linking the poems—all these contrive to suffuse the book with an atmosphere of trance.

It is a cliché that initiated shamans are specialists in spirit flight and ecstatic suspension between this and the other worlds they visit. Eliade and others have tabulated the co-ordinates of classical shamanistic topography, the souls of its practitioners deviating from horizontal relations in ordinary time and travelling up to worlds in the sky, or down through the earth or to underwater spirit regions. There is no sense in which Peter Riley's work suggests ethnographically defined ritual events like these; his voice is neither rhetorical nor ecstatic, but one of persistent self-extension into otherness, into regions of scarcely imaginable opacity. This is an important aspect of *Distant Points* and other late works: in them, the shamanistic element has moral and poetic meaning in the empathic relations of writer to the region of the elsewhere. Through study and meditation the poet creates for interred realities a parallel one, a voice which recalls them from their disintegration. And just as those realities are as ordinary as the poet's own, his voyaging is never separate from the movement of daily intercourse or a meditative walk.

It is hard positively to enjoy, probably easy to dislike a work at once so impressive and bewildering, as original and derived, as intense and apparently casual as *Distant Points*. The conjunctions are dazzling; the motifs universal; the shafts of lyrical or grey deathlike speech from both Riley and supportive structural apparatus often overwhelming. Unlike other recent work—*Alstonefield, Sea Watches, Noon Province* in particular—*Distant Points* is a recalcitrant, sometimes rebarbative text. Dislocated and restless, the eye forks over the paragraphs in search of connections that make sense, greedy for threads, veins, intercalations offering a route through the labyrinths of discord. And is this not the nature of an excavation? We follow a progression from eye to spade, trowel, specimen box, laboratory cabinet and finally museum—or its linguistic semi-equivalent, the published, catalogued and reviewed volume.

The archaeologist arrives at sense presumably when the rubble has been separated and classified. But we get perhaps only half the view to which Riley has invited us if we decontextualize ourselves from the confusion of unclassifiable clutter which, I think Riley suggests, societies extended in time but collective in experience inevitably give rise to. So as the eye forks round the paragraphs, that angular shadow still slopes fugitively inward, inviting the reader—scarified by the process—to his "wonderful labour" ("Ospita," *Noon Province* 108). It is a unique enterprise, and all the more satisfying for its fugitive and demanding nature.

Works Cited

Peter Riley. *Alstonefield.* London: Oasis; Plymouth: Shearsman, 1995.
————. *Distant Points*: *Excavations Part One Books One and Two.* London: Reality Street Editions, 1995.
————. *Noon Province et autres poèmes.* Bilingual edition, with translations by Lorand Gaspar, Sarah Clair and Claire Malroux. Saint-Pierre-la-Vielle, France: Atelier La Feugraie, 1996.
————. *Sea Watches.* Kenilworth: Prest Roots, 1991.
————. *Tracks and Mineshafts.* Matlock: Grosseteste, 1983.

TRAPPINGS OF THE HART: *READER* AND THE BALLAD OF *THE ENGLISH INTELLIGENCER*

Simon Perril

Peter Riley's 1992 collection *Reader*, despite its brevity, seems a central text within an oeuvre spanning 30 years. In a mere 14 poems it condenses a range of concerns, harking back to the early work from the time of *The English Intelligencer* while also anticipating the prose-poems to come in *Distant Points*. The latter collection sports a blurb claiming that "any singular voice" in the poems "is constantly interrupted by itself in another guise, and a whole theatre of masks jostles for position around the central condition of meditation: the hole in the ground and the human entirety it no longer holds, but which continues to exist in the history of script." *Reader* consists of mostly very short lyrics, often seemingly autobiographical, but for this reader they give the lie to any assumption that the lyric is a monologic form. The poem "Macclesfield" warns that "A provincial voice has / total age or falls to scraps." The title's naming of a location might suggest an autobiographical anchor, but the total age of this voice is due to its origins in a province that is also textual. Riley's essay "The Creative Moment of the Poem" talks of poetry in terms of a "zone," a "climate of possibility…consisting of the work of others past and present, which criticism is constantly trying to reduce to a fewness" (111–12). In *Reader* there is no theatre of masks jostling for position; poetry/language itself is the ancestral grave.

Reader opens with "Harecops," titled after a house in North Staffordshire that Riley in for several years. The poem culminates in a visit to the aforementioned grave:

> …a dark
> green mass strung with white stone walls

> At its highest point an ancestral grave,
> a circular fate capsule of long stones.

This evocation of the fate capsule begins and ends the collection, and its circularity is emblematic of how the book circles not just landmarks in Riley's life—Macclesfield, Denmark, Hastings—but also in his work. W.S. Graham's poetry frequently presents itself as an imagined land populated with real landmarks, even though these could not feature in one location, folding as they so often do his childhood home of Greenock in Scotland into his adult life in Zennor and its environs in Cornwall. Riley's work has rigorously anchored itself in place and landscape. Yorkshire, Derbyshire and the Peak Distrinct have all been duly excavated, in a career that took its initial impetus from the transatlantic crossing of Charles Olson's mantle of "archaeologist of morning" to the trustees of the fugitive *English Intelligencer* project (*TEI* from now on). However, *Reader*, from its opening page, opens a field that is as much intertextual as literal:

> Our front window looked two
> miles over pasture and woodlands thick
>
> With the sheen of equity that eschews
> greed or fantasy, its pale emblems still
>
> Shelved at the field edges and tending
> to fade to advantage.

This nostalgic gaze spans a semimythical landscape encompassing pasture and woodland that is "shelved" between field edges. The thickness is not so much an empirical attribute of the woodlands, as it is a rich density of allusion. The "sheen of equity" is a gloss of evenhandedness that taps into the rhetoric of the constitution of trust through the establishment of a "community of risk" that lay at the heart of the *TEI* project. And yet to then gloss this sheen as being a quality that "eschews / greed or fantasy" introduces what has been seen as a more problematic aspect of the legacy of *TEI*: the reluctance of certain British poets to enter a public discursive sphere of poetics debate in the decades since the breakdown of *TEI*'s "community of risk," a weighty stoicism which Drew Milne has called "agoraphobia."

In my reading, *Reader* is full of a sheen of equity that is very much a product of fantasy in the sense of the pursuit of traces of a vision of a utopian ethical community: a distant lustre to be endlessly pursued. Rosemary Jackson has noted that fantasy is "a literature of desire, which seeks that which is experienced as absence and loss" (3). The motif of the hunt is the buried narrative linking these poems, from the opening benevolent hunt for the human heart by the descending forces of "Grace and honour," to the later evocation of the emblematic image of the poet hunting the hart of Nicholas Moore's posthumously published final collection—a collection that owes its public existence to Riley's own hunting of the elder poet to his lair in a squalid flat near Orpington. Moore's *Lacrimae Rerum* was published in 1988. *Reader* was published in 1992, a year after Iain Sinclair's *Downriver*. In this novel, Sinclair uses Moore's final collection as a pretence to visit Riley and conduct an interview concerning what Riley diagnoses as the "slow haemorrhage of readership" that stranded the initially popular and acclaimed poet of the 1940s in a condition that rapidly became one of virtual exile within his own country (309). Sinclair's ruse is to get Riley to indirectly allude to his own condition:

I was trying to discover how much the contemporary Cambridge poet felt that he was ready to accept the role of scapegoat, the condition of exile. If the culture at large refuses to imagine your existence, how strong is the impulse to spit in its eye? Or: do you stick modestly to your last and wait (to the death) for a tap at the window? (316)

The sheen of equity that haunts *Reader* is that of an equity of redemption: the right which a mortgagor who has in law forfeited his estate has of redeeming it within a reasonable time by payment of the principal and interest. It seems natural that this equity of redemption, addressed to the reader, should keep circling back to *TEI* as a mythical forfeited estate, a fate capsule hidden in the woods waiting to be found. If this reading seems fanciful—and the *OED* lists "hare-brain" as one meaning of "hare-cop"!—then indulge me this observation: not only is the collection framed by an epigraph from J.H. Prynne, but the covers that house the text are of heraldic significance. The white chalk scraped down the buckram green card rhymes exactly with the recent hardback edition of Prynne's 1969 collection *The White Stones*, the book that most epitomizes the *TEI* project—just as the fate capsule inside Riley's text is "a dark / green mass strung with white stone walls."[1]

The purpose here is not to trace Riley's work back to Prynne's, but to show the extent to which the experience of *TEI* lies at the root of both writers' works, and the extent to which these roots still protrude in *Reader*. A consideration of *TEI*'s impact is still largely absent from the available range of criticism on Prynne, even though it might conceivably also provide a starting point for a consideration of Riley, Barry MacSweeney, Andrew Crozier, John James and Wendy Mulford amongst others. This is in startling contrast to the critical attention paid to the role of magazines such as *This* and *L=A=N=G=U=A=G=E* in the formation of a contemporary American avant-garde. Of course, these latter were fully fledged publications, whereas *TEI* was never commercially available—it consisted of a worksheet begun in 1965 that was passed on, in the form of mimeographs, to a list of people who were presumed to have an interest. The model was the San Francisco journal *Open Space*, initiated by Stan Persky to provide just that—a regular forum for the ongoing work of the community. The space was predetermined to be open for a year only, and its fifteen issues included work from Robert Duncan, Jack Spicer, Robin Blaser and Joanne Kyger amongst many others.

Riley completed his M.A. thesis, "A Commentary on the Serial Poems of Jack Spicer," in 1975 at the University of Keele under the supervision of the poet Roy Fisher, and Spicer is another intertextual presence felt in *Reader*. The title of his 1962 serial trilogy is part of the textual fabric of "Macclesfield," where "Little red tractors // Buzzed round the / heads of the town." The only published part of Riley's thesis is the chapter on *The Holy Grail*, which appeared in the Spicer issue of *Boundary 2* in 1977. In it he discusses the significance of the structuring of Spicer's serial poems around a quest narrative that he claims is established by the end of Spicer's serial experiments of the 1950s:

By *A Red Wheelbarrow* the substance of the poetry is clearly defined as a process of penetration (descent), confrontation, and renewal (ascent). It is an elliptical quest which departs from the known, comes to an engagement (flight, coition, barrier, etc.) and is thereafter a double journey: on the one hand gaining access to further fields and continuing, on the other hand returning to the known. The ending always holds a sense of gain and a sense of loss in perfect equipoise. (163)

Though Riley has said that "it can be dangerous to rely on a poet's prose, because it can so easily be marginal to the poetry" ("Spitewinter Provocations" 1), I would argue that *Reader* models itself around this sense of an elliptical quest. And anyway, my reading of it is by way of attending to what is marginal to the poetry in the sense of what is intertextually present in the margins of its pages.

Riley's take on the last book Spicer lived to see published, *Language*, is that it marks "his final ability to operate a book beyond obsession or preoccupation altogether, and to produce the complete book without any external defining or colouring factors" ("Narratives" 165). Whilst this may be true in the sense that the book is not anchored in the reference field of Arthurian romance or the focus of a single "ghost" figure (Lorca, Rimbaud, etc.), the unpublished chapters of the thesis stress that *Language* is strongly anchored in a social field. The recent biography confirms this, claiming that "in a real sense, *Open Space* kept Spicer alive in 1964—its very regularity helped provide a rhythm in which to situate his final two books" (*Poet Be Like God* 279). In fact this condition not only shapes the emergence of *Language*, but seeps into the text as a narrative of a social love and antagonism that flickers in and out of focus in the poems. There are the "Love Poems" directed at Larry Kearney, the "Intermissions" that ask "Dare he / Write poetry / Who has no taste of acid on his tongue" (*Collected Books* 231), and most obviously the "Transformations" sequence, which opens with Spicer's linguistic play on accusations made against him that he needed enemies to write poetry. Spicer was certainly not interested in any peaceful sense of community. I would suggest that, just as *Language* is a book shaped by *Open Space* and the social energies surrounding it, Prynne's *The White Stones* was shaped by *TEI*. One might even speculate that the famed gulf between *The White Stones* and *Brass* can be partly contextualized by the break-up of the *Intelligencer*'s communal project.

The imprint of *TEI* is not hard to locate in *The White Stones*: key poems such as "The Wound, Day and Night," "First Notes on Daylight," "Aristeas, in Seven Years" and the prose piece "A Note on Metal" all appeared in its pages. But what Ferry Press's 1968 publication *Aristeas* and the 1969 volume published by Grosseteste obscure is the extent to which such works emerged from within *TEI*'s communal debate, and in particular from Prynne's responses to issues raised there by Riley. Initially, Andrew Crozier's editorship of the *Intelligencer* was virtually invisible, in the sense that any material sent was printed. But this soon presented problems, owing to some of the contributors' mistaking the nature of the project they were involved in. At the root of the misunderstanding was the question of what status the journal occupied. From the outset, *TEI* requested response and criticism and yet got very little. It became obvious that the nature of the space on offer was being mistaken as that of a publication—something that the method of circulation and selection of audience had already implied was not the case. Preconceived attitudes towards the nature of the printed poem and the nature of the space it occupied were proving detrimental to *TEI*. The project was not supposed to be a display case for completed private acts of composition touting for future book publishers. Around the end of January 1967, Crozier felt the need to state that "The Intelligencer is hardly a magazine, and I've never regarded what has circulated in it as *published*" (204). This feeling was echoed by Prynne and Riley. Riley was particularly adamant that the crux of the *Intelligencer's* function was that it existed *prior* to the permanence of the printed magazine, and so was wholly concerned with the activity of exchanging information with a view to forging a communal direction:

This need to share something more than private correspondence can cope with…the language we can use has to be worked out in common, among however many will allow themselves to trust, respond, risk, REACT, move outside their private worlds. (207)

Here is the rhetoric of "risk" and "trust" central to *TEI* and still traceable—becoming some kind of quest/hunt motif—in the "sheen of equity" glimpsed in *Reader.* Prynne also noted the complete absence of "trust," pointing to the damaging effects of "decorums of privacy" whereby poets are encouraged to solely inhabit their own private world of language and experience (189–90).

The need to break such decorums became the occasion for the second series of the *Intelligencer* under the new editorship of Peter Riley. This second series (beginning April 1967) was heralded by an "Announcement" attempting to lay out an agenda by summarizing the achievements of recent American poetry—particularly that of Charles Olson. Though not directly quoted, Olson's crisis poem "In Cold Hell, in Thicket" provides the real starting agenda of the second series, with its question, "How can he make out, he asks, / of this low eye-view, / size?" (*Collected Poems* 156). When Prynne's "First Notes on Daylight" states "the ques- / tion is really what *size* we're in" (*Poems* 69), it is filtering Olson's preoccupation with "objectism" and a "human universe" through Riley's extended attempt in the pages of *TEI* to understand the present landscape condition of England as an island through what conclusions could be drawn from prehistory. In the opening "Announcement" of the second series, Riley defined the poem in terms of *"physiological presence + cosmological range,"* initiating a poetics deliberately vast in scope so as to necessitate a project only sustainable as a communal venture. Riley's attempt to lay some foundations for this project had come in the form of "Working Notes on British Prehistory," an enormously ambitious 19-page survey spanning the Mesolithic, Neolithic and early Bronze periods. His theme was that

something existed in the life of man, *as* the life of man on this island up to about 1500BC at the latest, that we've lost sight of and need to reconsider.

That we cd get it back is a thought that frightens with its possibilities. That
we could recover something of our inheritance *without* anachronism, through
if anywhere this thing I hold now, discourse. (234)

Claiming that "The Mesolithic is the ground we all stand on," Riley
expresses admiration for the hunter-gatherers dismissed by the "ex-
perts" as savagely primitive and uncivilized. His bitter mimicry of
the grounds for such dismissal gives a sense of the lost condition he
imagines they represented: "what cd be worse, having to fetch yr own
breakfast off the land! Filthy gipsies they shd all've been put in insti-
tutions" (235). The Neolithic period, beginning 3000 BC, is tradi-
tionally seen as the origins of a process of civilization akin to our
present. Riley states that many of the innovations this heralded were
"of dubious value," adding: "I prefer, for the moment, to think of the
growth of a real civilisation but leading into a turn about 1500 that I
can only see as disastrous, and which is what we really haven't recov-
ered from. Not that it wasn't, if you like, 'inevitable'" (235). Some of
these invading novelties from more "civilised" parts—"and we've no
reason for thinking what went on before wasn't completely adequate,"
he adds—included farming and herding, settlement, trade and the
beginnings of towns through the need for a place where produce could
be brought for disposal. Against these potential negatives, what Riley
seems to regard as technological erosions of man's self-sufficiency,
were the positives of a genuinely felt community wherein "the dis-
tinction between one man and the group was by no means a simple
matter. So that the group could act as one man, and the things it left
behind bear about them the features of having come from the human
body" (236).

The consequences of such a reading of prehistory seem consist-
ently relevant to Riley's later work, through *Lines on the Liver*, *Tracks
and Mineshafts*, and on into *Reader*:

> It was always there, though the light
> came and failed.
>
> White stone messengers
> pierced the night and
>
> Focused the day, calling
> to the mind, calling to the cusped heart
>
> Calling together the kind forces
> that hunt us to death.

The persistence of this "fate capsule" in "Harecops" seems to emblematize Riley's whole oeuvre's preoccupation with the enigmatic traces of humankind's extension into the landscape: the monuments still visible upon Britain's moorlands and hillsides, and the invisible traces buried below the topsoil—as revealed in the frontispiece photograph of *Tracks*. What message the white stones are emitting is obscure, but Riley's *TEI* vision of such monuments' representing collective "thought reaching out beyond the life of one man…as the evidence of past action" seems poignant (236). However, here it is a haunting call that assembles "the kind forces / that hunt us to death." It seems no formal accident that the third time the "calling" is registered in the above lines it has pushed its way to the beginning of the final stanza, forcing it to adopt a capital letter that announces the collection's preoccupation with the mystery of poetic vocation.

This preoccupation is most clearly evident in the poem "Nicholas Moore." In a collection in which so many of the poems take their titles from locations—"Macclesfield," "Denmark," "Egbert Street," "Hastings," "High Lane"—"Nicholas Moore" testifies to the place of poetry as a location, an intertextual field. The opening lines of the poem evoke this mythopoeic realm: "I repeat, the heart, the / the hart in the forest // The white one I would / pursue that forehead for // Ever…." The lurching enjambment enacts the ambivalent movement of the book's buried narrative of simultaneous quest and pursuit. It was Riley's own pursuit of Moore that resulted in the publication of the poem to which Riley's lines allude. The first poem in *Lacrimae Rerum* is "Yearning," where the Muse is figured as a hunted hind:

> Like a white hind, striding across the sky,
> Waiting for the pursuers, turning this way and that,
> Looking for the unspoilt places; aware
> Of the hunters in pursuit, of the corrupt, the cold,
> The doom-laden air; knowing to walk carefully
> Like the Muse must or be dead. (9)

Moore's figuring of the white hind as elusive muse has its roots in the yearning of Psalm 42: "As the hart panteth after the water brooks, so panteth my soul after thee, O God." Moore makes of this Christian symbol of purity and aspiration a figure of fulfillment—a mysterious agent that makes life palatable and truth believable. And yet the fulfillment it offers is that of perpetual yearning, for as Moore realizes, "What can we make with no clear aim in view, / And how can we live if we kill what we pursue?" The second section of Moore's

poem treats the hind as a clear aim corrupted when viewed "as /
Though in the sights of a drunkard" (10). The result is a blurring of
aim with the scene "Advancing and retreating, now distant now close, /
But always in the centre the beautiful hind, wavering, / Shimmering,
increasing, diminishing, fading to a whisper."

"Yearning's" quest narrative recalls that identified by Riley in Spicer's
The Holy Grail:

The Holy Grail is the summation of Jack Spicer's explorations into perception-
as-love; it is a complete phenomenology of purpose which culminates his
attention to the poetic act in all his previous books. *After Lorca* gained access
to the field and established the direction of the poetry by its penetration of a
pastoral remoteness to reveal the structure of an ontological quest. ("Narra-
tives" 163)

Riley would doubtless balk at my reliance upon his critical prose as a
way into his poetry, but *Lines on the Liver* and *Tracks and Mineshafts*,
as well as *Reader*, seem inescapably involved in "penetrat[ing] a pasto-
ral remoteness to reveal the structure of an ontological quest." What
is striking here is how pastoral, a mode that characterizes almost all of
Riley's work, is in this formulation a veneer to be penetrated. If my
image seems clumsily phallic, it only draws attention to the sexual-
ized metaphor of mining that runs through Riley's work—perhaps
most condensedly in the 1975 broadsheet *Following the Vein*. John
Hall suggests that "the miner becomes a figure of the self, economi-
cally, ontologically—an economic function embedded in all human
purposes and equivalent to those other individualized metaphors of
the self, the hunter, the gatherer, the pastoralist, the cultivator" (36).
Lines on the Liver seems particularly dense in the way it folds its medi-
tations upon landscape back into an ontological quest, even as it warns:

There is a false pastoral (which like all ways of writing is also a way of
carrying-on) which inhabits this gloss and attempts to mask the boredom in
short-circuited dreamwork, leafy parabolas, ontological egotism—a reductive
clarity that conceals the steps and claw-marks on the surface of language. (10)[2]

Much of the prose in *Lines* is "troubled" in a highly self-conscious
fashion. Its heightened self-scrutiny seems to owe much to the scru-
tiny of the categories of "harm" and "good" in Douglas Oliver's 1970s
trilogy *The Harmless Building, In the Cave of Suicession* and *The Dia-
gram Poems*. The preoccupation with harm in Oliver's work has its
origins in his early interest in the Buddhist Jain monks, and is linked
to a practice of interpersonal regard that extends to all forms of life.

It becomes a concern with the ethical consequences of individual actions, and beyond this to a concern with the complexity of human intention. Oliver's work is haunted by questions of the contribution to the intentional process of feelings and thoughts, or of involuntary action such as bodily movements and physiological process. Such preoccupations led Prynne, in a letter published in *Grosseteste Review* in 1973 on *The Harmless Building*, to connect it with Iris Murdoch's scrutiny of the ethical problem of good intentions in the lectures she gave at Oxford University in 1970, published as *The Sovereignty of Good*. Oliver's work often conducts its meditation in a narrative frame—the consultation with the oracle in *Suicession*, the activities of the Tupamaros in *The Diagram Poems*—that allows the consequences of individual actions to be seen to spiral through a social situation. By contrast, Riley's works are often situated in a socially barren landscape in which the speaker's meditations become painfully isolated and internalized.

This is most notable in *Lines*, a book full of troubled quests and questions. The opening prose text posits an elliptical quest "which is never allowed to arrive, since separation from the questor's own being is the motivation and stay of the journey" (1). This quest is not for the authenticity of self-knowledge, but in fact a bid to escape from such confines; Riley seems to be positing an antiquest in which the "self-seeking…human image finally eradicates itself, and occupies only the gap in the torque, the emptiness before the mirror (the mirror shows a beautiful garden or a child who dutifully responds to us or any form of office) and is indeed the nothing masked by writing" (1).

In Riley's work, "The quest remains, not to find yourself but precisely to lose yourself into the interrogation" (2). *Lines* self-consciously engages with the issue of poetic vocation, charting a movement through which "the luxuries of denouncing wrong give place to the duties of tracing harm" (7). The evocation of "duties" is, however, very far from being an unproblematic assertion of vocation. This is largely because *Lines* is less a fully fledged poetics statement, and more a Beckettian endgame of quests and questions:

In the meanest version of activity there is always a counter-valency, and the effort is to raise the balance rather than tip it;…I can't see this as anything but a personally lived act, taking the form of an answering quest. The movement of quest and the stasis of leverage and balance cohabit finely, in fact this paradox is one of our best tricks. (8)

The text constantly cancels its own assertions through its awareness of its own tricks. The unresolved conflict seems to be over questions of human and poetic agency: what is the relation between poet and poem? poet and person? poem and world? The book's preoccupation with "Spitewinter Edge"—a limestone dome constituting the southern half of the Peak District, and described as "a white capsule of sedimentary patience 12 miles across, patinated thin green" (3)—seems again a pastoral veneer upon the text's preoccupation with

the edge of the person, which is where writing, among other things, takes place. This edge is furbished to a seemingly inhuman sheen as it extends into script, but the resulting compaction makes possible an entity which as it is so completely itself can begin to act helpfully.... Then surely the central disclaimer holds us together: what on earth do you think you can act *with* but who you are? (14–15)

The question mark that ends the line seems overburdened by the force of the assertion, backed up as it is by the weighty "Then surely." For what can it mean to be held together by a disclaimer—to be anchored by a renunciation of responsibility? The return question that troubles the book would seem to be: but who are *you* in poetic discourse? How do action and human agency—that of writer and reader—figure in poetry?

The focus then turns to a scrutiny of the process by which the poet's script literally figures the person writing:

There is a single point where the pen touches the paper, which is, as it moves into its fate, the mark of the whole person. The "whole person" is a fiction dependent on actuality, i.e. the movement of the authentic signature under trust. (17)

Although this seems to acknowledge the necessary inauthenticity of the single point of script as being only a representation of the whole person, the above formulation is quick to offer its own disclaimer: the necessarily fictional self of writing is underwritten by an authenticity—an "actuality" itself underwritten and authenticated by trust. The presence here of this talismanic *TEI* notion of "trust" indicates the extent to which Riley's whole oeuvre seems underwritten by the early communal explorations. *TEI*'s editors drew attention to its peculiar status as existing apart from a published, therefore public, space. In *Lines*, Riley's scrutiny of the relationship between person and script forces him to attend to his own use of the typewriter and its significance for a consideration of the status of his writing within accepted conceptions of public and private:

Meanwhile, this rectangular machine, rattling through the night, this bone-box, crashes a fully formed stigmata onto the skin at every stroke: the standard letter. On what model? Who licences these chunks of meaning? The sign is at once a shield and a majority verdict cut off from the beauties of any particular human visage as it reels through time. I insist that the heartscript is cursive, bearing difference at every point and unwinding its messages like a sledge-track in the snow; errant, and subject to the contours, but aligned. This stamping machine reduces the act to a package deal—alas it is public from the start, it is set already in the rigid star-track of ordered appearance. I never use anything else, indeed I no longer possess an ink pen. Every word fights against its publication for access to the heart, as indeed it should. (17)

Here, the typewriter is envisaged as a rectangular "bone-box," a coffin packaging the intimacy of cursive "heartscript" into the reductive violence of the "standard letter." The elegiac tone of "alas it is public from the start" is undercut by the implied acknowledgement that it is itself a rhetorical flourish; the writer doesn't even own an authentically intimate ink pen to contrast with the barbarously public type.

A subtle reassessment of previous preoccupations is notable in Riley's more recent work. If *Lines* sometimes lapses into a Prynnean register—"The lines on the window are thick with this question in the conditional modes, the yearning again, the fall into possibility" (19)—the essay provided for *Poets on Writing*, published the same year as *Reader*, rethinks some of the earlier concerns. Rather than following *Lines'* yearning for authentic intimate communication, "The Creative Moment of the Poem" rethinks that book's elegiac suspicion of the typewriter. Riley briefly discusses diverse metaphors used by poets for the poetic process—Rilke, Shelley and Mandelstam are mentioned—and suggests that the common factor is death. He claims that "The poet dies constantly into the poem," seemingly using death to indicate an enabling disconnection between poet and poem (102). In *Lines*, this disconnection is registered as a shock. The prose pieces permit an inauthentic, fictional self as long as it is underwritten by an authentic signature of trust. The indeterminacy surrounding the "central disclaimer" that "holds us together" is partly answered in the second of the poems titled "three disclaimers, which break the rules":

> I'm not this filled person you idealize.
> If we drank it, The Grail, would it act
> like warm milk on instant potato and some
> inner substance swell up and fill us to the
> inner surface of the skin, so as then to
> coincide with the form of the person and

> we'd act as nothing but that, whatever
> it is, poetry, love, truth, heart? (45)

Here the earlier ideal of the fictional "whole person" authenticated by the moving signature of trust is recognized as an essentialist idealization: an instant person whose manifestation is dubiously akin to the far from authentic glory of the packet meal. The question mark is again heavily weighted with a frustrated sense of incredulity. When it occurs on the same page for a third time it is attendant upon a realization that the emptiness discovered in place of the initially desired wholeness is necessary and perhaps even enabling:

> But what of the space, the empty
> and tough vacuities which the heart needs
> in order to function, and what is that function
> anyway but a stopgap device between our ends?

The essay "The Creative Moment of the Poem" acknowledges that the fall of "heartscript" into type is not the occasion for elegy and rhetorical pining, but that "poetry gains a lot of its energy from the tension between the person who in fact writes it and the non-person it evidently comes from" (94). Instead of a conduit carrying messages from writer to reader, the poem is now conceived of as "an object between poet and reader which is both a means of communication and a barrier to communication. It is neither opaque nor transparent" (93).

The parallel with W.S. Graham is productive. Graham envisaged the poem as a constructed space that becomes an object, both a meeting place and barrier between poet and reader. In "The Constructed Space" reader and writer view each other across the "abstract scene" that the poet describes as "a public place / Achieved against subjective odds and then / Mainly an obstacle to what I mean" (152). Graham's work is an ongoing wrestling with the "dark dialogues" of the printed words that trek across his white spaces, working towards an autonomy that will erase his intentional control over them. It is a process he finds both alarming and fascinating: "I would like to see where they go / And how without me they behave" (170). Riley's anxiety over the fall of heartscript into type is prefigured in Graham's playful/painful experiments with pressing intimate address and his anxiety over audience up against the formal linguistic register of letter-writing in poems such as "Yours Truly," "Dear Who I Mean" and the moving elegy "Dear Bryan Winter." Issues of distance and communication haunt Graham's work, and even in the frozen wastes of "Malcolm

Mooney's Land" is the incongruous presence of the telephone:

Enough

Voices are with me here and more
The further I go. Yesterday
I heard the telephone ringing deep
Down in a blue crevasse.
I did not answer it and could
Hardly bear to pass. (144)

Riley's work is informed by parallel preoccupations. Though *Lines* is not anchored in Graham's metafictional polar landscapes, its cover and the closing pages of the text are concerned with the incongruous presence of a telephone box. This box is situated by the side of a road that runs through the middle of nowhere. Riley is amazed by the decision of the GPO to install a public telephone box here:

It stands there alone in acres of moorgrass heather & peat groughs, precisely 1519 feet above sea level, exposed to the constant wind. Was it put there for the sake of the army, or the sheep farmers, or even weekend hikers? Who could actually have been conceived as requiring it, walking or riding down the vast horizons clutching his few pence? Anyway it does not work now. The 'phone is completely dead and there is no light in it at night. The G.P.O. decided at some stage no longer to keep it in repair. (55)

The incongruous presence of this box, once in the public service of communication and now in a state of disrepair, becomes emblematic for Riley of the position of the poet. It is no Tennysonian palace of art, but it is situated 1519 feet above sea level. It originally served a public function, but nobody can quite envisage the kind of public it might have served. The fact that the GPO (General Post Office) installed the phone is part of the book's bitter irony. *Lines* contains several puns on the term "Post Office," teasing it into a figure of the poet in (very) late capitalism. The late-twentieth-century British poet is deemed post-office in the sense of his coming so self-consciously *after* a culture that could conceive of poetry as holding any prospect of public office. "No one listens to poetry" repeated Spicer in *Language*, and even before this he had—in imagery akin to Graham's— situated his fake Rimbaud as being born in the Dead Letter Office of "Charlieville post-office" (149). In a markedly Spicerian twist, *Lines* ends with a text titled "Blackshaw 289: THE REPLIES" which, in my reading, positions the poet as receiver of incoming calls from the disused phone box—a perhaps bitter British take on Spicer's dictated Orphism:

> 15. This box is my office. There is
> No remission, no getting through without paying.
> I pay me till there's nought left and stride off again. (59)

The broken payphone provides a perfect vehicle for Riley's post-*TEI* discourse on counting the "cost" of a poetic calling. But again it recalls Graham. "What is the Language Using Us for?" contains a stanza strikingly similar:

> I am in a telephoneless, blue
> Green crevasse and I can't get out.
> I pay well for my messages
> Being hoisted up when you are about. (191)

Reader is a lot less pessimistic than *Lines*, and seems to find a form of service that is at peace with the idea that it is not immediately "public." The centre of the book is "Nicholas Moore"—fittingly, as Moore marks Riley's contact with a generation which he seems to consider the last to hold any truly "public" office. Moore's commitment to his craft through to the end of his life is a sustaining presence. That the poem bears his name as a title is significant, as the poem "Egbert Street" explains that "A name becomes a heart / and maintains life." "Nicholas Moore," the poem, pumps a series of homonyms and homophones around the book that transforms *Lines'* post-*TEI* discourse of hurt into something else: heart/hart/deer/dear/reader. It is as if Riley had reread the opening poem of Spicer's *Language* to discover the transformation of the pessimistic "No one listens to poetry" to the defiant assertion "No / One listens to poetry."

The poem that follows "Nicholas Moore" reflects the change:

Irish Drones

All those chanters
all faring well enough

And along he comes, what's
his name, Willie Clancie, Billy

Pigg, not Irish either and
plays as if

His heart's cut in
two. It isn't. Somebody's is.

Maybe it's mine, the
listener, maybe it's us.

The as if
is a long acquaintance with the sky.

This poem is in part a continuation of Riley's concern with the relationship between poet and poem. By extension, it is also concerned with the role of emotion in poetry, and more particularly with the arguments over authenticity that dog *Lines*. Relinquishing that book's weighty rhetoric of harm and hurt, authentically borne by the poet as stigmata translated into type, "Irish Drones" instead speaks of an emotional impact registered by the poem without needing authentication by the poet's signature. "The Creative Moment of the Poem" separates itself from a model of communication between poet and poem based upon the "urge to 'share' realisations of time/place" (96). Such a model, Riley claims, "offers a comfort which can only be retarded pain." The emotion registered in "Irish Drones" is all the more potent for its inauthenticity: the musician isn't Irish, his name is uncertain and he only plays *as if* his heart is cut in two. The significant fact is that "it isn't," that emotion can feature without a locatable confessional anchor; neither the poet nor the reader is the owner of experience here, hence the confusion generated by the false grappling over ownership: "Maybe it's mine, the / listener, maybe it's us." The false quest is halted by an assertion that seems finally at ease with the public anonymity of type: "The as if / is a long acquaintance with the sky." The implication is that whatever force it is that enables the musician to play *as if* his heart is broken, it is larger than his person. The musician taps a wider source, a drone that is a sustained note of no specific origin.

Reader is a book haunted, hunted even, by its own past—most immediately the poet's biographical traces dispersed across various specific locations, but also the total age of its provincial voice as it is hunted by textual provinces recognizably not merely its own. In the penultimate poem, "What The Fate Capsule Told Me," the oracular fate capsule calls back the poet as the quarry "rises / white against the green hill" and beckons as a "heraldic / creature with / open arms." The hunt motif is concluded and "there is // No further pursuit." And yet the Fate Capsule's message is unrecorded. The pursuit is ended in a poem that stretches this very pursuit into the only three-line stanzaic pattern in the collection—and across a line break that itself stretches to reach the final stanza. For this reader, the yearning outruns the provided conclusion.

The final poem, "Golden Slumbers," returns us to the ancestral grave, but its status is problematized by its title, which evokes the mythic dreamworld of the supernatural ballad and the fairy tale. Perhaps it is a tale that is told by the Fate Capsule, and therefore the "heraldic / creature with / open arms" is the Fairy Bride who enjoyed such eminence in the literary ballad. In "Thomas the Rhymer" she is the "Queen of fair Elfland" who wears a shirt "o' the grass-green silk" and is "mounted on her milk-white steed," thus displaying the heraldic colours of *Reader* and *The White Stones*. After successfully securing a kiss from Thomas, the Queen whisks him off to fairyland, where he is obliged to serve her for seven years. In Scott's popular nineteenth-century edition and addition to this traditional ballad, Thomas returns after this time, having learned to sing of Arthurian legends. The appearance of a white hart and hind during a night of such song is a signal summoning Thomas back to fairyland to forsake forever the "haunts of living men." A hare-brained reading once again, but only partly prompted by the irresistible temptation to cast Prynne as a fairy godmother.

"Golden Slumbers" is a devotional poem of service that seems to conflate amorous, poetic and even quasi-religious forms of vocation. Its yearning conditional tense, with its repeated "I would," seems restless even as it revisits the ancestral grave that opened the collection. Such a return suggests the book follows the elliptical quest that Riley identified as the underlying structure of Spicer's serial poems, which progress through a double journey of gaining access to further fields and simultaneously returning to the known. In my reading the quest motif is also a redemptive fantasy, a gleaming equity of redemption anticipating return to the mythical forfeited estate of the *Intelligencer* project as exemplified by the Prynne epigraph. I don't see this as mere nostalgia, but rather as a poetic acknowledgement of the sustaining presence of the *TEI* project of exploring the question of "what *size* we're in."

The Prynne epigraph, dated 1985 and presumably from a letter to Riley, seems still consistent with this project. In it he claims an "aspiration…to establish relations not personally with the reader, but with the world and its layers of shifted but recognisable usage; and thereby with the reader's own position within this world." Riley's "The Creative Moment of the Poem" similarly breaks away from a model of poetry that proposes the reader–writer relation as a direct and personal sharing. The sense of the lyric that emerges from the essay doesn't claim authenticity for it as direct address, but instead figures it as an act that cuts off the direct vocal transmission of the poet. Riley claims that the "raising of the voice from speaking to singing" is a "device which halts direct transmission in favour of a postponed and circumscribed message, the music itself a retardation of transmissive time-sense, sent floating into the world rather than directed, bomb-like, to the target at which it expires" (95). Consequently he suggests that "'Song' informs all poetry with a sense of vocal attenuation and isolation." This might account for the note of yearning tinged with loss in "Golden Slumbers":

> To have you I would bar the fields
> and turn the ores into the stream
>
> I would occupy the eyrie of my failure
> far into the night night after night

The final serial entry in Spicer's bittersweet "Love Poems" in *Language* is a reproach: "For you I would build a whole new universe but you obviously find it cheaper to rent one" (229). Spicer, at least initially, is aiming at a specific "you": Larry Kearney. Riley's poem of courtly service is to an indeterminate "you" that is a direction, but a direction he knows he cannot reach. This is why the yearning is twinned to the ambivalent "I would occupy the eyrie of my failure." An eyrie is the nest of any bird of prey, and most particularly an eagle's. It is a building high in the air, and figuratively a human residence perched high on a rock or mountainside. Is this eyrie the residence of the "kind forces / that hunt us to death"? This paradoxical being-at-home-with-failure more generally suggests that poetry is the home of failure. In this formulation, a poetic vocation is predicated upon failure: the writer can only write *into*, but never *through* the poem. For Riley, a poem is born of, and borne by, a failure at the level of direct transmission of authorial intention across to the reader. This failure seems to be for Riley a happy fall whereby "The words die into the page, and the future is replaced by hope" ("Creative Moment" 94). The replacement of the future by hope might seem an odd formulation, but it is one underpinned by a belief that "a much greater field of possibility is opened in the name of hope, which inhabits only the present tense, and cannot see through it" (94). The occupation of failure far into the night is Riley's rethought position on poetic vocation and his earlier play with the idea of being "post-office": now it has become a happy fall cushioned by "the ancestral bones" that form "a nest for my patience."

In its figuring of poetic creation as visit to/visitation by a place, the poem recalls Robert Duncan's "Often I Am Permitted To Return To A Meadow." Duncan's meadow is, like Riley's pasture and woodlands "thick / with the sheen of equity," a place to which entrance is not always "permitted." Both are uncanny utopian fantasies that fuse the familiar and the unfamiliar; hence *Reader's* sense of being haunted/ hunted by its own intertextual past, and Duncan's meadow that is "a scene made-up by the mind, / that is not mine, but is a made place" (7). Duncan's adaptation of Olson's composition by field transformed its focus upon kinetics and energy transfer into his notion of an intertextual field in which the self-consciously derivative poet would wander—Duncan likely would have had in mind the French word *dérive*, "drift." Duncan's meadow is also a place of yearning like that of the hart of the Psalms pursued by Moore and Riley. Duncan's made place that is both "mine" and "not mine" is "so near to the heart, / an eternal pasture folded in all thought / so that there is a hall therein" (7). This folded inner chamber parallels the nest of patience at the heart of Riley's "Golden Slumbers."

Patience and trust have a talismanic significance for Riley, whose roots stretch back to the ancestral grave of *TEI*. Prynne's "First Notes on Daylight" opens "Patience is truly my device, as we wait / for the past to happen" (*Poems* 69). But what is disguised by the poem's publication in *The White Stones*, and eventually in both editions of the collected *Poems*, is the extent to which it was conceived in the communal environment of *TEI*. The poem was printed in *TEI* after a letter by Prynne claiming for it the status of "enclosed notes" in response to issues raised in Riley's "Working Notes on British Prehistory." Riley had presented his notes as an attempt to "recover something of our inheritance *without* anachronism, through if anywhere this thing I hold now, discourse" (234). He saw the nature of the difficulty of such an exercise in terms of "our" distance from this inheritance, and how this forces him back "on instinct as a form of explanation." The letter in which Prynne responds to this approach manifests a suspicion of this notion of instinct.

Prynne suggests that the difficulty of recovering "our inheritance" does not simply arise out of historical and cultural distance. Instead, he suggests a difference in consciousness which inevitably infuses even the implied ideational neutrality of "instinct" with a hidden methodology. Therefore, to explore "origin as a type of primal purity" can only be unbalanced by the very distance that necessitates the instinctual approach (284). For Prynne this becomes an issue of motive. He agrees with Riley that "taking it as distant *does* entail a motive for enquiry," but is conscious that motive itself warps the inquiry's attempt at avoiding anachronism: "sustaining a motive is like making tools to make other tools, the first emergence of process as end-determined in the structure of intermediate forms" (284). The implication is that we are caught up in modes of analysis which constantly distort what we are addressing because of our inability to avoid post-humously assembling *cause* from what we assume to be its *effect*. The above quotation points to motive as an active force which is itself a constructed tool that alters what it touches and therefore makes "other tools."

I come back to this old discussion partly to re-emphasize the role of *TEI*, and Riley's editorship, as stimulus for Prynne. But also because these materials seem still to form part of the ancestral bones that line Riley's nest of patience in *Reader*. This is a nest

> In which I would sit and couple the numbers
> of my life without regret
>
> And remember with
> uncertainty the world
>
> In which we were and not, all
> our loves in vain.

There are aspects of this writing that I am not sure what to do with; and perhaps this awakening of a sense of uncertainty over readerly responsibility is itself significant, as the reader is hunted by the demands of the poem. My own uncertainty is over how to respond to the counterstatement to the above lines from "Golden Slumbers" on the last page: "No love is in vain, / reader." The key *TEI* abstractions of "love," "trust," "patience" and "truth" are still invoked in Riley's work, at the same time that they seem self-consciously aware of their distance from this originally communal context. Riley has asserted that "*There is no audience:* there is one reader at a time," and that "You have to trust the poem in reading it as you have to trust it in writing it. Any direct transfer of gain from reader back to writer breaks that trust" ("Creative Moment" 105, 104). The reader is figured as a distance the poet is in love with, but who can only be served as a distance; hence the infinite demands of "trust."

In his commitment to the poem as a trapping of the hart/heart, Riley writes a poetry of service which recalls that of Wyatt. Thomas Greene has written about how "In Wyatt our sense of an external presence in any given poem, an object of desire and of trust is very strong.... Within the poetic fiction, the speaker is truly responding to a second person who is responding to him, and the guarantee of this mutuality is the uncertainty" (247). That uncertainty should be the guarantee of mutuality seems akin to Riley's sense of the poet's "occupation" of failure as a guarantee of hope. Greene is especially pertinent in this context because he treats Renaissance poetry's interest in imitation as being part of a wider anxiety over "the newly perceived problem of anachronism" (2). The Riley–Prynne *TEI* debate over how to recover a prehistoric inheritance without anachronism finds an echo in Renaissance literature, where a growing awareness of cultural and linguistic distance was, as Greene points out, also a source of increasing disquiet and a profound sense of loss: the discovery of antiquity was also a registration of remoteness from it.

Greene's interest in *imitatio* is prompted by his awareness that the rise of the new science of philology coincides with, and responds to, the Renaissance's anxious awareness of cultural—and therefore linguistic—historicity. He cites Wilhelm von Humboldt's realization that we are always in the middle of a nation and of a language that necessarily consists of "material transmitted by earlier generations from a prehistoric antiquity unknown to us" (15). Greene explains that "we are able to tolerate this fundamental linguistic ignorance because we habitually build up significations in time that carry so to speak their causal structures with them" (15–16). Therefore, Greene envisages linguistic change as a constant battle between alteration and stability enacted at the micro level of each word. This awareness that a word carries with it a story of its evolution and development allows him to pun on the concept of "derivation" as involving an "interplay between drift and evolution" (16). One revealing drift/evolution he focuses on is Wyatt's use of the word "trouth":

It is the word from which our modern words *truth* and *troth* are descended, having split apart at some point during the sixteenth century. In a philosophical context *trouth* meant "reality"; in a social context it meant a covenant, the kind of engagement on which the medieval system of fealty rested; ethically, it meant "integrity," a recognized continuity in word and act that renders a man authentic, which is to say real; psychologically, *trouth* meant "faith" or "trust," a disposition to credit realities, including the supreme Reality; in this sense, it was one of the three theological virtues. It also meant, as early as 1380, "a true statement, a true doctrine, an established principle" (*OED*). (254–55)

Riley's account of the creative process "emphasises truth-telling as an act of focus," even if it is a "truthfulness which, as I argue throughout, can only be poetically conceived" ("Creative Moment" 99, 97). For Greene, "Many of Wyatt's poems use the perceived leakage in this word as a focus of their moral disorientation" (255). Perhaps *Reader* posits a fate capsule that seeks to recontain the various drifts of "trouth." In which case, *Reader*'s intertextual field of service seems parallel to Greene's image of a historically self-conscious text that is a

temporary shelter where the word finds a kind of lodging in its errancy through time, because the text assigns it a history, an identity, that solace its orphanhood. This history can never be complete and it can never be in any verifiable sense accurate, but it will provide that fabrication of a provisional source which the word needs to function. When an allusion is organic rather than ornamental, when it is structurally necessary, then it begins to sketch a miniature myth about its own past, or rather about its emergence from that past. (17)

Riley is often associated with the lyric and pastoral modes—not least because his pronouncements upon poetry in interviews, catalogue commentaries and reviews so often wear a self-consciously purist costume of avant-garde-baiting. Perhaps the heady *TEI* debates about a community of risk, and that project's eventual breakdown, have made Riley more prone to suspicion. After trying to chart my way through this large body of work—albeit through *Reader*'s small entrance into it—I emerge unsure about what it means to talk of pastoral in relation to the work of a poet whose career begins by tracking a golden age back to the hunter-gatherers. As an assault upon the postlapsarian forces of modernity this project is certainly monumental in scope—perhaps even intimidatingly so. For this reader, Riley's work is not about claiming for itself a stake in a tradition, though neither does it feel bound to reject past poetry as a guarantee of its own modernity. The best of the work is closer to Robert Duncan's vision of derivation: of inhabiting a language, of bringing out a grain in the wood of a language that necessarily predates and postdates the author. As "The Creative Moment" puts it: "no one owns the language, or can prevent the slightest lyric statement reverberating out into the world" (113).

Notes

1. The unbound pages intended for the hardback edition of *The White Stones*, long thought lost, were only recently rediscovered and bound. Peter Riley has informed me that only the first 50 copies of *Reader* were decorated with chalk; later copies are in plain green covers.

2. *Lines on the Liver* is unpaginated; my page numbering begins with the first page of the main text.

Works Cited

Duncan, Robert. *The Opening of the Field.* New York: Grove, 1960.

Ellingham, Lewis, and Kevin Killian. *Poet Be Like God: Jack Spicer and the San Francisco Renaissance.* Hanover, N.H.: Wesleyan University Press, 1998.

The English Intelligencer. Serial. Ed. Andrew Crozier and Peter Riley. 1965–68.

Jackson, Rosemary. *Fantasy: The Literature of Subversion.* London: Routledge, 1988.

Graham, W.S. *Collected Poems 1942–1977.* London: Faber, 1979.

Greene, Thomas M. *The Light In Troy: Imitation and Discovery in Renaissance Poetry.* London: Yale UP, 1982.

Hall, John. "On *Lines on the Liver* and *Tracks and Mineshafts*." See pp. 35–42 of this journal. Reprinted from *The Many Review* 2 (Spring 1984): 12–18.

Milne, Drew. "Agoraphobia, and the embarrassment of manifestos: notes towards a community of risk." *Parataxis* 3 (Spring 1993): 25–39.

Moore, Nicholas. *Lacrimae Rerum.* Hebden Bridge: Open Township; Cambridge: Poetical Histories, 1988.

Olson, Charles. *The Collected Poems of Charles Olson.* Ed. George F. Butterick. Berkeley: University of California Press, 1987.

Prynne, J.H. *Poems.* 2d ed. South Fremantle, Western Australia: Folio/Fremantle Arts Centre; Newcastle upon Tyne: Bloodaxe, 1999.

Riley, Peter. "The Creative Moment of the Poem," in *Poets on Writing: Britain, 1970–1991*, ed. Denise Riley. Houndmills and London: Macmillan, 1992.

———. *Distant Points.* London: Reality Street Editions, 1995.

———. *Lines on the Liver.* London: Ferry, 1981.

———. "The Narratives of The Holy Grail." *Boundary 2*, 6:1 (1977): 163–90.

———. *Reader.* London, 1992.

———. "Spitewinter Provocations: An Interview [by Kelvin Corcoran] on the Condition of Poetry with Peter Riley." *Reality Studios* 8 (1986): 1–17.

Sinclair, Iain. *Downriver.* London: Paladin, 1991.

Spicer, Jack. *The Collected Books of Jack Spicer.* Ed. Robin Blaser. 1975. Santa Rosa: Black Sparrow, 1989.

PETER RILEY: A CENTO

Tony Lopez

Down vast horizons, clutching a few pence
at the centre of the person, coming and going,
eating and trading, such as anyone—
pointing to an unreachable island,
we accede to this political reduction
because it is never bad enough
packed with brigands and sultanas
before it has rusted into position
in acres of moorgrass, heather and peat.
"I'll blow your house down," says the wind
as surrogate parents
suddenly look up and want to know
the very voice of the not-self
a man in a long dark coat and black hat.
"This woman" the guide explained "is very sad."

It was a 1960s confusion from which
the slightest construct of care might cast
an industrial disposition of settlement
without wrecking the joys
in their manifold capacities
with the sheen of equity.
The numbers are there whatever you do,
invasions of ore-bearing countries—
the hill, the limestone ridge
and the meaning of these paltry ruins,
cutting between actual production
and ecstatic finality
to install a public telephone box
in the name of freedom.

A person finds him/herself, year after year,
in the very singularity of the structure
by no means evident from the wooden church
and south of the town, across your brain
alternating blindness and rage
focused onto this encounter
families cooling and drifting apart
in their manifold capacities
a shelter against blizzards and driving rain.

People you meet in trains and buses,
the ribbons of tarmac
never to be relinquished,
starlight on steel rubbish bins
and ordinary things as we are
drafted in a pocket notebook,
squeezed into a segment.
Denmark was entirely my own fault.

The west pales the sky behind me
tending his beach barbecue
and the small concrete shop,
the very breath of patience
exposed to the constant wind.
This happened twice.

PETER RILEY:
A SELECT BIBLIOGRAPHY

This bibliography was prepared by Peter Riley, and expanded by Nate Dorward. It lists all separately published poetry, prose and translations; all magazines edited by Riley; and a selection of work that only appeared in periodicals. All places of publication are in the UK unless otherwise stated. Books published "with" another author contain individual poems by that author and Riley, not co-written texts. Periodicals with "curtains" in the title are various issues of Paul Buck's *Curtains* magazine, which changed its title with each new issue.

I. Works by Peter Riley

Books and booklets: poetry

Love-Strife Machine. London: Ferry Press, 1969. Cover by Michael Craig-Martin. 1/500. 26 signed with additional poem in holograph.

[with John James] *10-Ball Tennis: a demonstration match by Peter Riley and John James.* Issued as *The Curiously Strong* 3.4 (8 December 1970).

The Canterbury Experimental Weekend. Gillingham: Arc, 1971. 1/250, 15 numbered and signed.

The Whole Band. Lancaster: Sesheta Press, 1972. Drawings by Adrienne Riley. 1/250, 25 numbered and signed.

The Linear Journal. Lincoln: Grosseteste Press, 1973. 1/350, the first 50 signed.

Strange Family. Rhode Island, USA: Burning Deck Press, 1973. 1/250.

Five Sets in Two Sessions. Issued as *The Curiously Strong* 4.8 (Summer 1973).

Five New Poems. Durham: Pig Press, 1978. Cover drawing by Barnaby Riley. 1/200, 10 numbered and signed.

The Musicians The Instruments. London: The Many Press, 1978. Drawings by the author. 1/200.

Preparations. London: Curiously Strong, 1979. 1/200.

Lines on the Liver. London: Ferry Press, 1981. Ordinary edition, plus 12 copies signed and with additional holograph text, different in each copy.

Tracks and Mineshafts. Matlock: Grosseteste Press, 1983. Frontispiece from a photograph by Paul Hill. Ordinary edition plus about 20 cased.

Ospita. Poetical Histories no. 4. Cambridge, 1987. 1/200, plus about 12 copies on medium grey paper. Reprinted in *The New British Poetry*, ed. Fred D'Aguiar et al. (London: Paladin, 1988), *Noon Province et autres poèmes* (1996; see below) and *Contemporary Criticism* 19 (1997).

Noon Province. "Provisional Edition." Cambridge: Poetical Histories, 1989. 1/150, 10 with additional holograph text. Revised reprint in *Noon Province et autres poèmes* (1996; see below).

Sea Watches. Kenilworth: Prest Roots Press, 1991.

Reader. London, 1992. Frontispiece by Helen Macdonald.

This Carol They Began. Provisional edition of pages from *Excavations* Part One, issued by the author for CCCP3. Cambridge, 1993. 13 sheets in plastic folder. 1/50.

Sea Watch Elegies. Poetical Histories no. 27. Cambridge, 1993. 1/200.

Lecture. Cambridge: Equipage, 1993. Frontispiece from a photograph by Beryl Riley.

Royal Signals. Cheltenham: Short Run Press, 1995. 1/60 of which 6 signed and with additional text in holograph.

Distant Points: Excavations Part One Books One and Two. London: Reality Street Editions, 1995.

Alstonefield. London: Oasis Books; Plymouth: Shearsman Books, 1995.

Noon Province et autres poèmes. Saint-Pierre-la-Vielle, France: Atelier La Feugraie, 1996. Parallel text in English and French; translations by Lorand Gaspar, Sarah Clair and Claire Malroux.

Between Harbours. Artist's book by Colin Whitworth. Barton (Cambridge), 1996. Edition of 40 signed by author and artist.

Small Square Plots. South Croydon: Grille, 1996.

Snow Has Settled [....] Bury Me Here. Plymouth: Shearsman Books, 1997.

Author. Cambridge: Folio (Salt), 1998. 1/100. Second edition, with small changes, 1/50.

Untitled Sequence. Bray, Co. Wicklow, Ireland: Wild Honey Press, 1999. The discarded fifth section of *The Linear Journal*; first published in *Perfect Bound* 4 (1977).

The Gravel Paths. Manchester: Carcanet, forthcoming. Selected poems, excluding *Excavations* and *Alstonefield.*

Books and booklets: prose

A Bibliography of T.F. Powys. Hastings: R.A. Brimmel, 1966. 1/200.

Two Essays. "Published to elucidate some of the imagery of the poems in *Tracks and Mineshafts.*" Matlock: Grosseteste Press, 1983. Ordinary edition, plus about 20 copies case-bound; an errata slip is called-for.

Spitewinter Provocations. Interview with Riley conducted by Kelvin Corcoran. London: Reality Studios, Occasional Papers no. 4, 1986. 1/50. Previously printed in *Reality Studios* 8, 1986.

Company Week. London: Compatible Recording and Publishing, 1994. 1/350. An "extended commentary" on Company Week 1977, reproduced in the author's hand.

A Poetry in Favour of the World. Review of R.F. Langley's *Twelve Poems,* with two new poems by Langley. London: Form Books, Occasional Papers no. 6, 1997.

Small publications and very small limitations (poetry and prose)

[with Andrew Crozier] *Romney Marsh.* London: Ferry Press, 1967. 4pp leaflet. 1/100.

[with Andrew Crozier] *Two Poems.* Hand-printed by the poets. Hastings, 1968. 1/5.

Edward III: a patriotic drama after William Blake. Odense, Denmark: privately issued, 1972. A4 sheets stapled. Very few copies.

From "Marine Life." Odense, Denmark: privately issued, 1972. About 20 copies.

Statement About Poetry. Oxford: Museum of Modern Art, 1974. 1 sheet.

Following the Vein. London: Albion Village Press, 1975. Broadsheet. 1/300, 25 signed.

[with Helen Dennis] Untitled booklet. Leamington: Other Branch Readings, 1982. 1/100. [Riley's poems were later published in *Tracks and Mineshafts,* with revisions.]

Two poems issued as *Infolio* 78 (Cambridge, 1987). 4pp card.

Walking. Cambridge: privately issued, 1991. 4pp leaflet. 1/30.

Flyer for *Sea Watches.* 1991.

Manchester. Cambridge: privately issued, 1992. 8pp. 1/25. Second issue of 12 copies, 1997.

The Forest of Bowland. Cambridge: privately issued, 1994. 4pp leaflet. 1/50.

È questa vita un lampo. Cheltenham: Short Run Press, 1995. 4pp card. 1/26.

Three Pastoral Poems. Glasgow: The Plague Press, 1996. 5pp. 1/50.

Parallel Ninths. Cheltenham: Short Run Press, 1996. 4pp card. 1/54.

Two Romanian Sketches. Cambridge: privately issued, 1998. 4pp leaflet. 1/30.

Two More Romanian Sketches. Cambridge: privately issued, 1998. 4pp leaflet. 1/30.

Three Romanian Towns. Cambridge: privately issued, 1999. 8pp leaflet. 1/40.

Translation: books and booklets

Lorand Gaspar. *Ground Absolute.* Great Works Editions, 1976. 1/200.

Lorand Gaspar. *Four Poems.* London: Oasis Books; Plymouth: Shearsman Books, 1993.

Editions

T.F. Powys. *Two Tales.* Hastings: R.A. Brimmel, 1966. 1/200.

Nicholas Moore. *Lacrimae Rerum: last poems.* Hebden Bridge: Open Township; Cambridge: Poetical Histories, 1988.

Nicholas Moore. *Longings of the Acrobats: selected poems.* Manchester: Carcanet, 1990.

Periodicals edited

The English Intelligencer. First series, pp. 276–533. [This journal began under Andrew Crozier's editorship in 1965; Riley took over in April 1967, and continued to the end of that series. A new series began on 6 December 1967, with issues mostly unpaginated or separately paginated, and assembled (rather than edited) by Crozier, John James and J.H. Prynne.]

Collection. Seven issues. Hove, then Odense (Denmark), 1968–70.

Crust. Issued as *Spanner* 1.7 (1976).

Musics 10 (1976).

Selected periodical contributions: poetry

"The Melting-Pot." *Collection* 3 (1969).

"Archilochus." *Grosseteste Review* 3.1 (1970).

"The Last Ten Poems of *Marine Life*." *Turpin* 6 (1973).

Six poems. *Grosseteste Review* 7.1–3 (1974).

"Did the C.I.A. Kill Albert Ayler?" *Poetry Review* 65.2–3 (1975).

"From *Marine Life*." *New Directions* 32 (New York, 1976).

"Poems from the End of III." From the projected continuation of *Tracks and Mineshafts*. *Perfect Bound* 3 (1977).

"Birth Prospectus. The End of Us." *Grosseteste Review* 10 (1977). Reprinted in *A Various Art*, ed. Andrew Crozier and Tim Longville (Manchester: Carcanet, 1987).

"To the Tune of 'John Riley.'" In *For John Riley*. Wirksworth and Leeds: Grosseteste, 1979.

"Other poems written on 28th May 1968." *The Atlantic Review*, n.s., 3 (1980).

"Prelude: Night Lights." In *CCCP2: Cambridge Conference of Contemporary Poetry*, 1992.

"The Translations of St. Columba's Sea-Watch." *PN Review* 102 (March–April 1995).

"From *Excavations* Part I Book 3: *Vacated Thrones*." *Chicago Review* 43.3 (1997).

Other excerpts from *Excavations* Part I Book 3: *Pharos* 4.1 (Paris, 1998) and 5.1 (1999), and *Sub Voicive Poetry* 4 (1998).

Excerpts from *Alstonefield* Part V: *Salt* 8 (Applecross, Western Australia, 1996), *Salt* 10 (1997), *Salt* 11 (1999), *Involution* 5 (1997), *Shearsman* 41 (1999), *Gare du Nord* 2.2 (Paris, 1999), *Salt* 13 (forthcoming).

"Dioscuria: Six Preludial Flotations." From *Excavations* Part II. *The Gig* 1 (Toronto, Canada, 1998).

"Absent from Llŷn." Four poems. *Pharos* (Paris, forthcoming).

Selected periodical contributions: prose

Review of *Megalithic Sites in Britain*, by Alexander Thom. *Journal of Further Studies* 5 (Buffalo, undated [c. 1968]).

"Review of three unspecified books." *Collection* 5 (1969).

"Some Considerations of the Playing of Derek Bailey." *Great Works* 2 (1973).

Review of *Modern Poetry in Translation* 16 and two books by Kenward

Elmslie. *A Range of Curtains* (undated [c. 1973]). The Elmslie review was actually about John Wieners.

"Derek Bailey: Improvisor." *Guitar* 2.12 (London, 1974). The first two paragraphs are editorial, the rest an interview with Bailey.

"The Mist." *Turpin* 9 (1975).

"Old European Music." *Musics* 1 (1975).

Review of *Manchester Square,* by Ed Dorn and Jennifer Dunbar. *Poetry Information* 15 (1976).

"From *A Green Book Written at the Places Mentioned*: Three cave sections over the new year." *Perfect Bound* 1 (1976).

"The Narratives of *The Holy Grail*." *Boundary 2*, 6.1 (1977). Derives from Riley's MA thesis.

Review of *Notes for a New Culture*, by Peter Ackroyd. *Poetry Information* 17 (1977).

Review of *Science and Society in Prehistoric Britain*, by E.W. Mackie. *Perfect Bound* 4 (1977).

"Peak District Mine Names: a preliminary survey." *Bulletin of the Peak District Mines Historical Society* 6.5 (1977).

"From *Blake*, I." *bal:le:d Curtains* (1978).

"Slow Music: A Thesis." *Musics* 17 (1978).

"T.F. Powys at Mappowder." *The Powys Review* 3 (1978).

"Some Notes on Notation, Vocal Setting, and George Crumb." *Prospice* 10 (1979).

"From *Blake*." *Spindrift* 2 (undated [c. 1979]).

"Blake." *Great Works* 7, 1979.

"Incus Records." *Coda* 167 (1979). A history of the label and a disc-by-disc survey of its first 26 releases.

"'With You' by Anthony Barnett: Observations." *Grosseteste Review* 12 (1979). Revised reprint as "The Kind of Poem that 'With You' Is," in *The Poetry of Anthony Barnett*, Lewes: Allardyce Book, 1993.

"Some Notes Marginal to Douglas Oliver's *In the Cave of Suicession*." *Grosseteste Review* 12 (1979).

"Granite Flowers." Review of *Collected Poems and Plays*, by Wyndham Lewis. *Poetry Information* 20/21 (1979–80).

"High and Low Orders." *Palentir* 15 (1980). On improvised music.

"Brief Report from the Shires." *Not Poetry* 2 (1980).

"Further pages from *A Green Book Written at the Places Mentioned*, 8–16." *Figs* 2 (undated [c. 1980]).

"From *The Green Van*." *Grosseteste Review* 15 (1983–4).

Review of *Continual Song*, by Michael Haslam. *Reality Studios* 9 (1987).

"On Andrew Crozier's Poetry." *Archaeus* [2] (1989).

"Afterword." In *Spleen,* by Nicholas Moore. Second edition. Menard Press, 1990.

"The Guilty River," part 2. Interview with Riley by Iain Sinclair concerning Nicholas Moore. In *Downriver*, by Iain Sinclair. London: Paladin, 1991.

"The Creative Moment of the Poem." In *Poets on Writing: Britain 1970–1991*, ed. Denise Riley. Houndmills and London: Macmillan, 1992.

"A Sounding Dome." Review of *Four Poems*, by Michael Haslam. *Parataxis* 6 (1994).

"Nicholas Moore in the 1960s and 1970s." In *Conductors of Chaos*, ed. Iain Sinclair. London: Picador, 1996.

Review of *The Book of Demons*, by Barry Macsweeney. *Poetry Quarterly Review* 9 (1998).

Review of *Pauper Estate* and *Switching and Main Exchange* by Andrew Duncan, *What Suzy Was* by Kelvin Corcoran, and *Interviews through Time* by Roy Fisher. *Poetry Quarterly Review* (forthcoming).

Review of *Jack*, by R.F. Langley. Forthcoming.

Selected periodical contributions: translations

Claude Royet-Journoud. "For Enigma" and "Manual." *French Curtains*, 1973.

Claude Royet-Journoud. "Colloidal Suspension" and "Neuter." *A Range of Curtains* (undated [c. 1973]).

Miscellaneous

Derek Bailey. "Dead She Dances." Track on *Takes Fakes & Dead She Dances.* Incus CD 31. 1998. Performance by Bailey of selections from *Distant Points* to guitar accompaniment.

II. *Works about Peter Riley*

Cornall, John. "Mutated Muse." Review of *Human Capital* by Andrew Lawson, *Cut Memories and False Commands* by Andrew Duncan and *Sea Watches* by Peter Riley. *Marxism Today*, October 1991: 44.

Fine, Milo. Review of *Company Week. Cadence* 21.6 (June 1995): 12.

Freeman, John. "Being and Becoming." Review of *Five New Poems* by Peter Riley and *Down where changed* by J.H. Prynne. *Vanessa and One* (Spring 1981): 23–30.

Hall, John. Review of *Lines on the Liver, Tracks and Mineshafts* and *Two Essays*. *The Many Review* 2 (Spring 1984): 12–18. Reprinted in this issue as "On *Lines on the Liver* and *Tracks and Mineshafts*."

Healy, Randolph. "Personal Objectives." Review of *Clean and Well Lit* by Tom Raworth, *Five Easy Pieces* by Billy Mills, *Larksong Signal* by Ric Caddel, *Snow Has Settled [....] Bury Me Here* by Peter Riley and *Greeting Want* by John Welch. *Orbis* 107 (Winter 1997): 67–70.

Jordan, Andrew. "My Placeless Heaven." Review of *Alstonefield*. *10th Muse* 7 (1996): 49–50.

Keery, James. "The Bloodsoaked Royston Perimeter." Review of, *inter alia, Sea Watches*. *PN Review* 93 (September–October 1993): 42–47.

———. "Warmth with Honour." Review of, *inter alia, Distant Points* and *Alstonefield*. *PN Review* 119 (January–February 1998): 63–66.

Labrusse, Hughes. Preface. In *Noon Province et autres poèmes*, by Peter Riley, 7–9. Saint-Pierre-la-Vielle, France: Atelier la Feugraie, 1996.

Lawson, Andrew. Review of *All Fours* and *Catacoustics* by Tom Raworth, *Sea Watches* by Peter Riley, and *Prospect into Breath*, ed. Peterjon Skelt. *fragmente* 4 (Autumn–Winter 1991): 116–18.

Lopez, Tony. Review of *Sea Watches*. *Parataxis* 2 (Summer 1992): 45–47.

Manson, Peter. Review of *Distant Points*. *Object Permanence* 6 (January 1996): 65–66.

Maud, Ralph. "Thanksgiving for a Habitat." Review of *Sea Watches*. *Planet* 95 (October–November 1992): 104–5.

Philpott, Peter. "Lines on Lines." Review of *Lines on the Liver*. *Grosseteste Review* 14 (1981–82): 128–32.

Purves, Robin. Review of *Alstonefield*. *Object Permanence* 6 (January 1996): 61.

Smith, Simon. Review of *Selected Poems* by Eric Mottram and *Noon Province* (1989) by Peter Riley. *fragmente* 1 (Spring 1990): 38–40.

Stannard, Martin. "Quite Excellent." Review of *Snow Has Settled [....] Bury Me Here*. *Poetry Quarterly Review* 8 (Winter 1997): 11.

Tuma, Keith. "On Peter Riley's Lyric Excavations." *Chicago Review* 43.3 (1997): 8–17. Reprinted in Keith Tuma, *Fishing by Obstinate Isles: Modern and Postmodern British Poetry and American Readers*, 215–22. Evanston, Ill.: Northwestern UP, 1998.

AFTERWORD

John Hall's 1984 piece, which opens the essay section of this collection, says that "just as the reading that meets [the poetry] is a lonely reading—no one in my daily life talks to me about the latest Peter Riley text—this is a lonely writing that knows its own urgency from within and has lost any easeful nonchalance about the political vacuousness into which it might place itself" (36). Hall's essay has remained something of a lonely reading: this volume's bibliography lists a respectable number of reviews of Riley's books, but Hall's piece is one of the few extended critical accounts to appear there. (Its importance is implicitly recognized by its citation in a number of this volume's essays—citations made, I should point out, without most contributors' being aware that it was to be reprinted here.)

Riley's more recent work has maintained the sense of urgency Hall spoke of; and it often speaks out of, and about, the condition of loneliness. That combination of urgency and loneliness has often been figured in the poetry as the interior chamber of the heart, and with that image in mind I'd like to turn briefly to Riley's, *Noon Province* (Atelier La Feugraie, 1996). There's no sentimentality involved here: *Noon Province* is hauntingly aware of the transience and fragility of the human, seeing it as perpetually under erasure from the landscape's harsh sun and the "scouring wind": "we think we hear faint voices // In the ground and between the stones, / Dealing and deciding in a lost tongue / A far and fragile history, though no-one / Ever passed this way, save people, and us" (28, 20). That last line's self-contradiction speaks of how little trace we can leave of our *selves*, our hearts; what is left is as desolate and impregnable as the fortresses that dot the book's landscape. *Noon Province* is written from a self-consciously post-Christian moment, one that lacks a nostalgia for the remnants of the absolute. But neither is it content with the "ordinary things" of the day and of social life: the self inhabits them and is consistuted by them, but not necessarily comfortably or unanxiously: as one of the book's most resonant lines puts it: "We are together, we are lost" (60). So if Riley looks for "justice," he finds its ground in the heart, that solitary place: "Stretched in the stone chamber / Awake and listening / To the dark stone silence that / Grew from nothing. Final justice / Lives in our hearts" (74). And the heart is of course no ground at all: Riley knows that it may pulse with harm, and that its justice may be that of heated courtroom battle: "Mutual enemies debate in the / Chambers of the heart" (36). It's not an absolute ground but a focal point, a "cavern of image" which does not, cannot, avoid the contingencies of the ordinary social world but tries to pace them out, maintaining its "modest expectation" and keeping a slow "pulse" (14). Poetic labour is thus "a solitary and quiet wish / To line a space" (24). That solitude is importantly figured as "neglect," a condition of especial fertility, of "separation... / With you there and you there" (30). (One thinks of Nicholas Moore, whose neglect by the literary establishment Riley feels enabled the enormous creativity of his later years—though that neglect was leavened by the care of poets such as Riley, Roy Fisher, Barry MacSweeney and others.) Riley is not positing a defensive solitude, as he knows that any isolation is illusory: he stresses that "the films and ads of the / Town" are "deep in us" even when they neglect and alienate us; they are "a politics of matching / By which we are neglected / And rightly so, calling us out / From mind-grid to the fruited flesh" (30). The social world's double "calling... out" and "neglect"—another beautifully paradoxical sentence!—pushes the poet outside of his solitary "mind-grid" to a new fruitfulness.

I've been sketching out how Riley both insists on the patient and lonely nature of poetic labour and avoids that concept's potential dangers of self-pity and self-importance by setting it inside the larger durations and processes of history, the natural world, and social and political life. As I write, though, I'm conscious that this account (which in any case only picks a few threads out of a complex weave) doesn't stress enough the great ease and joyfulness that is often to be found in the poetry. Or other aspects: its technical resourcefulness and beauty, for instance. Or Riley's long involvement with improvised music, which has resulted in fine books like *The Musicians The Instruments* and *Company Week*, books that place him among the select company of those who have produced great writing about music, a notoriously recalcitrant subject-matter. That the latter topic is not specifically dealt with in this volume's essays indicates how much this volume remains only a beginning, an attempted instigation.

I want to return to one of the key words of *Noon Province*, "neglect." It's a term one often hears used in connection with literary reputations; often it is shorthand for "critical neglect," a term containing within it a certain potential for contradiction when applied to experimental or modernist poetries. Poetry such as Tom Raworth's or Maggie O'Sullivan's, for instance, would seem designed to evade or dismantle conventional modes of critical reading. There are serious arguments (perhaps deriving from Adorno) that poetry such as J.H. Prynne's is intended precisely to resist instrumental or institutional co-option, so that to treat a Prynne poem merely as a particularly difficult text in need of decoding is to miss its true point. Peter Riley's poetry does not, by the author's choice, present such obstacles, yet has not been much discussed in print up to this point. I do not know the reason for this, or why other poets from the UK and Canada are similarly little talked-about in print. For instance, the critical bibliography on UK poets other than J.H. Prynne and Roy Fisher is surprisingly thin, though essays in journals such as *Pages*, *Reality Studios*, *fragmente*, *Angel Exhaust* and *Parataxis*, and books such as Clive Bush's *Out of Dissent* and *New British Poetries: The Scope of the Possible*, edited by Robert Hampson and Peter Barry, have been valuable exceptions. And while it's important to note that experimental poetries can make conventional critical exegesis or explication irrelevant or impossible, and that the critical modes now available may be inflexible or tone-deaf (see Charles Bernstein's essay "Frame Lock," in *My Way*, Chicago: University of Chicago Press, 1999), the benefits of critical discussion are plain. One needs to be sometimes (though not always) articulate about why one admires or dislikes what one does; the process of articulation might in fact help break down a monolithic "avant-garde" into particular poets, poems…stanzas, lines, words. It's particularly necessary to do this when the conventions of small-press reviewing and criticism can seem unduly weighted towards the enthuse. And the "politics of form" in my experience often can't explain why one poem is a graceless and limiting short-circuiting of language (what Riley has called "word-salad"), another a truly valuable reorientation of one's linguistic expectations and horizons.

I've moved away from Peter Riley's work in the paragraph above; I'd like to conclude this afterword with some particulars about this collection. It has had a long gestation, and I therefore want to thank Nigel Wheale and Keith Tuma for their early enthusiasm, counsel and encouragement. I would also like to thank Peter Riley himself. The bibliography relies to a great extent on his information; he participated with enthusiasm and thoughtfulness in Keith Tuma's interview (conducted via e-mail this past fall and winter); and he answered many questions that arose from the essays. Riley was unfailingly patient and modest in his consultant's role; like myself he harboured no taste for "authorized" criticism. I also want to thank Tony Baker, Ric Caddel, John Kinsella, Ralph Maud, Laure Millet, Billy Mills and Lissa Wolsak for their assistance with details of items in the bibliography.

I lastly wish to acknowledge the financial assistance of the many people who subscribed in advance to this issue, or dug into their pockets for donations. Small-press publishing is a labour of love; it is important to recognize that many people who make these contributions do not have a lot of money. I want to thank everyone who helped out; and in particular acknowledge donations from: the Dalhousie English Department, Allen Fisher, Jeremy Green, Alan Halsey and Geraldine Monk, Randolph Healy, Victor Li, Michael Mann, Peter Manson, Stuart Mitchell, Robin Purves, Pete Smith and Lyn Richards, Harold Teichman, Ian Vickers, Jeffrey Twitchell-Waas and Candice Ward (plus one anonymous donor). My parents Tom and Marla Dorward deserve a special thanks for their assistance, both with the issue itself and more generally in the past year.

Essays have been arranged in roughly chronological order according to the published text they discuss, though I often diverged from strict order for reasons of variety or juxtaposition. Quotations from Riley's poetry throughout are from individual published texts (though printing errors are silently corrected). *The Gravel Paths*, Riley's selected poems, will be appearing from Carcanet, and will incorporate a certain amount of authorial revision; but given the retrospective nature of this volume I thought it most appropriate that the essays deal with the texts as they first appeared. Readers who wish to acquire the books discussed here should contact Peter Riley's own bookselling business; the address is given in the front matter to this volume.

Nate Dorward, 26 March 2000